3 - "Latourette once wrote that Mott had done "more for evangelization of the world than any other single person since St. Paul."

BREAKTHROUGH

4 - "Organize as if there is no prayer; pray as if there is no organization." - Mott

21 ff. H. R. Niebuhr said some liberalism like "A God without wrath brought men without sin into a kingdom without judgment through the ministrations of a Christ without a cross."

61 - Rolle 1951 Central Committee: "ecumenical" defined as "everything that relates to the whole task of the whole church to bring the Gospel to the whole world."

73 - Visser 't Hooft hurt people around him.

103 - Lund description report - "act together... except where diff of conviction compel to act separately"

105 - New Delhi report on nature of unity - "as all in each place..."

NCMC
BX
8.2
B44
1989

#1955042

BREAKTHROUGH

The Emergence of the Ecumenical Tradition

Robert S. Bilheimer

WILLIAM B. EERDMANS PUBLISHING COMPANY
GRAND RAPIDS, MICHIGAN

WCC PUBLICATIONS
GENEVA

Copyright © 1989 by Wm. B. Eerdmans Publishing Co.
255 Jefferson Ave. S.E., Grand Rapids, Mich. 49503

First published 1989 jointly with WCC Publications,
World Council of Churches, 150 route de Ferney,
1211 Geneva 2, Switzerland.

All rights reserved
Printed in the United States of America

Library of Congress Cataloging-in-Publication Data

Bilheimer, Robert S., 1917-
   Breakthrough: the emergence of the ecumenical tradition /
Robert S. Bilheimer.
     p.   cm.
   ISBN 0-8028-0296-6
   1. Ecumenical movement. 2. Bilheimer, Robert S., 1917-
I. Title.
BX8.2.B44 1989
270.8'3—dc20   89-7705
                                                   CIP

WCC ISBN 2-8254-0955-3

This book is dedicated in gratitude to my colleagues on the staff of the World Council of Churches and the close collaborators from the varied committees and Assemblies who together showed me new heights in our common calling in the Body of Christ.

Contents

Preface

The ecumenical movement has a memory, and this book has been written to contribute to it. It is not likely that the history of events and institutions which constituted the movement will be forgotten, for they are all well documented. Mine is an account of what the early ecumenical movement believed in, what it stood for, and how it understood the times in which it lived. The story is told in the first person, because I was there, believed in it, and felt called to serve it throughout my ministry.

A chief purpose in writing has been to make materials accessible. Many of them are contained in fugitive pamphlets, dull documents, drier minutes of meetings, and not very exciting biographies. Others are contained in books written from conviction in the midstream of ecumenical discussion and development. The official sources are listed in the Official Ecumenical Corpus, pp. 224ff. below; all are named in the notes. Most everything needs to be "unpacked." If my attempt to do so stimulates others to do the same, I shall be glad.

As I have not written a history of the development of ecumenical events, so also I have not written an account of the intellectual history, whether of church traditions or of theologians, which lies behind the thought here presented.

To avoid too much subjectivism in a first person account, I have turned to numerous critics, and am especially grateful to the ecumenical veterans among them, namely Paul Abrecht, Alan Booth, M. M. Thomas, and Oliver S. Tomkins. I have also turned to critics of younger generations and record here my appreciation of their time, insight, and knowledge: Joan Chittister, O.S.B., Patrick Gillespie Henry, John Long,

S.J., Douglas M. Meeks, Richard Mouw, Margaret O'Gara, Dolores Schuh, C.H.M., Thomas F. Stransky, C.S.P., Anthony Ugolnik, and Michael Vertin. Their contributions, together with those from members of my family, especially my wife Dorothy, have been of high value.

For many courtesies at Alcuin Library at St. John's University, the Library of Yale Divinity School, and the Library of the World Council of Churches, I am grateful, as I am to my editors and especially to Audrey Abrecht, by whose knowledge and determination a host of documents from the WCC Archives were found, copied, and sent across the Atlantic.

Collegeville, Minnesota

1

The Event

At 10:00 a.m. on Monday, August 23, 1948, I sat in the place reserved for staff behind the table of presiding dignitaries on the stage of Amsterdam's Concertgebouw, a hall known to music lovers the world over. The imposing auditorium was filled. The people, from countries on every continent, represented 145 churches.[1]

Amid the ruins of a war that had revealed the extent of perversion and disintegration in contemporary civilizations, they were embarking on a new venture; and they shared the sense of a grave turning point in human history. In Europe, it had required a herculean effort to defeat a preposterous "new order." Moreover, people understood that Hitler's "order" had not really been new, but had been the terrible expansion of some of the worst characteristics of human disorder. And now devastated cities, crippled economies, refugees and displaced persons in forlorn millions attested to the hardships and suffering of the war, while further outbreaks appeared in the catastrophic division and bloodshed of newly independent India and in the armed struggle for independence in Indonesia. The atomic bomb gave an apocalyptic cast to all.

At the same time, there were signs of a vigorous, hopeful response in 1948. The United States, emerging from the war intact and energetic, stood at its high point of liberal leadership. The Marshall Plan had just been authorized; the occupation of Germany and Japan had

---

1. W. A. Visser 't Hooft (ed.), *The First Assembly of the World Council of Churches,* Vol. V: "Man's Disorder and God's Design" (New York: Harper and Brothers, 1949), p. 27. This volume contains "the official documents of the Assembly together with a general description of its work and life" (p. 7).

1

sought reconstruction rather than revenge. The United Nations had been founded three years earlier. A vision of "one world," though often affirmed too romantically, nevertheless pointed to a new sense of worldwide interdependence.

The Nazi period and the war had severely tested the faith of Christians. Many had failed. But heroic examples of steadfastness in obedience to God had become widely known. Despite outward isolation, new and unforgettable experiences of Christian unity had occurred. During and just after the war Christians had demonstrated a desire to stand in solidarity with the agony of humanity.

Many of those in the Concertgebouw on that August Monday morning had suffered and stood firm, transcending battle lines to respond to human need during the war, thus coming to know the enabling bonds of true unity in Christ. Although such an experience had not been mine, as I had listened to and worked with these people in preparing the meeting, I too was swept up by the conviction that this was a landmark occasion for confessing the faith held in common and for relating the Good News to the present conditions of this new world within which the churches were set.[2]

The meeting on Monday morning had been preceded by a Sunday worship service in Amsterdam's Nieuwe Kerk. The force of unspoken gratitude rising to God for the grace by which all were gathered was almost palpable. John R. Mott preached, and if many recognized in the sermon of this 83-year-old pioneer "once more the old phrases which we had heard so often," Mott was the incarnation and to a large extent the cause of the forces and events which had brought everyone to that place.[3]

Born in 1865 and active until his death in 1955, Mott was a layman from the Pentecostal branch of US Methodism. His life spanned the imperial expansion of Europe and the USA, two world wars and the dawning age of "one world." Working from a base in the YMCA, he founded three worldwide ecumenical movements—the Student Volunteer Movement for Foreign Missions, the World's Student Christian Federation, and the International Missionary Council—and was closely associated with the founders of the Faith and Order and Life and Work Movements.

In my home, "Dr. Mott" had been a household name. My father had a YMCA career, and for a period in the early 1920s worked with

---

2. This paragraph reflects *The World Council of Churches: Its Process of Formation*, the minutes of the meeting of the Provisional Committee of the WCC in Geneva in February 1946 (Geneva: WCC, 1946), pp. 32-33, 106-12.

3. W. A. Visser 't Hooft, *Memoirs* (Philadelphia: Westminster Press, 1973), p. 208.

John R. Mott

Mott. At the Nieuwe Kerk, I recalled how often my mother would ask at the dinner table, "Did you see Dr. Mott today, dear?" Especially now, I realized that Mott had then been at the height of his career and seeing him was no routine matter.

Kenneth Scott Latourette, the great historian of the expansion of Christianity, once wrote that Mott had done "more for the evangelization of the world than any single person since St. Paul." I myself had heard the utterly compelling power with which Mott spoke of Christ. "From the moment of his youthful commitment to the Lordship of Christ that winter morning in his room at Cornell," wrote C. Howard Hopkins, "the certainty of the Resurrection had been the guiding light of his life. . . . To convey his meaning he would use such phrases as 'the larger Christ,' the 'great gospel,' the 'larger evangelism,' the 'whole gospel,' a 'synthesis between the old and never-to-be-neglected individual gospel and the equally true and indispensable social Gospel of Christ.'"[4] "Live," Mott

4. C. Howard Hopkins, *John R. Mott, 1865-1955, A Biography* (Grand Rapids: William B. Eerdmans, 1975), p. 628.

was fond of saying, "on the utmost limits of your faith, not on your doubts."

Mott was no theologian, but theologians paid tribute to him. To update himself on trends in American theology, Mott once convened a meeting which included the Niebuhrs, Tillich, Van Dusen, Calhoun, and others. At the end, wrote Henry Nelson Wieman, Mott

> thanked us for coming and for our participation and then stated those simple convictions which had carried him through the great labor of his life, up the long mountain, through the dark sea. But he was not trying to persuade us. He was not arguing with us. He was scarcely talking to us. He was simply stating what he had so often stated, the simple faith by which he lived. Then he went away with that calm, unhasting step, with that manner that seems never ruffled, never excited, never anxious. There is something like the mountains and the sea in John R. Mott. He will always be the same, very simple and a bit sublime.[5]

In Amsterdam — and later — at times when things were not so sublime, I would recall his injunction: "Organize as if there is no prayer; pray as if there is no organization."[6]

The tribute paid to Mott in the Concertgebouw came — with the force of British understatement — from another layman, Mott's longtime colleague Joseph H. Oldham: "One can say of him in a much more far-reaching sense than of any of his contemporaries that, had he not lived, the ecumenical movement would not have taken the form that it has done, and many fruitful growths in many different countries would not have taken place."[7]

But if the past had made possible the gathering in the Con-

5. *Ibid.,* pp. 632f.

6. Norman Goodall, *The Ecumenical Movement: What It Is and What It Does* (London: Oxford U.P., 1961), p. 10.

7. Hopkins, *op. cit.,* p. 697. In 1955, upon Mott's death WCC Central Committee chairman Franklin Clark Fry paid the following tribute to Mott: "It was given to him to play a decisive and creative role among the generation of those who laid the foundations for the ecumenical movement, among the generation of those who actually gave shape to the movement and among our present generation, which is called to make sure that the movement may be used meaningfully and fruitfully by the churches. The life of John R. Mott embraced all the concerns which in their togetherness keep the ecumenical movement alive: mission and evangelism, Christian unity, the witness of the church in and to society and the world of nations, the mobilizing of the laity and of youth for the cause of Christ. In him we have lost a truly 'catholic' and 'apostolic' soul, and as we think of him again and again we will let ourselves be reminded of the large dimensions of the Kingdom of God about which he has spoken to us with true authority." A tribute by an ecumenical lay leader is found in the autobiography of Sir Kenneth Grubb, *Crypts of Power* (London: Hodder and Stoughton, 1971), p. 138.

D. T. Niles (WCC Photo)

certgebouw, the orientation was toward the present and future. The young D. T. Niles of Sri Lanka (then Ceylon) had also preached in the Nieuwe Kerk the day before, immediately following Mott. Slight of stature but radiating energy, possessing a voice that went into action and a mind both profound and brilliant, Niles, a leader of the "younger churches" of the non-Western world, bespoke the future. "Who am I, that I should go unto Pharaoh?" (Exodus 3:11), he asked, speaking of the contemporary powers and of the power with which God confronts them and sends us forth. In a moment when everyone's sense of place and history was being changed, it symbolized the deep concerns of this gathering for the church's unity and mission that the oldest and the youngest of evangelists had been chosen to open it.

The delegates and alternates, consultants and observers, accredited visitors and youth delegates who had worshiped in the Nieuwe Kerk and were now present in the Concertgebouw embodied

Early World Council officials (l. to r.): Eivind Berggrav, Athenagoras of Thyateira, Marc Boegner, Geoffrey Fisher, and G. Bromley Oxnam (WCC Photo)

Christian history. Joined in the company were ancient churches of the Orthodox East, Greece, Constantinople, and the Malabar coast of India; Anglican and Old Catholic churches with ancient roots in the West; Protestants from the time of Luther and of the eighteenth- and nineteenth-century missionary expansion into Asia, Africa, and Latin America. Their different personal and church histories during the war and their hopes for the post-war world reflected contemporary reality. All were silently mindful of the absence of representatives of the Roman Catholic Church, which had not participated in preceding ecumenical work.

Presiding in the Concertgebouw, Archbishop of Canterbury Geoffrey Fisher asked US Presbyterian Samuel McCrae Cavert, who had chaired the committee on arrangements, to explain the three aspects of the Assembly program — work, worship, and study. Later, I would marvel at how Benedictine was this trio, built into the structure of virtually all ensuing ecumenical work. Cavert, the general secretary of the Federal Council of the Churches of Christ in America, of distinguished presence, quick in motion of body and mind, was wisely concise, allowing the assembly to get to the main business of the morning.

Samuel McCrae Cavert (WCC Photo)

The chair called on Pasteur Marc Boegner, who had chaired the Provisional Committee for the World Council of Churches, to present the long-awaited resolution.[8] Boegner, in his sixties, was an imposing figure, tall, erect, white-haired, with a marvelous snow-white handlebar mustache. He spoke a French so magnificent that even I, who knew no French, sat spellbound by its rhythms and enunciation. During the war, Boegner had held major offices within French Protestantism, and had been its recognized spokesman. Whether under the Vichy government or the German Occupation, Boegner had stood stoutly in Christ, protesting, mediating, defending, protecting, and assisting many in the Re-

8. This account is based on the Amsterdam report, pp. 27-28; the resolution is on p. 28.

sistance.[9] Later he would be made a member of the Academie française, an unheard-of honor for a Protestant church leader.

Before a hushed assembly, Boegner moved the resolution:

> That the first Assembly of the World Council of Churches be declared to be and is hereby constituted, in accordance with the Constitution drafted at Utrecht in 1938 and approved by the churches; that the Assembly consists of those persons who have been appointed as the official delegates of the churches adhering to the Council; and that the formation of the World Council of Churches be declared to be and is hereby completed.

A Church of England delegate raised an objection, but he failed to secure a second. The motion was called for, put, and carried *nemine contradicente.* A somewhat awkward moment of silence followed, as the meaning of the vote began to dawn; and it became obvious that no preparation had been made for celebrating its passage. Fisher, quick to sense the situation, called for silent prayer and concluded with fine, spontaneous words of petition for God's blessing.

Six years earlier another Archbishop of Canterbury, the late William Temple, had paid tribute to the ecumenical movement in his enthronement sermon, saying that "almost incidentally the great world-fellowship has arisen; it is the new fact of our era."[10] So, too, in the Concertgebouw the decisive vote was taken "almost incidentally," with neither fanfare nor pageantry. In this strange simplicity, the event stood by itself.

---

9. Marc Boegner, *The Long Road to Unity: Memories and Anticipations* (tr. René Hague; London: Collins, 1970).

10. F. A. Iremonger, *William Temple, Archbishop of Canterbury* (New York: Oxford U.P., 1948), p. 387.

I

FORERUNNERS

2

Ferment

The event at Amsterdam had precursors. One was the Student Christian Movement, the earliest of modern-day ecumenical enterprises. Explosive for those engaged in it, though virtually unknown outside of it, the SCM had been a remarkably influential force for more than half a century, creating the ferment and vision from which twentieth-century ecumenical Christianity emerged.[1] To a large extent the SCM explained my own presence at Amsterdam.

On a resplendent day in the autumn of 1936, at the beginning of my sophomore year at Yale, Fay Campbell, secretary of Dwight Hall, the local SCM, and I were strolling along a walk on the Old Campus toward Battell Chapel. I was vigorously denouncing the church.

"What do you mean by the church?", he asked.

"These local churches and their denominations."

"But that is not what I mean by the church," he responded.

"What do you mean by the church?"

"The church," he answered, "is the Body of Christ."

I stood still, dumbstruck. I had never really heard that before. In some inchoate but undeniable way, that concept of the church as the Body of Christ burned its way into my mind and soul. A hitherto un-

---

1. Ruth Rouse and Stephen Neill, *A History of the Ecumenical Movement*, Vol. I (Philadelphia: Westminster, 1968), pp. 341ff.; cf. William Richey Hogg, *Ecumenical Foundations — A History of the International Missionary Council and Its Nineteenth Century Background* (New York: Harper and Brothers, 1952), pp. 81ff. The SCM continues in New England, but as a national entity in the USA (but not elsewhere) it died out in the early 1950s, supplanted by church foundations, Youth For Christ, the InterVarsity Fellowship, and others.

known reality struck my consciousness. That new vision produced a wholly new seriousness about "church," "ministry," and the Christian faith itself. I no longer saw these as optional or peripheral. The thought that the church is the Body of Christ, and that we are members of it put these matters of faith and life into a new configuration.

I had had, quite unwittingly, a classic SCM experience.

The Student Christian Movement was a generic term for national Christian student movements, however organized, in many countries. They were brought into association with one another in the World's Student Christian Federation, founded in 1895 by John R. Mott. It was the first of the modern, worldwide ecumenical movements.[2] In the USA, the student divisions of the YMCA and YWCA, associated in the National Intercollegiate Christian Council (NICC), largely formed the Student Christian Movement. Dwight Hall at Yale was the local unit of the New England SCM and of the NICC.

Dwight Hall, including the wider SCM, became the focal point of my undergraduate years. Here in discussions and debates, in prodding and questioning by Fay Campbell, in exposure to experts from the faculty and the outside, we could engage the issues of the time. All of us were products of the shock and fear of the depression years. In the late 1930s we were in the midst of the Roosevelt revolution and the growing threat of war. The depression, Roosevelt, the Reuthers, Norman Thomas and socialism, *The Grapes of Wrath*, transient poor at the Yale Hope Mission, as well as voluntary poverty, the Catholic Worker movement centered in New York's lower East Side, the relative importance of political activity and direct relief of poor people all occupied us, whether by day or into the night. And we were intense about the primacy of Christian faith: what should Christians think, be, and do in these matters? My vote for Norman Thomas was the first Socialist vote ever recorded in the Connecticut Yankee town of Bethany.

War and peace were equally pressing. War had begun between Japan and China, the earth shook in Spain, appeasement appeared and ended in Europe. The United States, neutral, began "preparedness." How, we asked ourselves and one another, should Christians react? Fay Campbell, a staunch pacifist on Christian not pragmatic grounds, belonged to the Fellowship of Reconciliation. His challenge was a healthy one for those like me who were too influenced by the "horror of war" argument, an unsure foundation for pacifism. There was much discussion of Gandhi, with some highly attracted, others puzzled by his

---

2. For the history see Ruth Rouse, *The World's Student Christian Federation* (London: SCM Press, 1948).

nonviolence. I wavered between the two, unable to see how it would work against bombs and artillery.

Though following Fay Campbell in the view that pacifism must result from a conviction about what one must do and not do, accompanied by a willingness to pay the price, I was haunted by the thought that this removed me from the political arena. Activity in the United Student Peace Committee took us into the United Front, where we struggled in argument and parliamentary procedure with the Communists until the Hitler-Stalin nonaggression pact.[3]

At the same time, I could not escape the challenges of the secularism of the university. If I could deplore the secularism prominent among students and faculty, I could not deny the benefits of the broad humanism of the culture. A tug of war began between the humanism of "the secular" and Christian faith which would find some resolution only much later.

One root of this lay in a theological turnaround which originated in the classroom. Intrigued by the title of a book in the reading list for a philosophical ethics course—*The Ethics of Power*, by Philip Leon[4] —I turned to it one evening. I was engrossed by Leon's psychological-philosophical analysis of the ego and its pervasively aggressive and receptive function. Immediately I saw the optimistic assumptions about the human condition underlying the liberal theology I espoused demolished. With one spark, the dry wood of an ideological house went up in flames. Secular philosophy had provided a revelation that started a revolution. Scripture took on new meaning, and my own apprehension of Christian faith was radically changed.

Bible study at Dwight Hall took place largely in small groups, frequently accompanied by prayer. Though using historical criticism, it was not concerned with that discipline as such. Sometimes a faculty member joined us, not so much to teach as to share a competence. Thus Scripture began to "speak." A world opened up. The Bible ceased to be a "religious book," a mere vision or ideal or refuge, but came to be seen as the delineation of reality, placing life and one's outlook on life within inexhaustible dimensions of meaning.

There was talk at Dwight Hall about the work and promise of the ecumenical movement. The conferences at Oxford and Edinburgh in 1937 and Madras in 1938 (to which we shall turn in the next chapter) were much discussed. It was clear that the sort of community and

3. Irving Howe, in *A Margin of Hope: An Intellectual Biography* (New York: Harcourt Brace Jovanovich, 1982), gives a moving account of the Hitler-Stalin pact's devastating effect on the left in the USA (pp. 61ff.).
4. Philip Leon, *The Ethics of Power* (London: George Allen & Unwin, 1935).

fellowship which made Dwight Hall meaningful and was embodied worldwide in the WSCF, was also connected with the growth of the ecumenical movement.

At the annual midwinter conference of the New England SCM in 1938, my junior year, Henry P. Van Dusen, then professor of theology at Union Theological Seminary in New York, gave a powerful address on the ecumenical movement.

Already prominent, he would become even better known within two years for his self-confessed conversion to world missions, announced boldly in his book *For the Healing of the Nations*. At the time, of course, I could not know that as mentor and friend and colleague he would be decisive in my own ecumenical career from 1945 until his death in the 1970s. A commanding presence and personality, he seemed to me always to choose the high road, perceived with a masterful sense of strategy, while remaining acutely aware and caring of the person with whom he had to deal.

During the preceding summer he had attended the famed Oxford Conference on Church, Community and State. One morning, he told us, a group of the leaders on the platform had caused him to reflect. There were about a dozen—from England, Europe, Asia, and the USA — all prominent in their own countries and internationally. Van Dusen knew they were all old friends.

"How had they come to know one another so intimately?" he asked.

> Suddenly the answer flashed upon me. They had learned to know and believe in one another through a common devotion in student days. It has been said that in the third and fourth centuries, when the Bishops of Christendom assembled in ecumenical conference, it was like a reunion of old school-fellows; almost all had been trained in the theological college at Alexandria. Today, when the leaders of Protestant Christendom come together, it is like a reunion of old school-fellows. The great majority have been trained in the World's Student Christian Federation.[5]

Van Dusen described the fellowship in the WSCF as exceeding all others "in depth and strength of ecumenical understanding and vitality." To me, that meant that Dwight Hall was not a merely pleasant place for extracurricular religious activities. There we were connected

---

5. Henry P. Van Dusen, *For the Healing of the Nations: Impressions of Christianity Around the World* (New York: Charles Scribner's Sons, 1940). This portion of the address appears on pp. 140f.

with the most exciting development in contemporary, worldwide church life.

The SCM showed us a valuable, even indispensable, but too much neglected element in "church." Perhaps its most enduring contribution was indeed to enable generations of students to discover or rediscover the meaning and power of "church." Primarily a *movement*, the SCM always made it clear that it was not the church, but an arm of the church. For some the arm took us into the Body. For others the arm showed that it was part of the Body. In any case, we received an enlarged view of the church as not merely institution—which it was and always would be—but as movement combined with institution. Either side without the other suffered.

Toward the end of my junior year, notice was abroad that a World Conference of Christian Youth would be held in Amsterdam in the summer of 1939. I was one of those chosen to represent the New England SCM there.

"Amsterdam '39" met from July 24 to August 2 in the Concertgebouw. Later I would realize that the sense of confusion I felt there afflicts virtually everyone attending an international ecumenical conference for the first time. Cultural and historical backgrounds make human beings very different from one another, raising barriers among them. From its opening worship service onward, however, a conference is an intensely intimate event. Unexpected conflict and bewilderment ensue.

The breakthrough came for me in part through listening to the addresses, but especially in the group Bible studies. The leader of my group was the Frenchman Théo Preiss, who would later refuse to be an officer in the French Army in order better to witness to the men along the Maginot Line, notably by conducting Bible studies there. A brilliant leader, his early death was one of many which impoverished the church in the 1940s. At Amsterdam, he helped us to understand each other's interpretation of Scripture and to allow it to speak for itself, so that barriers were overcome and strangeness gave way to community.

Mine was not an isolated experience. By universal testimony the lasting significance of Amsterdam '39 lay in the affirmation of its theme and the sense of community that accompanied it. The theme was *"Christus Victor."* The affirmation, overwhelming to each of us, was made in singing a hymn. Visser 't Hooft wrote later, "I have never heard *'A Toi la Gloire'* sung as it was sung at the closing meeting in the Concertgebouw. It was a cry: *Kyrie Eleison,* but also a clear commitment to the faith that had brought us together and would hold us together."[6] "Thine be

6. Visser 't Hooft, *Memoirs,* p. 103.

the glory, risen, conquering Son" would become the great hymn of the ecumenical movement, and Visser 't Hooft in his lifetime may have sung it more often than anyone else, although some of us were not far behind.

The Statement of the conference affirmed

the task of the Church to proclaim the truth as it is made known in Jesus Christ and experienced in the life of the Christian community, and to test all human institutions in the light of this truth. We realize that if we live up to this calling, we will enter into conflict with the world, just as some who belong to our fellowship have already had to pay high prices for their loyalty to Christ.[7]

During the darkest days of the war that was soon to engulf much of the world, Visser 't Hooft wrote, "young men and women in armies, in prisoner-of-war camps, in resistance movements, remembered that they belonged to the family gathered by *Christus Victor.*"[8]

I returned from Europe on the *Queen Mary,* sailing September 2 on what would be her last civilian voyage before the war. On the high seas the next day we learned that, following the German invasion of Poland, Britain and France had declared war. The lights went out on the *Queen Mary* and the decks were closed off.

For the ecumenical movement and for me, a period of ferment had ended and a time of focus was at hand.

7. *Christus Victor,* Report of the World Conference of Christian Youth, p. 237.
8. Visser 't Hooft, *op. cit.,* p. 103.

3

Focus

In the autumn of 1945, when the US war effort was at its height, I sat on an oversold train, westward bound, in an overcrowded Pullman car. Four men, three in uniform and I in civilian clothes, sat, knee to knee, thigh to thigh, in a section intended for two. I had set aside this day to get through some research for my last remaining course in divinity school, and was deep in the preparatory volumes for the 1910 Edinburgh world missionary conference,[1] briefcase, book, and notepaper balanced on my knees. My unease amid the train full of soldiers in uniform increased as I noticed that they kept looking at the book I was reading. The dreaded plunge into explaining the esoteric was inevitable: "What are you reading?", one of them asked.

I explained that I was a divinity student and that these books had been written to be discussed in 1910 at a worldwide conference on Christian missionary work. A few questions and a little ensuing discussion led me, now less hesitantly, to talk about the ecumenical movement.

"What are you doing now?", they asked. I told them I was executive secretary of a national movement of students at some 100 Protestant theological schools in the USA; that its purpose was to secure their participation in the ecumenical movement; and that we hoped thus to have an ecumenical effect on their churches later on.

Encouraged by their intent listening, I said: "Tell me something. Here I am, as a theological student, along with ministers, deferred from

1. *World Missionary Conference, 1910,* nine volumes (Edinburgh: Oliphant, Anderson & Ferrier, 1910).

the draft, together with Congressmen, criminals and others, out of the war. How does all this sound to you?"[2]

The answer was immediate: "Stay out. Do what you are doing. That's what we're fighting for."

I might have taken umbrage at that, had it been spoken in an ideological tone, but it wasn't and I didn't. The atmosphere was not jingoistic as in World War I, and these men were not crusaders. They had the attitude, more typical of World War II, of the "sad and mournful warrior" who had a dirty job to do and wanted to get it over forthwith, but had not lost their sense of values.

The atmosphere and extraordinary faculties of academic training, the intensity of missionary concerns in employment, and the influence of the ecumenical church leadership made it inevitable—as I would later see — that "ecumenical" would form my realm of life.[3] And, as I came to reflect, how, if not through these factors, does God communicate a calling and vocation?

Graduation from divinity school brought the approach of ordination. It was clear to me that I should not pursue a Ph.D. and an academic career. A "church vocation" was indicated, but what of the attitude of the Presbyterian Church toward an ecumenically oriented ministry? There was no credal prohibition; on the contrary, the Westminster Confession used "Church" to mean the universal church and the particular churches that were parts of it. (This fundamentally ecumenical ecclesiology may explain why the Reformed tradition in general and the US Presbyterian Church in particular provided many of the ecumenical pioneers.) The inherent breadth and freedom of this doctrine fostered ecumenical ministries, soon to be formally recognized. I was ordained in 1945 in my home church at White Plains, New York, with Fay Campbell, a Presbyterian, giving the charge and Kenneth Latourette, an American Baptist, preaching the sermon.

Except for those who bore a pacifist witness, the churches supported but were not engulfed by the war. Many leading laypeople,

---

2. When I had to register for the draft in 1940, I had been unable to refuse and go to jail, as a considerable group of friends had done, including David Dellinger, whose pacifism would be lifelong and prominent, and James Alter, who became one of the most respected missionaries in India. Stirred by the gallant defensive fighting of the Finns, I had finally yielded to the idea that absolute pacifism removed me too much from the world's political history.

3. To my primary seminary work at Yale, under Bainton, Calhoun, Latourette, and H. R. Niebuhr, I was able, through a wartime "accelerated program" at Union Seminary, to add a year's work in one summer, with courses under Knox, Muilenburg, Terrien, Tillich, van Dusen, Bennett, and Coffin (R. Niebuhr was away!). During divinity school, I had worked part time in the Student Volunteer Movement.

clergy, and theologians showed a high capacity both to support and transcend the war at the same time.

The core of this transcendent quality in Christian life, prayer, and witness in wartime had been formed during the three decades since the Edinburgh Conference. A vital new concept of the church had increasingly been at work among Christians. This was partly a matter of the mind, partly of spirit, partly an articulated perception, partly a vague vision. Originating in one of the great movements of church history, it did not lead to a new denomination, but was taken up within ecclesiastical structures and brought to bear upon them.

This extraordinary period, embracing the closing years of Western imperial expansion, wartime, the interwar pause, and then more devastating wartime years, also witnessed an emerging consciousness of the People of God in the world as a whole.

Three ingredients composed this new consciousness of church-in-the-world: first, a movement from "foreign missions" to the world mission of the church; second, a movement that sought the renewal of the church by confessing the faith in relation to society and culture; third, a movement from the historical denominations to an undefined vision of visible church unity.[4]

MISSION

The movement from "foreign missions" to the world mission of the church was born of the tension between the final, universal saviorhood of Christ and the virtual confinement of Christianity to Europe (including Russia, where it seemed to be dormant), North Africa (where it was a tiny minority), and North America. The universality of Christ contrasted with the Western locus of Christianity. And that tension, built into the history of nineteenth-century missions, was complicated by a virtually inevitable factor: the passionate conviction that Christ must be made known throughout the whole world was colored by conviction about the benefits of "Western Christian" civilization. Through the range of missionary activity, from the mission compound, to church worship, to education, agriculture, and medicine, to morals, manners, and life-

---

4. Among summary accounts of ecumenical history, as the growth of cooperation in mission, Faith and Order, and Life and Work, are Samuel McCrae Cavert, *On the Road to Christian Unity* (New York: Harper and Brothers, 1961), pp. 15-36; Norman Goodall, *The Ecumenical Movement: What It Is and What It Does*, chs. 1-3; Ruth Rouse and Stephen Neill, *A History of the Ecumenical Movement*, chs. 8, 9, 12.

style, Christ was interpreted strongly in terms of the benefits of Western civilization.[5]

The presentation of Christ in Western clothing is strikingly apparent in the literature of the Edinburgh conference. For the most part, the 1910 conference affirmed both sides of the tension between the universal Christ and Western civilization as the business of Christian missions. Christ was to be preached and the benefits of Western civilization inculcated. Yet, at the same time, a different vision animated some, namely that the real business of "missions" is to help to create an indigenous church in the non-Christian lands, which would then take up the evangelistic task.[6]

Crucial to this latter vision was the leadership of Mott, exercised in travel, speaking, writing, organizing, and inspiring colleagues. Through him and many others, impelled by the thrust of Edinburgh, the missionary enterprise was led to concentrate on the goal of preaching the gospel and assisting those who responded to evangelize their own people.[7]

Moreover, during these years the horizon broadened, backwards. Less and less did the West appear as the home of an enduring

5. See Kenneth Scott Latourette, *A History of the Expansion of Christianity,* seven volumes (New York: Harper and Brothers, 1937-1945), especially Vol. IV, chs. 1-4; Vol. V, chs. 7-9, and Vol. VI, chs. 3-7. Chapters 1 and 2 of William Richey Hogg's *Ecumenical Foundations: A History of the International Missionary Council and Its Nineteenth Century Background* shows the depth of the tensions in the early cooperative movement.
"Missionary biographies," especially of the pioneers, form a genre in themselves; see Latourette's extraordinary bibliographies. The classic is S. Pearce Carey, *William Carey, DD: Fellow of Linnaean Society* (New York: George H. Doran Company, 1923). All this literature makes it evident that missionaries were among the most severe critics of perceived evils within Western civilization and the practices of Western governments and businesses, but this does not remove the overall Western coloration of missionary effort.

6. Hogg described Edinburgh as coming "on the eve of the mood-change from the nineteenth to the twentieth centuries. It was part of the metamorphosis from 'ecclesiastical colonialism' to global fellowship. In large measure Edinburgh and its radiating impulses helped to shape the new Christian world community with its growing recognition of inner unity and outer hostility" (*op. cit.,* p. 101). Among the impressive addresses at the conference were those by V. S. Azariah of India (Edinburgh Report, Vol. IX, pp. 306-15) and Cheng Ching Yi of China (Vol. VII, pp. 195-97); see Hogg, *op. cit.,* pp. 126, 128.

7. The Edinburgh Conference created a Continuation Committee, chaired by Mott. Under its aegis, continuation committees were organized by Mott in many countries, forerunners of the present national councils of churches. See Hogg, *op. cit.,* pp. 151-60. Although many missionaries shared Mott's goal, the turn from "missionary compound" to "indigenous church" was slow. Even after World War II, I heard a report from a leading US mission board executive of an extensive trip to Asia in which he never mentioned having stayed with or consulted a national. Asked about this, he replied that he was "concerned only with missionaries."

Christian civilization, more and more as the source of a radical secularism. By 1928 at the world missionary conference in Jerusalem, the missionary forces who had spoken in 1910 of the benefits of Christian civilization were pointing to the urgent need to challenge the secularism and the racism of the west.[8]

After another decade, with war being fought in China and threatening in Europe, the missionary forces went further. Under the banner of "The World Mission of the Church," missionaries, now joined by a significant number of people from the "younger churches," gathered in Tambaram, near Madras, India. The statement of that conference on "The Faith By Which the Church Lives" is an ecumenical classic, affirming that "to the gift of Christ, God has added the gift of His Holy Spirit in the church. Christ's true Church is the fellowship of those whom God has called out of darkness into His marvelous light. . . ."[9]

In 1938 the darkness was not only the darkness of paganism; it was the darkness of Peter's letter and of John's gospel, the darkness of the world, growing thick.

A CONFESSING MOVEMENT

The second ecumenical thrust of the period, arising in the 1920s, was analogous. The missionary movement, with its eyes on the ends of the earth, operated through special agencies within the institutional churches, drawing from them money, people, and, increasingly, sanction. The second thrust of this period also operated within the institutional church, but, under heavy pressure from the surrounding society, expressed the meaning of life in Christ by a confessing movement.

The WSCF had confronted secularism since the turn of the century. The highly varied expression of the social gospel in Europe and North America attacked crucial issues within industrial society. Somewhat later the Confessing Church of Germany stood in opposition to Hitler. These were all loosely linked in outlook, sense of calling, and

8. Hogg, *op. cit.*, pp. 244-58. The Jerusalem Meeting of the International Missionary Council, March 24-April 8, 1928, eight volumes (New York and London: International Missionary Council, 1928). On secularism, see Vol. I, pp. 401ff.; on racism, Vol. IV.

9. *The World Mission of the Church: Findings and Recommendations of the International Missionary Council, Tambaram, Madras, India, December 12-19, 1938* (New York: International Missionary Council, 1939), p. 15. See also *The Madras Series*, seven volumes (New York and London: The International Missionary Council, 1939).

personnel. With many differences, they all manifested a basic form of renewal in the church, namely renewal by confessing the faith in relation to society and culture.

In the 1920s and early 1930s, however, there was a division of theological approach among those concerned about renewal of church and society. It corresponded roughly to the divergence between Anglo-Saxon and continental European viewpoints. The British and Americans reflected an optimistic view of progress in human social affairs. They held that the Kingdom of God may be realized in the application of the social gospel. The European (especially, perhaps, German) view had a pessimistic estimate of human progress, believing that the Kingdom of God is eschatological, promised for the future end-time. Meanwhile, the Christian lives within two realms: the kingdom of this world, the scene not of upward progress but, at least in the West, of decline; and the realm of the church, in which there is a foretaste of the Kingdom of God to come.

From the early 1920s, however, a theological renaissance had been spreading. Associated in large part with Karl Barth, it neverthless included a wide spectrum from Orthodox to Anglican to Protestant, and from continental Europe to Britain, the USA, and Asia.

This renaissance affirmed two important fundamentals for the ecumenical movement. The first was a turn to Scripture as the primary source of Christian thought and life, giving rise to "a new biblical theology." The second was the discernment of a radical difference between the claims of Christ and those of society and its processes. This discernment had two components: the biblical affirmation of God's transcendence, in the sense of God's ways being, not "far off," but different from —indeed "wholly other" than—human ways; and the biblical presentation of the human condition and sin. From this arose much creative analysis of society, as the international impact of Reinhold Niebuhr attests.[10]

At the same time, the conflict within the church of Hitler's Germany was bringing momentous consequences. This epic struggle entered ecumenical consciousness in various ways, but notably in the Life and Work movement, whose leaders were close to leaders in the German Confessing Church. At a meeting of Life and Work in Fanö, Denmark, in 1934, the issue was whether the ecumenical leadership and

---

10. There were many others. Visser 't Hooft (who could himself be included) lists William Temple (*Memoirs*, p. 11), Emil Brunner, Paul Tillich, Berdyaev, Hoskyns, Schniewind, and C. H. Dodd, who rediscovered "the inner cohesion of the Bible"; *Has the Ecumenical Movement a Future?* (Belfast: Christian Journals Limited, 1974), p. 17.

movement would take their stand with the Confessing Church of Germany. Their favorable decision, after much debate as to the wisdom of a neutral position, proved crucial.[11]

To have opposed the Barmen Declaration and the Confessing Church — or even to have remained neutral — would have been comparable to the martyrs of the early church being overlooked by their contemporaries or later historians. As it was, the position affirmed early at Fanö was decisive in maintaining the inherent connection between the renewal of the church and its ecumenical expression, and thus crucial for the concept of the church on which the whole ecumenical enterprise depended.

By 1937 the time was at hand for an examination of the fundamentals. Ancient assumptions concerning the function of the church in society, and therefore the relation of the church to society, had largely broken down. The Christian world needed guidance. Prophets had arisen and among the most powerful, as Van Dusen had noted, were those who had met and learned of Christian fellowship and community in the WSCF.[12] Perhaps their experience in the ecumenical student movement led church leaders, theologians, and laity to use "ecumenical conferences" as their vehicle. In any case, can it be other than by the hand of the Spirit that the array of experience, conviction, acuity, and vision assembled at the Oxford conference in 1937 provided both substance and power?

Two things were clear. First, "corrections" or "improvements" in Western society along the traditional lines of the social gospel would no longer suffice. Far-reaching historical developments and a theological awakening had made reexamination of the historic relation of church to society urgent. Second, it was time for a close look at the fundamentals. Accordingly, the Oxford Conference was convened to consider three: Church, Community, and State.

Seldom if ever has an ecumenical conference been so carefully prepared or conducted. Seven symposium volumes[13] were issued in advance of the meeting as preparatory material. The table of contents of

---

11. *Ibid.*, pp. 16f.

12. Visser 't Hooft called the WSCF the "Nursery and Brains Trust of the Ecumenical Movement" (*Memoirs*, ch. 6).

13. *The Official Oxford Conference Books*, seven volumes (Chicago & New York: Willett, Clark & Company, 1938). J. H. Oldham, an English, Anglican layman, originated this technique in collaboration with Mott at the World Missionary Conferences in 1910 and in 1928, and brilliantly developed it at Oxford. It was taken over by Visser 't Hooft and further developed by Henry P. Van Dusen and Nils Ehrenstrom in preparation for the First Assembly of the WCC.

each reflects a well-thought-out unity; the list of contributors reads like an intellectual Who's Who of ecumenical Protestantism, Anglicanism, and Orthodoxy. The conference itself met in carefully organized sections, each intended to produce a report for consideration by the conference as a whole in plenary session. The resulting overall report[14] "won a recognition and influence, if without authority, comparable to those of the papal encyclicals on similar issues in the Roman Church."[15] A major reason for the intrinsic authority carried by these writings was the collaboration among laity, clergy, and professional theologians in addressing the issues of church and society of the time.[16]

A central result was a conviction concerning the church. "The first duty of the church, and its greatest service to the world, is that it be in very deed the church—confessing the true faith, committed to the fulfillment of the will of Christ, its only Lord, and united in him in a fellowship of love and service."[17] This duty requires the church to be engaged with society. The message and reports from Oxford discussed problems, trends, issues as realms of life in which the church is or should be engaged: the community (especially race), the world of nations, the state, the economic sphere, and education. Only in regard to the last of these does the report read today as though it were speaking in a bygone age; for the rest, clear insight and competent knowledge indicate the task of the church in societies living under increasing threat.

The conference bequeathed a legacy. The world missionary conference of 1938 (Madras) admittedly stood in its debt, affirming the same sense of "church" in its own sphere of concern. Through the war and into the postwar period, Oxford and Madras stood together. During suffering and change beyond comprehension, the final meaning of both was caught by the watchword which went forth from Oxford: "Let the church be the church."

CHURCH UNITY

During my work in the Interseminary Movement (basically the SCM in theological schools) from 1945 to 1948, I developed a speech, given at

14. *The Oxford Conference: Official Report* (Chicago & New York: Willett, Clark & Company, 1938).

15. James Hastings Nichols, *History of Christianity, 1650-1950* (New York: The Ronald Press, 1956), p. 443.

16. Visser 't Hooft, *Memoirs*, pp. 71-75.

17. "A Message From the Oxford Conference To The Christian Churches," Oxford Report, pp. 45-52.

many seminaries, based on the two world conferences on church unity in Faith and Order: in Lausanne in 1927 and in Edinburgh in 1937.[18]

I sketched what each conference had said about the cardinal points of Christian theology: God, Christ, the human condition, and the church. The important matter was not only the general agreement in these realms of Christian faith, but especially the conviction that there was no reason for the churches to be divided over these basics. At each point, no one in the Faith and Order conferences had contradicted (the famous *nemine contradicente*) the statements from which the material in my address was drawn. The speech was always well received; yet it had little impact either on my audiences or on me.

The same was true when I came to the one point on which there *was* disagreement: the question of the fundamental order within the various churches, especially the issues of ordination and the legitimization and authority of the ministry. It was an issue about which Henry Van Dusen was wont to snort in derision: "For heaven's sake, agreement on all the big points of the living faith, and a group of ministers gathered in a world conference cannot agree on their own authority!"

Everywhere there was admiration and hope for the Faith and Order movement, founded by US Episcopal Bishop Charles Brent, a man dedicated to social action and consumed with missionary passion, and by the leadership of his church.[19] In the fact that Brent was the originator of Faith and Order also lay a speech on the connection between mission and unity, for Brent had been in Edinburgh in 1910 and there derived much of his ecumenical vision. Yet secretly I did not generate much enthusiasm for Faith and Order.

Still, my own lack of excitement was chastened by the steady conviction of pioneers. In addition to Brent, there was William Temple,[20] an emerging giant of the ecumenical movement, to die too young during the war years, and others closer to home—Douglas Horton, Angus Dun, Abdel Wentz, Floyd Tomkins, John Mackay, and others.

Fortunately for me, two of my divinity school professors had

18. H. N. Bate (ed.), *Faith and Order, Proceedings of the World Conference, Lausanne, August 3-21, 1927* (Garden City, NY: Doubleday, Doran & Company, 1928); Leonard Hodgson (ed.), *The Second World Conference on Faith and Order held at Edinburgh, August 3-18, 1937* (New York: Macmillan, 1938). Preparation for the Faith and Order Conferences was largely done through monographs. For a complete bibliography see Lukas Vischer (ed.), *A Documentary History of the Faith and Order Movement, 1927-1963* (St. Louis: The Bethany Press, 1963).

19. Alexander C. Zabriskie, *Bishop Brent: Crusader for Christian Unity* (Philadelphia: Westminster Press, 1948); Tissington Tatlow, "The World Conference on Faith and Order," in Ruth Rouse and Stephen Neill, *op. cit.*, pp. 405-407.

20. F. A. Iremonger, *William Temple, Archbishop of Canterbury*, pp. 387-427.

Henry P. Van Dusen (WCC Photo)

imparted broad perspectives as well as much information. Church historian Roland Bainton had for years drawn overflow crowds to his magnificent lecture on Abelard and Eloise, until the faculty forbade visitors because of the effect on other classes. And students of Robert Calhoun tape recorded, edited, and published two mimeographed volumes of his lectures on the history of doctrine. From their truly catholic surveys, I come to appreciate the origins and depth of the differences among the church traditions and the tenacity imparted by the origins to the present divisions.

Clearly, some sort of revolution would need to take place, in order to turn the *nemine contradicente* into a committed "Yea!" Was it the sweep of missions that Latourette had given us, and the depth of church ethics coming from H. Richard Niebuhr that had somehow to be vitally connected with Faith and Order—perhaps in some shift of perspective and approach? That shift would come later. In the meantime Faith and Order was kept alive and powerful, not by the likes of me, but by the committed and far-seeing who knew that its work, whatever its shortcomings, was fundamental.

*   *   *

I undertook my work in the Interseminary Movement because it was a wide open ecumenical opportunity and also because Van Dusen, who then chaired it, assured me that it would be "superb" for testing the vocational waters.[21] Was my enthusiasm a commitment? Would the ecumenical movement have power with theological students of my generation?

The surprising "yes" to the latter was explained by various factors. The ecumenical program was more attractive to those from denominational seminaries than to those from the relatively few large interdenominational schools: denominational isolation appeared to be confining. In addition, the "movement" aspect of the program appealed, because most theological students had been nurtured and trained to view the church in a more structural sense.

Also, it was clear that traditional liberalism had left many needs unmet. As Theodore Wedel wrote, "modernist Christianity" seemed to want to rewrite John 3:16 to read "God so loved the world that He once inspired a certain Jew to inform His contemporaries that there is a great deal to be said for loving one's neighbor."[22] It was not only that Barth

---

21. For the history of the movement see W. Richey Hogg, *Sixty-five Years in the Seminaries: A History of the Interseminary Movement* (New York: Interseminary Movement, 1945). The movement's annual conferences in nine regions across the country were surprisingly well attended; and a national conference of some 700 theological students and faculty was prepared by a series of five volumes published as *The Interseminary Series* by Harper and Brothers in 1946. Ninety theologians collaborated in producing the volumes, edited by Clarence Tucker Craig, Randolph C. Miller, Kenneth Scott Latourette, O. Frederick Nolde, and myself. The whole series may be taken as a representation of US Protestant and Anglican theology at the time.

22. Theodore O. Wedel, *The Coming Great Church* (New York: Macmillan, 1945). Two further devastating descriptions came from H. Richard Niebuhr: "A God without wrath brought men without sin into a kingdom without judgment through the ministrations of a Christ without a cross"; *The Kingdom of God in America* (New York: Harper and Row, 1959); and Oliver Tomkins: "The Kingdom of Heaven often seemed to be identified with a society of psycho-analysed socialists"; *A Time for Unity* (London: SCM Press, 1964), p. 41.

in Europe and Reinhold Niebuhr in the USA had a wide influence; theological renaissance was associated with the ecumenical movement. There was theological power in the broad convergence of thought arising from scriptural foundations and being tested in ecumenical forums of many kinds, one of which was the Interseminary Movement.

In this general renaissance, there were three themes.[23] One was the discernment of the crisis of European and American civilization, which pressed on everyone. The second was the gospel itself. The inadequacy of the old liberalism required an answer, which was found by using the techniques of biblical criticism to speak, usually in highly orthodox terms, about the person and work of Christ. The third theme concerned the nature and responsibility of the church. At this point, thought shifted back and forth between analysis of the crisis of the West and the nature and responsibility of the church. Overall, thought was dominated by the two poles which, by this time, had come to characterize the ecumenical enterprise itself: the nature and the mission of the church.

Four of the five ecumenical conferences between 1937 and 1939 —Oxford, Edinburgh, Madras, and Amsterdam—attracted much notice. The fifth, at Utrecht in 1938, did not. Composed of seven persons named by Life and Work at Oxford and seven by Faith and Order at Edinburgh (the Committee of Fourteen), together with a representative group of people drawn directly from the churches, it was convened to draw up a constitution for a proposed World Council of Churches. The conference completed its work and sent the constitution to the 196 churches which had been invited to send delegates to Oxford and Edinburgh, asking them to a first assembly, which it was hoped would be held in 1941. A Provisional Committee was constituted, with W. A. Visser 't Hooft of Holland and William Paton of England as general secretaries, and Henry Smith Leiper as secretary in the USA. This arrangement was called The World Council of Churches in Process of Formation. In the war years and after, until the Amsterdam Assembly in 1948, it became a large and influential agency.[24]

In early 1947 the WCC's Provisional Committee met in Buck Hill Falls, Pennsylvania. During the meeting, I received a telegram from Van Dusen. It contained a question, together with a virtual command to appear at The Inn at Buck Hill Falls the next day. An invitation for

---

23. W. A. Visser 't Hooft, "The Genesis of the World Council of Churches," in Rouse and Neill, *op. cit.,* pp. 697-724.

24. *Ibid.* Upon Paton's death in 1943, Visser 't Hooft was appointed General Secretary.

an advance look at the gateways of heaven could scarcely have attracted me more than going to the meeting of the Provisional Committee! The question, outlined by Van Dusen in person and discussed for about 60 seconds with Visser 't Hooft: would I be willing to go to Geneva in May 1948 to organize the visitor's program for the forthcoming Assembly of the World Council of Churches? Subject to my family's response, I replied, Yes. And the family had no objection.

II

THE END OF CHRISTENDOM: RUIN AND COVENANT

4

The End of Christendom: Covenant

Hans Hoekendijk, a young, large, ruddy-faced Dutchman, stood with me on the lawn at the Ecumenical Institute in Bossey, near Geneva, in the summer of 1947. My invitation to go to Geneva had included attendance at the preparatory commission meetings for the Amsterdam Assembly. Everywhere in evidence were giants in theology, survivors of the Battle of Britain, heroes in the resistance movements, exemplars of the USA, whose worldwide stock was very high, and vibrant voices from Asia. Hoekendijk, a figure of the resistance who would leave a lasting imprint on the ecumenical movement, waited patiently for me to get through with something I was saying. Then, with the enormous force of which he was capable, he said: "Bob, it is the end of Christendom. Traces of it are still around, but don't count on them. Christendom itself is gone."

That Christendom had been under attack for some time anyone who had read Kierkegaard knew full well.[1] Moreover, the books from the Oxford Conference had made it clear that ecumenical thought was largely finished with the concept of "Christendom." Hoekendijk broke through that consciousness with force: Christendom *itself* is *finished.* As I was increasingly to realize, the demise of "Christendom" mattered. It was a fact of world history that would have a decisive influence on Christian identity, the churches, the ecumenical movement, and the World Council.

1. Søren Kierkegaard, *Attack on "Christendom"* (Princeton: Princeton U.P., 1944).

33

What was this "Christendom" whose disappearance had such far-reaching consequences? When people first spoke of the disintegration and then of the end of Christendom, they meant the basic settlement of the early church at the time of Constantine, which evolved into a structured whole—a comprehensive *corpus Christianum*, consisting of the church, the emperor or state, the culture, and the society. The Reformation and the rise of nationalism eventually introduced change, but neither produced a shift at the crucial point, the relation of church to society and the state. Nationalism meant a change in the concept of the state, but there was no fundamental change in the relation of church—whether Protestant or Catholic—to the state thus newly defined. The Reformation settlement, expressed in the formula *cuius regio, eius religio*, meant that the same relation of state-society-church obtained where there was a Protestant prince as where the prince was Catholic. Both embodied the preceding *corpus Christianum* or Christendom.

The death of Christendom had been preceded by a long process of disintegration.[2] Beginning with the Renaissance, through the Enlightenment and the scientific, political, and social revolutions of the eighteenth and nineteenth centuries, secularism had loosened and frequently broken the bond between church, society, and state. Even so, the vehemence with which Hoekendijk and other prophets of "the end of Christendom" spoke and wrote could not be accounted for simply by the disappearance of a once-powerful synthesis of church and society. They believed that the *corpus Christianum*, whatever its values, not only *could* not but *should* not be restored.

One reason was the imperialism of the *corpus Christianum*. The

2. Among influential ecumenical contributions on this subject see Emil Brunner, "And Now?", Amsterdam Vol. 3, pp. 176-80; Jacques Ellul, "The Situation in Europe," Amsterdam Vol. 3, pp. 50-60; Georges Florovsky, "The Church—Her Nature and Task," Amsterdam Vol. 1, pp. 43-58; Kenneth Scott Latourette, "An Historical Survey and Interpretation," Oxford Vol. 5, pp. 3-17, and "What Can We Expect in the World Mission?", *International Review of Missions*, XL (1951), 141-48; Hans J. Margull, *Hope in Action* (Philadelphia: Muhlenberg Press, 1962); Lesslie Newbigin, *The Household of God* (New York: Friendship Press, 1954), p. 1; The Oxford Conference Official Report, p. 183; Paul Tillich, "The World Situation," in *The Christian Answer* (New York: Charles Scribner's Sons, 1945), pp. 1-44; M. M. Thomas, *Recalling Ecumenical Beginnings*, Ch. II (Delhi: Indian Society for Promoting Christian Knowledge, 1987); Oliver S. Tomkins, *The Church in the Purpose of God*, Faith and Order Paper No. 3 (Geneva: WCC, 1950), p. 42; and W. A. Visser 't Hooft, "The Church and the Churches," Oxford Vol. 1, pp. 47-99; "The Ethical Reality and Function of the Church" (unpublished paper; Geneva: Study Department of the Universal Christian Council for Life and Work, June 1940); *Has the Ecumenical Movement a Future?*, pp. 78f.; *None Other Gods* (New York: Harper and Brothers, 1937), pp. 84ff.; "The Significance of the Asian Churches in the Ecumenical Movement," *Ecumenical Review*, XI (1959), 365-76; *The Wretchedness and Greatness of the Church* (London: SCM Press, 1944), pp. 19-26.

"Christian West" had become missionary—in the secular sense of creating empires throughout the world, as well as in the Christian sense of preaching the gospel, sometimes in advance of the emissaries of trade and government, sometimes along with them. These Christian missionaries were virtually always perceived by Asians and Africans as representatives of the "Christian West." The missionaries themselves were less clear. To be sure, they spoke of taking the benefits of "Christian civilization" (that is, Christendom) to these lands, but they also spoke with conviction of Jesus Christ and sought to build indigenous churches within the varied countries. Frequently, too, they strongly criticized the behavior of people engaged in Western business in Asia and Africa, as well as practices of colonial governments.

Yet from the mid-1930s a new passion animated those who spoke and wrote of "the end of Christendom." The reason for it was the German experience. In the middle of Europe, in the very heart of the old *corpus Christianum,* the horror of the Nazi ideology had arisen. One does not find in ecumenical literature an explicit statement that Christendom itself somehow led to the rise of the Führer. But one does find the conviction that the secularism of both the Renaissance and the Enlightenment took on demonic power in Nazi totalitarianism.

In the dark days of 1940, Visser 't Hooft wrote from his lonely desk in Switzerland that "it cannot be said that the West represents 'Christian civilization.'"[3] What could be said was that the West "represents the possibility of a Christian impact upon civilization." Politically, this "West," including Christian influence on it and within it, translated into "democracy" and the various democratic revolutions in Europe and the US.

Germany had never experienced such a revolution, and in the 1930s it took a different course. The Third Reich embraced instead the concept of *Herrenvolk* and all that it implied. Thus arose an "irreconcilable difference of national idiom between Germany and the democratic nations." But it was not until the invasion of Czechoslovakia that the West recognized National Socialism as "a fundamental break with the European tradition, including the German version of it." Even the secularized remnant of Christendom was trod under booted foot.

There was, however, another part of the German experience. The Confessing Church in Germany realized in 1934 what it took the rest of "the West"—aside from a few prophets—five intense years of Nazi oppression and expansion to perceive. The Nazi policy of "posi-

3. "Germany and the West" (unpublished paper; Geneva: Study Department of the Universal Christian Council for Life and Work, March 1940).

tive Christianity" and of being "protectors of the church" was only a propaganda device to sanctify what the state wanted to do. This policy, combined with many illegal attacks on the churches, sowed great confusion. As clergy and laity defected, often with an easy conscience, it was clear that the membership of the church was weaker and more bourgeois than previously realized. "The kingdom of this world had become to a large extent either confused with Christ's Kingdom or completely cut off from it. . . ."[4] In this situation, the gathering at Barmen in May 1934 was the occasion on which new life arose from the surrounding sickness.

Edmund Schlink described the Confessing Church as "one of the strongest Bible movements in the history of the church."

> People gathered afresh around the sacraments. People realized, to their strength and consolation, that the Church was not a mere collection of like-minded persons, but a concrete, local reality. Jesus' promise that when two or three were gathered together in His name, He would be there in the midst of them, proved to be a great force.

Under such circumstances, discovering kindred spirits in other Christian churches did not remove the confessional differences, but it did change the emphasis, so that "opposition paled in the face of the reality of God."

The rise of a confessing (or "confessional") church involves two factors: utter seriousness in confessing Christian faith, a willingness, as Luther wrote, to "let goods and kindred go, this mortal life also"; and pressure, even persecution, by the surrounding society against those who make a serious confession of their faith. In the Europe of the 1930s, as in South Africa today, these two elements produced a distinct community over against the regular, established churches.

Visser 't Hooft saw the formation of confessing churches as the "great ecumenical event of our time."[5] Not only did confessing churches

---

4. Edmund Schlink, "The Witness of the German Church Struggle," Amsterdam Vol. 1, pp. 97-108. About the Confessing Church, Reinhold von Thadden (Amsterdam Vol. 2, pp. 106-108) said it was the only really audible voice, though some groups in the free churches dared to oppose the Nazis. A substantial number of people who participated in renewal movements of various kinds made up a kind of passive resistance. But large numbers of clergy were neutral. See also Martin Fischer, "The Confessing Church and the Ecumenical Movement," in *The Sufficiency of God: Essays on the Ecumenical Hope in Honor of W. A. Visser 't Hooft*, ed. Robert C. Mackie and Charles C. West (Philadelphia: Westminster Press, 1963).

5. Quotations in this paragraph are from W. A. Visser 't Hooft, *The Wretchedness and Greatness of the Church*, p. 64. See also, on the Confessing Church, the message to "Brethren in the Evangelical Church in Germany," Oxford Report, pp. 259-60; Arne Fjellbu,

or the confessing church spirit arise in other European countries, but these formed a fundamental spiritual base for the ecumenical movement because they left the static condition which Kierkegaard had protested so vehemently. No longer could a bourgeois church exist comfortably as though the *corpus Christianum* were still in force. The confessing churches entered "into the dynamic reality of the work of God in the heart of His Church. A confessional church is one which allows itself to be set in motion by the living word of God."

Moreover, the confessing churches knew that they had won. Obviously, they were grateful for the Allied military victory, but theirs had been a more profound triumph over Hitler, the archenemy, the essence of demonic force. The Nazi apparatus of cruelty had failed in its effort to confine them and stamp them out. "Blessed are the meek" appeared not only as a lesson in humility but also a key to ultimate power. Thus brought to a living fire of witness, the churches were "suddenly in the center of the great battle for Europe's soul."[6]

Even so, another act was required from within the German experience. That came at a crucial meeting of the leaders of the Confessing Church at Stuttgart in 1945. Stuttgart was a rubble, the scene of some of the most severe of the "carpet bombing" by the Allies. Its people were destitute, scrambling for food and fuel. Many who attended the meeting had just been released from prison or concentration camp, and bore scars of their long struggle. Gathered together, they understood the need of the hour and received the clarity and courage to meet it.

Speaking to the world (symbolically represented by an invited delegation from the WCC-in-process-of-formation), they said:

> We with our people know ourselves to be not only in a great company of suffering, but also in a solidarity of guilt. With great pain do we say: through us has endless suffering been brought to many peoples and countries. What we have often borne witness to in our own congregations, that we declare in the name of the whole church. True, we have struggled for many years

---

"Witness in Occupied Europe," Amsterdam Vol. 1, pp. 89-96; Kenneth Slack, *George Bell* (London: SCM Press, 1971), pp. 56ff.; Ronald C. D. Jasper, *George Bell: Bishop of Chichester* (London: Oxford U.P., 1967), chs. 11 and 14; W. A. Visser 't Hooft, "Bishop Bell's Life Work in the Ecumenical Movement," *Ecumenical Review*, XI (1959), 133-40. Walter Freytag, "Meeting Christians in China," *International Review of Missions*, XLVI (1957), notes that Chinese Christians invited as a first visitor to the People's Republic someone from the Confessing Church in Germany.

6. W. A. Visser 't Hooft, *The Kingship of Christ: An Interpretation of Recent European Theology* (New York: Harper and Brothers, 1948), p. 8.

in the name of Jesus Christ against the spirit which has found its terrible expression in the National Socialist regime of violence, but we accuse ourselves for not being more courageous, for not praying more faithfully, for not believing more joyously and for not loving more ardently. Now a new beginning is to be made in our churches.[7]

Radically different from the situation after World War I, this German initiative made it possible to begin ecumenically in 1948.[8]

The combination of the end of Christendom and the lessons of the confessing churches meant a shift at the very foundations of the relationship between the church and society. Just what this shift would entail was the subject of a great deal of further ecumenical work. The main point, however, seemed to be clear. A new form of Christian identity and a new mode of Christian living were emerging. Three people, each to have a creative role in the new World Council of Churches, may be seen as symbols of this.

Despite an unexceptional physical stature, Martin Niemöller had extraordinary energy and force of presence. I first heard his name in 1937 and met him in Geneva in January 1948 during a planning meeting for the Amsterdam Assembly. But although I worked with him for several years in WCC committees, it was not until the 1950s, on a ship in the Mediterranean, that I grasped the symbolic power of his life. Up early one morning, I saw Niemöller in the bow. Joining him, I could feel a preoccupation even as we chatted. Suddenly he became intent, looking straight ahead. Conversation ceased. Soon he pointed: "There, there is where we surfaced, and fired, and got 'em!"

I was amazed. The flood of memory had transported him to World War I, when as a U-boat commander he was known by the British as the Scourge of Malta. In the Kaiser's Germany, he had represented the old Christendom, fighting fiercely in good Christian conscience for the Fatherland. Yet he became an unswerving opponent of Hitler, spending seven years in a concentration camp as a result. He had been a leader

---

7. G. K. A. Bell, *The Kingship of Christ: The Story of the World Council of Churches* (Harmondsworth: Penguin Books, 1954; repr. Westport, Conn.: Greenwood Press, 1979), p. 46; *The Formation of the World Council of Churches*, p. 13.

8. Visser 't Hooft's assessment of the contribution of the Stuttgart meeting to the WCC is in *The Genesis and Formation of the World Council of Churches* (Geneva: WCC Publications, 1982), p. 59. At the end of World War I, the churches had been "identified with nations so that they prayed against one another" (*ibid.*, p. 14). Mott had aroused hostility in German missionary circles by accepting membership in the Root Commission; and Germans had been absent at the founding of the International Missionary Council; cf. W. Richey Hogg, *Ecumenical Foundations*, pp. 172f., 203f., and Hopkins, *John R. Mott*, pp. 476-519, 576f., 581, 592f.

Martin Niemöller (Popperfoto, London)

of the Stuttgart meeting, and a short while later undertook a lonely, dangerous trip to Moscow to visit the Russian church but also to plead with the government on behalf of millions of German troops being held prisoner there. In his life one saw the world history and the church history of the twentieth century united in a living symbol.[9]

Of his first meeting with the Bishop of Chichester, G. K. A. Bell, Visser 't Hooft wrote that "he was a young-looking Anglican clergyman with a most innocent look."[10] The look remained into his old age. One is tempted to say that there was more there than innocence. That would

9. A report of Niemöller's trip to Moscow is in the minutes of the WCC's February 1952 Executive Committee meeting, item 6.
10. Visser 't Hooft, *Memoirs*, p. 24.

World Council officials at faith festival at Soldier Field, Chicago (l. to r.): W. A. Visser 't Hooft, Marc Boegner, G. Bromley Oxnam, Athenagoras of Thyateira, G. K. A. Bell, and Eivind Berggrav

not be true, but Bell's innocence was the innocence of the gospel. "To love him," wrote Marc Boegner, "was indeed a blessing from heaven."[11] The Church of England was (and is) "established." In its relation to the state, it maintains the pattern of the ancient *corpus Christianum*. For that reason Bell was a member of the House of Lords. At the same time, the Church of England nurtures and supports a strong prophetic tradition.

An early advocate of church unity[12] and a spokesman for the pre-war peace movement, Bell was deeply linked with the Confessing Church in Germany, especially through a close friendship with Dietrich Bonhoeffer. Visser 't Hooft had written to Archbishop of Canterbury William Temple that many Europeans felt that in the massive bombings the Allies were "equally if not more, totalitarian in their warfare

11. Marc Boegner, *The Long Road to Unity*, p. 75.
12. See G. K. A. Bell, *Documents on Christian Unity, 1900-1924*, First Edition (London: Oxford U. P., 1925).

than the nazis."[13] On February 9, 1944, the Bishop of Chichester spoke in the House of Lords presenting a direct challenge to the bombings.

London was in ruins. Canterbury (except for the cathedral), Coventry, and Portsmouth had been all but levelled. Every person in Britain was straining at the war effort. Now the tide was beginning to turn, chiefly because of the bombings.

Bell began. The innocence showed forth. It was a carefully reasoned, well-documented speech exhibiting knowledge of the military situation. He granted that "military, industrial, war-making establishments in Berlin are a fair target." But he protested the bombing of civilian populations and cultural centers. Of the bombing of Berlin he said:

> Through the dropping of thousands of tons of bombs, including fire-phosphorus bombs, of extraordinary power, men and women have been lost, overwhelmed in the colossal tornado of smoke, blast and flame. It is said that 74,000 persons have been killed and that 3,000,000 are already homeless. The policy is obliteration, openly acknowledged. That is not a justifiable act of war.[14]

Bell was intensely unpopular because of his speech. But Visser 't Hooft could write to him later, acknowledging wide discussion in Europe, "I think that all family members [a code word for church people] are most grateful that you have broken the silence on this point, which for many had become an intolerable silence."[15] The bishop had shown the dimension of transcendence, required of Christian identity in the ecumenical age.

D. T. Niles, from a third-generation Christian Tamil family, was converted from nominal to committed Christianity at a conference of the Indian SCM under the impact of a speech by Visser 't Hooft, then on his first trip to Asia. Niles entered the world ecumenical scene at the Madras Conference, where he was among the youngest delegates. From the wartime years in India and Ceylon, the new independence of India, and expected independence of Ceylon, he emerged as one of the world's foremost evangelists, preachers, and interpreters—of Asia to the West, the West to Asia, and, in later years, of Asia to Asia.

With Niles in the Nieuwe Kerk pulpit immediately following John R. Mott, no one needed to be told about the end of Christendom and the emergence of a new Christian identity. Niles spoke of its roots:

13. Visser 't Hooft, *Memoirs,* p. 183.
14. *Hansard,* Feb. 9, 1944, pp. 744-46.
15. Visser 't Hooft, *Memoirs,* pp. 183f.

Christ tells us it is not for us to "know the times and seasons," but sends us forth in the strength that springs from God's continuation in us and through us of what He has begun. He says to us, "The power you will show is the power of the leaven which I have already hid, the harvest you will reap is the harvest of the seed which I have already sown, the passions you will rouse are the passions of the fire which I have already kindled, the love you will share is the love of the deed which I have already done, and the end you will proclaim is the end of the end which I have already accomplished."[16]

THE COVENANT

In the Message of the WCC's First Assembly are these words: "Here at Amsterdam we have committed ourselves afresh to Him, and have covenanted with one another in constituting this World Council of Churches. We intend to stay together."[17] These oft-quoted sentences capture the mood which impregnated the vote of the Assembly at its first plenary meeting. It was an action not merely to create another ecclesiastical organization but to seal a covenant.

At each WCC Assembly the message is intended, not as an attempt to formulate dogma, but as an affirmation. To be sure, each has been a considered, thoughtful affirmation, carefully drafted, read, pondered, debated, and voted on. An Assembly message is a common word of faith soaring up out of the cultures, politics, loyalties, and traditions of the Christian world represented there. It pertains to its own moment in human affairs, but also to the great abundance of the traditions present at the Assembly. It speaks of the unchangeable, affirmed in the succession of those who have gathered in Christ's name since the Council of Jerusalem.

Although the Amsterdam Message addressed the world situation and the churches' response to it, its core was the understanding of the constitution of the WCC as a covenant. In 1946, at the first postwar meeting of the WCC Provisional Committee, Eivind Berggrav of Norway closed his sermon at a packed service in Geneva's Cathedral of St. Pierre with a statement of conviction tested and confirmed by wartime experience: "My Christians you are one."[18] That is the spirit of the Amsterdam covenant. It does not represent a narrow "covenant the-

16. Amsterdam Report, pp. 23f.
17. *Ibid.*, p. 9.
18. See "World Council Diary," *Ecumenical Review,* XI (1959), 324.

ology," but it reflects the biblical movement from grace to covenant and the biblical revelation of grace in covenant. Far from applying the scriptural text in a merely academic fashion, the phrase "covenanted with one another" described a re-enactment, led by the Holy Spirit, of the personal and corporate relationship of God and God's people.

The Assembly was well aware of two important elements in this "covenanting." The first concerned the authority of the World Council. The letter of invitation sent to the churches after the Utrecht conference included an "Explanatory Memorandum" in which a phrase of Archbishop Temple's proved to be of enduring import: the proposed Council would have no constitutional authority over its member churches, but "any authority that it may have will consist in the weight which it carries with the churches by its own wisdom."[19]

The second element was related. The vote in Amsterdam implied a commitment of the churches whose representatives were present. Churches joining the WCC later would also enter into a commitment. But the commitment and obligation of this covenant was never thought of in legalistic terms as something which could be enforced, for that would imply a central authority to secure compliance, which would have ushered in the unthinkable—a "super-church." The founders wanted a council of churches. They understood that it would have churchly importance. But they did not want an ecclesiastical agency with authority capable of deciding issues no one was ready to have decided, such as the divisions over apostolic succession or the authority of the ministry.[20]

Everyone at the Amsterdam Assembly was gratified by the number and range of the churches which entered into the covenantal relation with one another. Protestantism, Anglicanism, and Eastern Orthodoxy were all represented. But there were uncertainties. How solid were the Eastern Orthodox in their membership? Would the great body of Orthodox come in, especially after the Russian Orthodox Church had refused participation? Would "younger church" representation increase? Could there be any rapprochement with conservative Protestantism? Would Rome *ever* respond? The covenant would need to grow.

The covenant invited an unceasing alternation of thought between the calling of God in Christ and the response. Some had objected to the idea that the church sins and needs to repent. To this, H. Richard Niebuhr's article in preparation for Amsterdam gave a substantial reply:

> The disorder to which our attention is called in repentance is not so much the disorder *of* the Church as disorder *in* the

19. Visser 't Hooft, *Genesis and Formation*, pp. 48ff.
20. Visser 't Hooft, *Has the Ecumenical Movement a Future?*, p. 44.

Church. . . . The church as the community and Body of Christ, as the holy and whole people of God, as the City of God in heaven and on earth, is the mediator of grace and not of sin, of order and not of disorder. Disorder resides in ourselves and not in it. Yet disorder is in ourselves not as individuals only but also as organized parts of the Church, as vocational, national, ethnic and historical organs of its body. . . . Today we learn of our disorder not only as national or denominational parts of the Church, but also as the part of the Church located in the twentieth century.[21]

Within that realism, however, there was notable response. None wrote more eloquently of it than Olive Wyon in a substantial survey prepared for the Assembly. Looking at the church as a whole, she remarked that elements of renewal may seem insignificant when taken in isolation, but "gain a certain coherence when seen as part of a spiritual pattern which is emerging out of the mists of confusion and disorder. . . . We do not forget the darkness; but we look thankfully at the gleams of heavenly light; for they are a promise and an assurance that we possess a Kingdom that cannot be shaken."[22] Promise and assurance formed the absolute ground upon which those who made the covenant stood. We are driven together, wrote Oliver Tomkins, by the pressure of history; we are drawn together by love born when we see Christ in separated fellow-Christians.[23]

The Amsterdam message was part of an intense work process. The covenant arose not only from being, but from doing. The "Amsterdam agenda," prepared during two-and-a-half years following the end of the war, articulated enduring themes. For the first 15 years of the Council's life those themes, with evolving variations, were those of the WCC. Part of the work was action, part reflection. The two interpenetrated one another as the member churches fulfilled their intention to stay together.

From my seat on the stage of the Concertgebouw, I could not escape the impression of a pageant of the peoples. Returning home, delegates made speech after speech about the Assembly, talking of the races, colors, clothing, nationalities, and cacophony of languages. And

---

21. H. Richard Niebuhr, "The Disorder of Man in the Church of God," Amsterdam Vol. 1, pp. 78-88. See also W. A. Visser 't Hooft, *The Renewal of the Church* (London: SCM Press, 1956), pp. 69, 124; "The Asian Churches in the Ecumenical Movement," in *A Decisive Hour for the Christian Mission* (London: SCM Press, 1960), pp. 65f.; and Gustav Aulén, Amsterdam Vol. 1, p. 21.

22. Olive Wyon, "Evidences of New Life in the Church Universal," Amsterdam Vol. 1, p. 110.

23. Oliver S. Tomkins, *A Time for Unity* (London: SCM Press, 1964), p. 46.

Franklin Clark Fry (WCC Photo)

even if the vividness of the pageantry would lose some of its luster for me after many such meetings, the import of these meetings grew deeper. Traditions, institutions, cultures, and manners of life lie deep in human consciousness. These elemental components of peoples and nations also shape the consciousness of Christians and their institutions. In 1949, Franklin Clark Fry—a US Lutheran who would later play a large role in the WCC—speaking about "What the churches expect from the World Council," said: "The modern age is dominated by vigorous forces. It needs vertebrate religion in vertebrate churches, churches which know what they believe." The Bishop of Chichester, answering the same question, said: "The World Council has begun when nationalism is on the increase and the world is divided, economically, politically and spiritually. The very existence of the World Council is a demonstration of a supra-national unity. The Churches expect the Council to do everything in its power to emphasize this supra-nationality."[24]

Fry had pointed to the principalities and powers, the "forces" of the modern post-Christendom world. Bell had indicated the nascent yet clear sense of transcendent Christian identity in this same world of many peoples. Thus the Amsterdam pageant endured in the form of a working faith from which the ecumenical tradition would be constructed.

24. Central Committee minutes, 1949, pp. 75-79.

5

The Covenant:
Stress and Growth

Almost immediately the covenant made at Amsterdam was threatened. Yet the vigor of the commitment produced not only survival but growth over the next decade and a half. Stress afflicted the nerve center of the covenant, and growth became visible both qualitatively and numerically.

THE COVENANT AND THE CHURCHES

Within two years of its founding, the infant Council was strained to its limits.

One might have anticipated problems with the affirmation made by churches as a condition of joining the Council. In the WCC Constitution adopted at Amsterdam, this read: "I. Basis: The World Council of Churches is a fellowship of churches which accept our Lord Jesus Christ as God and Saviour."[1] It was not satisfactory; a case could be made that its lack of emphasis on the humanity of Christ verged on the heretical; almost everyone was mildly uneasy and some were strenuously opposed.

At the same time, the Basis was too important to warrant early tampering with its wording. Since accepting the Basis was the chief criterion of membership, the affirmation indicated the nature of the fellowship and its specific source in Jesus Christ. Moreover, it gave an orien-

1. Amsterdam Report, p. 197.

tation to the Council's work: a point of reference for ecumenical dialogue and a guide for already various activities. In short, the Basis made it clear that the fundamental criterion for the Council is acknowledgment that the Lord is the Second Person of the Trinity.[2]

Furthermore, the specific formula of the Basis had been used by Faith and Order since its founding. Faith and Order had come into the proposal for a World Council of Churches somewhat reluctantly in 1937-38, and a certain nervousness was still evident, meaning that it would not be politic to change the Basis too soon after the WCC was constituted.[3]

But more was at stake than politics. The perceptive and statesmanlike secretary of Faith and Order, Oliver Tomkins, wrote that the ecumenical founders had meant to root the movement in the worship of God incarnate in Jesus Christ and made known in the Holy Spirit. Although the formula was not trinitarian, its purpose was to ensure the trinitarian tradition in the WCC. So established, the WCC conveyed the conviction that a Christian meets Christ in a different mode than a merely denominational one, that fellow-Christians could not be ignored without ignoring Christ; and that this in no way puts down or minimizes what one believes about the God-ordained means of grace in one's own tradition.[4]

The difficulty with the wording of the Basis was met with a "both-and" solution: the original Basis was kept, but the Central Committee appointed a "Committee on the Basis." Finally, the Third Assembly at New Delhi in 1961 adopted the wording which remains until today:

> The World Council of Churches is a fellowship of churches which confess the Lord Jesus Christ as God and Saviour according to the Scriptures and therefore seek to fulfil together their common calling to the glory of the one God, Father, Son and Holy Spirit.[5]

But the problems were deeper than disagreement over the Basis. By the beginning of 1949 already, the WCC had become "a sign of contradiction" in "our nervous and divided world," its purposes misunderstood and attacked.[6] A meeting of Roman Catholics seriously interested

---

2. *The First Six Years: Report of the Central Committee to the Second Assembly,* pp. 11f.; Evanston Report, p. 306; Goodall, *The Ecumenical Movement,* p. 69.

3. W. A. Visser 't Hooft, *Memoirs,* pp. 80f.; *Genesis and Formation,* pp. 49f.

4. Oliver S. Tomkins, *The Wholeness of the Church* (London: SCM Press, 1949), p. 26; cf. Goodall, *op. cit.,* p. 69.

5. The New Delhi Report, p. 152.

6. General Secretary's report, Central Committee minutes, 1949, p. 63.

Oliver S. Tomkins (WCC Photo)

in the ecumenical movement had posed some especially searching questions. In particular, the triad of "the Church, the Churches and the World Council of Churches" caused a question to arise like steam from a bubbling surface: what does the WCC mean for the views which the member churches hold concerning themselves and their relation to the church universal?

Hoping to allay fears in some quarters, Visser 't Hooft told the Executive Committee in February 1949 that: "it is definitely possible for a Church which considers itself the true Church to enter into the Council. . . . Ecumenism does not mean ecclesiological relativism or syncretism."[7] But stilling the questions required more than a "definitely possible" from the general secretary.

The storm broke at the 1950 Central Committee meeting in Toronto. There are not many theological questions which have not been

7. *Ibid.,* p. 67.

formulated and debated before, but this new and relatively inex-
perienced committee had one on its agenda: "What is the ecclesiological significance of the World Council of Churches?"

A preparatory document had gone through four drafts, the last
of which was the subject of the key discussion.[8] This raised two viewpoints. The first, stated by Henry P. Van Dusen and supported by
John A. Mackay, both US Presbyterians, held that the WCC expressed
the adequate form of Christian unity, on the grounds that the churches
in it were all relative to one another and to a unity higher than any
possessed. This position was based on the conviction that varying church
orders may be found in the New Testament, that the order of a church
is in this way relative, and that other churches may be equally true and
full churches.[9]

The threat to the WCC emerged in an impassioned speech by
Fr. Georges Florovsky, a Russian emigré living in Paris, one of a group
of Orthodox theologians who had substantially influenced the general
theological renaissance of the time.[10] A learned and passionate priest
and professor, the bearded, black-robed Florovsky was a beloved veteran in ecumenical gatherings and an undoubted friend of the ecumenical movement.

That perhaps accounted for his emotion: he foresaw a head-on
collision between the ecclesiology of Orthodoxy and the WCC, both of
which he loved. Nearly everyone present was aware of the Orthodox
position — other churches are *essentially* incomplete (the negative side
of the conviction that the Orthodox Church is the true church). Five
anxious and largely futile interventions later, Pierre Maury of the Reformed Church of France, a man strongly influenced by Barth, broke
the deadlock. As the record has it: "He [Maury] did not consider his
own Church a full and true Church. Nor the 'High Churches' either!
Nor the Roman Church! Why then should any family of Churches be
afraid because that fact is so stated in this document? He wanted the
document sent out as the *minute* of one stage or moment in the movement of the Churches seeking their unity and each other."[11] And so it
was sent, a momentous "minute," indeed.

---

8. The origins of the basic idea of the "Toronto Statement" were in a 1945 paper
by Visser 't Hooft, revised and published as "The Significance of the World Council of
Churches," Amsterdam Vol. 1, pp. 177-200. In preparation for the Toronto discussion,
another paper by Visser 't Hooft went through two drafts, with substantial help from Oliver
Tomkins, then Secretary of Faith and Order; Visser 't Hooft, *Genesis and Formation*, p. 70.

9. Central Committee minutes, 1950, pp. 15-17.

10. Visser 't Hooft, *Memoirs*, pp. 64, 200.

11. Central Committee minutes, 1950, p. 16.

Georges Florovsky (WCC Photo)

The Toronto Statement, as it was called, outlined a basic ecumenical "ecclesiology." I had always had trouble with that word. It sounded extremely technical and very dry. Technical it is: it means the doctrine of the church. Dry it is not: how one conceives of the church in reference to one's self, one's world, one's own church, and other churches is the very stuff of Christian living. Seen, for instance, in the context of the confessing churches and their significance for Christian history, ecclesiology becomes a gateway to inspiration and commitment.

The ecclesiology of the Toronto statement begins with a statement of the problem: how to describe the implications of "church" in its universal sense for the churches belonging to the WCC without using the categories of one of its members or groups of members? In the debate, Van Dusen and Mackay were actually urging on the Council a Presbyterian ecclesiology (with no little American Protestant flavor to it)—without the name. The statement disavowed this approach.

Having defined the problem, the Toronto Statement contains several disavowals. The WCC is *not* a super-church; it is *not* the world church; it is *not* the Una Sancta; it *cannot* make decisions for its members; its purpose is *not* to negotiate unions between churches, although it witnesses to the unity of the church of Christ.

That said, the statement moves closer to the center of its position. "The World Council cannot and should not be based on any one particular conception of the Church. It does not prejudge the ecclesiological problem." Being in the WCC, in other words, does not force a church to compromise its own doctrine of the church, or even imply that it has. Nor does it imply that a church must treat its own conception of the church as merely relative. This met the chief concerns of the Orthodox, for they would not admit that the Orthodox church is any but the true church. Accepting the proposition that WCC membership does not prejudge or minimize that claim opened the way ahead.

The argument went beyond the self-conception of the member churches to the doctrine of unity. Membership in the Council does not imply the acceptance of a specific doctrine of the unity of the church. "The whole point of the ecumenical conversation is precisely that all these conceptions enter into dynamic relations with each other." In particular, the WCC does not define unity as the unity of the invisible church: it includes churches which believe in spiritualized unity and churches which do not.

What then does the Council believe about these matters? That rests on three crucial assumptions. First, the member churches base their participation in the work of the Council on "the common recognition that Christ is the Divine Head of the Body." Second, on the basis of the New Testament, the church of Christ is one. Third, the membership of the church of Christ is more inclusive than the membership of their own church body.

Two crucial affirmations form the climax of the document.

First, "the Member churches of the World Council consider the relationship of other Churches to the Holy Catholic Church which the creeds profess as a subject for mutual consideration. Nevertheless, membership does not imply that each Church must regard the other member churches as Churches in the true and full sense of the word." In other words, Orthodox churches could be in the WCC while believing and saying that other churches were not churches in the true and full sense of the word. They could keep their own ecclesiology in good conscience. And churches whose ecclesiology said that the Orthodox go too far could also believe and say that within the World Council.

Second, "the member churches of the World Council recognize

in other Churches elements of the true Church. They consider that this mutual recognition obliges them to enter into a serious conversation with each other in the hope that these elements of truth will lead to the recognition of the full truth and to unity based on the full truth." Frequently, this idea of *vestigia ecclesiae* had been used negatively, in the sense of "only traces." Toronto turned the idea around and made it the basis of dialogue. "Traces," in ecumenical usage, do not call forth condescension, but are welcomed as "hopeful signs pointing toward real unity."

The genius of the Toronto Statement lay in these two points. The Council had forbidden any imperialism of ecclesiologies, whether Van Dusen's (and my own), which wanted to level all down to it, or Florovsky's, which said there are no true churches except the Orthodox. At the same time, the existence of these ecclesiologies in the WCC did not imply that they were being reduced by simply being in the Council together. Finally, the agreement about the *vestigia ecclesiae* made it more than an agreement simply to "live and let live." Capping the whole was the conviction that no ecclesiology should remain in isolation from the others.[12]

At the time, I did not grasp the full significance of what had happened in the Toronto debate. Basically, the Orthodox had threatened to withdraw from the WCC. This would have been a terrific blow to the new Council. In world figures, the Orthodox had perhaps 130 million members, the Protestants 220 million, and the Roman Catholics 500 million. That I could understand. Moreover, it would have meant that on the "catholic" side the WCC would have had only the Anglicans, and many of them were heavily influenced by Protestantism. That I could understand, too. But there was something deeper in all of this—an almost total unfamiliarity with this ancient Orthodox Christian tradition.

Samuel McCrae Cavert would later write frankly of his own ignorance, which many shared:

> My textbooks in church history made little or no reference to Eastern Orthodoxy after the Great Schism between East and West in 1054 — or at least after the fall of Constantinople in 1453. I assumed that the Orthodox Church was static and impervious to renewal, weighted down under the dead hand of the past. I thought of it as preoccupied with an endless repeti-

12. See the discussion by Yngve Brilioth, Peter Brunner, H. van der Linde, Lesslie Newbigin, and Oliver Tomkins, in *Ecumenical Review*, III (1951). Newbigin, a champion of organic union, felt that the "provisional neutrality on ecclesiology" may need to be abandoned in the future. See the rebuttal, with cautious agreement, in Visser 't Hooft, *Genesis and Formation*, p. 80; see also Visser 't Hooft, *The Pressure of our Common Calling* (Garden City, NY: Doubleday, 1959), p. 25.

tion of ancient rituals unrelated to the ongoing currents of life in today's world. The practice of invoking the saints and reverencing icons appeared to me to be expressions of unenlightened credulity. The ascetic and monastic forms of life looked like outmoded medievalism. The long centuries of subservience of church to the state struck me as intolerable. A sacramental mysticism seemed to me to have taken the place of a prophetic mission in contemporary society.[13]

The Orthodox had challenged the WCC, helped it survive a potentially fatal crisis, and decisively contributed to a broadened self-understanding. How could this be? What was it in Orthodoxy that impelled its representatives to challenge, not to walk out, but rather to deepen? I came, in time, to feel that the answer lay in three words: history, *koinonia*, and truth.

Islam had swept through Orthodox territories from the seventh century onward, leaving only pockets of Orthodoxy in the Mediterranean world. The growth of the church in Russia had culminated in the end of the Constantinian period for Orthodoxy with the Russian revolution of 1917. Tragedies like these meant that the Orthodox churches, decimated and confined to themselves, had scarcely entered the stage of world history until the mid-twentieth century.[14] Islam was still regnant in many of the earlier territories of Orthodoxy; the Church of Russia suffered unimaginable persecution; the Ecumenical Patriarchate in Constantinople held only prestige; the Church of Greece, as a result of the two world wars, underwent severe deprivation.

Still, the ecumenical movement met with an Orthodox response from its early days.[15] The basic principle of Orthodox collaboration was set forth by the Ecumenical Patriarch Joachim III, in an encyclical in 1902. Although the Orthodox Church must primarily watch over its own doctrines, the letter said, "we must nevertheless be also concerned for our Christian brothers and never cease our prayers for the union of all into ONE . . . for they also believe in the all-Holy Trinity and take pride in being called with the name of our Lord Jesus Christ, hoping also to

---

13. Samuel McCrae Cavert, *On the Road to Christian Unity — An Appraisal of the Ecumenical Movement* (New York: Harper and Brothers, 1961), pp. 78f. Largely unsung, Cavert was one of the formative leaders of the ecumenical movement in the USA and of the WCC (it was he who first proposed the name, World Council of Churches). The quotation is an introduction to Cavert's own high appreciation of the Orthodox tradition.

14. Visser 't Hooft, "The Church and the Churches," in Visser 't Hooft and J. H. Oldham (eds.), *The Church and Its Function in Society* (Chicago: Willett, Clark and Company, 1937), pp. 52-54; J. H. Nichols, *History of Christianity*, pp. 15-28, 335-50, 351-64.

15. For the history, see W. A. Visser 't Hooft, *Genesis and Formation*, pp. 1ff.

be saved by the grace of God."[16] The Encyclical of 1920, proposing a league of churches, used the word *koinonia* (community, fellowship) in both an organizational and spiritual sense. The significance of the 1902 formulation was that it formed "the foundation of the ecumenical theory and practice adopted by the Constantinopolitan Patriarchate."[17]

The idea of *koinonia* was fundamental. In a remarkable speech to a 1956 conference of people involved in interchurch aid and service to refugees, Professor Alivisatos of the theological faculty in Athens talked about the 1.5 million refugees in Greece after World War I, the multitudes of refugees produced by the resistance and guerrilla warfare in World War II, and the sale of vast church property holdings to meet the needs of the two waves of homeless people. Earthquakes had added to the misery. "The needy in Greece reaches nearly 50% of the population." Then had come the response of substantial material aid, "collected by several churches for the needs of a sister church." What was important about this, Alivisatos said, was that "for the first time since the great schism of the 9th century, the various churches have felt the imperative obligation of coming to the rescue of other suffering churches." The work was "unblemished," he said, "simply because all the work of distribution is left to the good care of the receiving church."[18] That is, he saw that the non-Orthodox churches trusted the Orthodox, and did not seek to proselytize them. As the Patriarch in 1902 had reached out in *koinonia*, so the non-Orthodox churches had reached back in a different form of the same *koinonia*.

On another occasion, an Orthodox bishop said: "When you came and served us in our need, you used a language of manual signs, the sign-language of brotherly love in Christ."[19] Archbishop Iakovos (then Metropolitan James of Melita) put the same point in ecclesiological language: "The Churches of the East hold steadfastly to the Biblical assertion that nothing happens without the knowledge or the will of our Father in heaven. They believe that the WCC is a sign, through which God intends to say something to the world . . . understood as an instrument of the divine providence and economy."[20]

16. Cited by Archbishop Iakovos, "The Contribution of the Orthodox to the Ecumenical Movement," *Ecumenical Review*, XI (1959), 396ff.

17. *Ibid.*, p. 397; Visser 't Hooft, *Genesis and Formation*, pp. 1ff.

18. H. Alivisatos, "The Significance of Ecumenical Inter-Church Aid for the Witness of the Churches," in *Addresses and Reports to the 1956 Annual Consultation on the Church's Mission and the Role of Inter-Church Aid* (Geneva: WCC mimeographed document), pp. 65-70.

19. Cited by Norman Goodall, *op. cit.*, pp. 77f.

20. Metropolitan James of Melita, "The Significance of the World Council of Churches for the Older Churches," *Ecumenical Review*, IX (1956), 16-18.

It is little wonder that the Toronto struggle was intense. The covenant was threatened. But instead of breaking, it was deepened, largely on the initiative of the ancient churches of the East. Holding to both their conviction as to the one, true church and their commitment to *koinonia*, the Orthodox had made a signal contribution to the ecumenical enterprise.

Nikos Nissiotis, long a member of the WCC staff and later a successor to Alivisatos in Athens, put it this way:

> The Orthodox Tradition believes its witness is to help all the other historical churches to recover their own true life. This means in practice that Orthodoxy must give up its defensive, confessional-apologetic attitude and, in the glory of the Holy Spirit, become a mighty river of life, filling the gaps, complementing opposites, overcoming enmities, and driving forward towards reunion. This was how the Church lived in the time of the Fathers, creating new ways for achieving dynamic unity, richer forms of worship, a really ecumenical theology which regenerated the world through its authentic interpretation of the mission of the Church.[21]

The covenant also grew in influence and extent. A second world conference of Christian youth had been held at Oslo in 1947, and a third in Kotayam, Travancore (now Kerala), South India, in 1953, where the ecumenical movement "went local" with thousands at the daily meetings and continuous contact and conversation with the people of Travancore.[22] The East Asia Christian Conference came into existence at the initiative of the WCC and the International Missionary Council, followed shortly by the All-Africa Conference of Churches. At the WCC's Third Assembly in 1961, twenty-three churches were admitted—eleven from Africa; two from the islands of the Pacific; two Pentecostal churches; and four Orthodox churches, from Russia, Bulgaria, Romania, and Poland.[23]

Visser 't Hooft pointed to the significance of the simple sentence in the Toronto Statement in which the member churches "recognize each other as serving the one Lord." Of it he wrote: "Where there

---

21. Nikos Nissiotis, address in the New Delhi Report, pp. 22f. See also Edmund Schlink, "The Significance of the Eastern and Western Traditions for the Christian Church," and C. Konstantinidis, "The Significance of the Eastern and Western Traditions Within Christendom," both in *Ecumenical Review*, XII (1960), 143-56; and the report of the general secretary, in the 1962 Central Committee minutes.

22. Report of the Youth Department in *The First Six Years*, pp. 48f.

23. New Delhi Report, p. 9.

is a clear acknowledgment of the common calling, the forces of *koinonia* must begin to operate in spite of all obstacles."[24]

THE COVENANT WITHIN THE TENSIONS OF THE NEW WORLD

World tensions present when the Central Committee met in Toronto in 1950 were more acute a year later. North Korean forces had invaded South Korea on June 25, 1950, and captured Seoul. Anti-Communism was on the rise in the USA. Soviet pressure on Eastern European countries was severe.

The Central Committee met in 1951 in Rolle, situated amid the magnificent rolling vineyards along Lake Geneva, climbing toward the Jura mountains. The idyllic town is the home of Le Rosé, a renowned preparatory school for boys, largely from wealthy families, and it was there that the Committee gathered.

Beyond the natural beauty, the Committee perceived a divided world. North America, Western Europe, Eastern Europe/USSR, and Asia seemed to be moving away from one another, almost living in different stages of history. It was essential that the WCC keep aware of all four. The clear danger lay in the drive of each to make its own ideology the standard of outlook, policy, and conduct. Ecumenically, it was important to help the churches see beyond the ideologies and their limits.[25]

At its Toronto meeting the WCC had supported the United Nations peacekeeping action and force in Korea. T. C. Chao, a leading Chinese Christian theologian and President of the World Council, had resigned his WCC post in protest. In consequence, Bishop Bereczky of the Reformed Church in Hungary had published an open letter attacking the WCC for its support of the UN. Only two years earlier, the WCC had protested the arrest of the Lutheran Bishop Ordass of Hungary, who was still in prison.[26]

For the only time in a decade and a half, the Central Committee met in a prolonged closed session. At stake was the issue of the *koinonia:* would world tensions do the harm that confessional tensions had threatened but not accomplished? The basic issue took shape: would the Council move too far toward the general Western position, and if not, how would it demonstrate its capacity to transcend ideology?

24. Visser 't Hooft, *The Pressure of Our Common Calling*, p. 71.
25. Report of the general secretary, Executive Committee minutes, February 1952.
26. Central Committee minutes, 1948; see also Visser 't Hooft, *Memoirs*, p. 214.

The question was complicated by Bereczky's attitude. No one fundamentally doubted his Christian integrity, although Franklin Fry, President of the Lutheran Church in America, an erstwhile defender of Ordass, strongly doubted Bereczky's ability to discern reality. From a pronounced feeling of the churches' guilt in ignoring the poor, Bereczky seemed unable to take a strong position over against the Hungarian Communist regime, while seeming to bend over backwards in criticism of the West. Hence his attack on Visser 't Hooft and on the WCC's support of the UN in Korea.

Major deportations from Hungary had taken place in the preceding months. Questioned during the closed session about the church's response to these, Bereczky said they had ministered to the deportees, especially at the moment of their departure at the railroad station. Deep silence followed. Everyone saw the woeful weakness of the answer, but who would challenge him? No one else was in a similar situation. Then, from the head table, where he was seated with other presidents, Berggrav arose.

Everyone knew that this was the man who had been confined in Norway for much of the war by Quisling. "I was," he wrote to George Bell, the Bishop of Chichester, "confined in my cottage in the woods in Asker. I had 17 policemen on guard of which 3 were on duty at a time. A peasant's wife had the idea to bring me every day a bottle of milk. The guards were accustomed to her coming, but she was of course only allowed to go as far as to the fence, where the guard then took over the bottle. This day she didn't walk the path, but came through the forest, jumped the fence and was before my kitchen window before the guards observed it. She whispered to me in a hurry: 'My husband listened to London yesterday evening, and he heard the Archbishop of Canterbury pray for you, bishop!' Then the guards arrived and took her away, but what a difference with me! No longer left alone, but taken into the fellowship of Christian brethren, even in Great Britain. This moment is my deepest experience of 'Ecumenism' as a reality."[27]

Most of those in Rolle knew why Berggrav had been imprisoned; I had first heard the story when he preached at the World Conference of Christian Youth, in Oslo in 1947.

When Hitler and the Nazis came to power, the established Lutheran church in Norway had not been noted for its prophetic quality. Church and state formed the framework and much of the substance of the fabric of Norwegian society, a veritable *corpus Christianum*. Church life was marked by a profound piety.

---

27. This account is contained in a letter to Bell. See G. K. A. Bell, *The Kingship of Christ*, p. 38; cf. Goodall, *The Ecumenical Movement*, p. 66.

Eivind Berggrav (WCC Photo)

Of the few Norwegian church leaders who participated in various aspects of the ecumenical movement Berggrav was the most notable. Many felt that the mantle of the great Swedish churchman, Archbishop Söderblom, the chief figure in the Life and Work Movement, would fall upon Berggrav. He had been prominent in the inter-war peace movement within the churches, seeking as late as autumn 1939 to organize an initiative for peace with the German government.

Hitler struck Norway through the Fifth Column, headed by Quisling. By late autumn 1940, the brutality of the Norwegian Nazi regime had become evident. The bishops protested, and did so again in early 1941. Berggrav, as Bishop of Oslo a leader in the protest, received a summons from Quisling, who received him, but did not invite him to sit down. Standing, Quisling sharply demanded that Berggrav recant and support the Nazis. Berggrav replied, "And if I don't?" "In that case," Quisling replied, "I will shoot you." During a moment of pause, Berggrav looked his opponent in the eye. "Then shoot," he answered. Quisling backed down and put Berggrav under house arrest instead.

As Berggrav now arose at the meeting in Rolle, "intrinsic authority" was personified. To my surprise, he did not speak. Instead, he walked slowly to the seat of the Hungarian bishop. Quietly, levelling his finger, Berggrav put the question: "But did you protest the deportations?" Head down, Bereczky answered in barely audible tones: "No." Amid profound silence Berggrav returned to his seat. A necessary ecumenical act had been performed. The covenant had a strength which the world's divisions could not break.[28]

THE COVENANT—IMPERATIVE DIMENSIONS

The affirmation made near Madras in the foreboding moments of late 1938, that ultimate hope for humanity and final power within human turmoil alike reside in the church, found confirmation in excited sharing among a small international group gathered at Whitby, in Canada in 1947. As their reports were given, they found that the missions and small churches which had sprung up around the world had survived and in many cases were strengthened by the world cataclysm. As a result, they discerned a new pattern of missionary work, "partners in obedience."

But they and the people they represented had a question about the new World Council of Churches. Many, concerned with prophetic social action, had asked whether the "churchification" of the ecumenical movement would dull the demand for justice. Similarly, those committed to world evangelism now asked whether these ecclesiastical bodies, and the council they created, would embrace world mission. Their question was warranted, for "foreign missions" had historically been supported by a minority in the churches, many of whose leaders and members had been feeble in their support of, if not hostile to, the missionary movement.

With the WCC having clarified its ecclesiological basis and meaning, these people were asking it to make clear its convictions about world mission, specifically how it understood the relation between "unity" and "mission." The concern was not academic. Admittedly, a certain logic pointed to integrating the pioneering International Missionary Council with the World Council of Churches. For that to happen,

28. Visser 't Hooft refers to this incident in a single sentence in his *Memoirs* (p. 225), where he says that Bereczky was "strongly challenged."

however, the question pressed: Did the covenant at Amsterdam include "mission" as well as "unity," and if so, in what terms?

The issue was faced at the same Central Committee meeting in idyllic Rolle in 1951 when East-West world pressures were severe. A key figure was Lesslie Newbigin. His passions ran 100% in two directions at once: evangelism, as his *South India Diary* so marvellously revealed, and organic church union, as his defense of the South India Scheme of Union demonstrated. Newbigin had steered the drafting of the Amsterdam Message (and read it out in such majestic voice as to all but defy amendment). By talent, experience, and reputation, he was uniquely situated to assist in formulating the relation between mission and unity in the ecumenical movement.

Varied feelings could be discerned in both the "mission" and "WCC" constituencies. To an unprecedented degree, the new post-Christendom situation of the churches in the West had put them in a missionary situation. Would the ecumenical movement respond to this need? At the same time, some appeared to assume that the "missionary" era of the church had been superseded by the "ecumenical" era and that the worldwide missionary obligation had thus lost its urgency.

Many in younger and older churches alike felt that missions were connected with a bygone era of organizations controlled by the West. Others feared that if the WCC left missionary concerns to another agency and became the province of ecclesiastics, it would lose its openness and commitment to the world's needs. And, perhaps the weightiest problem of all, the WCC was in fact rejected by considerable numbers of Christians who, in the name of missionary concern, refused to be bound up with a council of churches.[29]

The response to these difficulties is contained in the statement, approved at Rolle, on "The Calling of the Church to Mission and Unity." This statement vigorously addresses confusions as to important terms, especially "ecumenical." Properly used, the word, coming from the Greek term *oikoumene* (the whole inhabited earth), describes "everything that relates to the whole task of the whole Church to bring the Gospel to the whole world. It therefore covers equally the missionary movement and the movement towards unity, and must not be used to describe the latter in contradistinction to the former."

The issue, however, goes beyond etymological precision. At stake is the gospel. Division in thought between mission and unity is overcome only "as we return to Christ Himself, in Whom the Church has its being and its task, and to a fresh understanding of what He has

---

29. Central Committee minutes, 1951, pp. 65ff.

Lesslie Newbigin

done, is doing and will do." This work is reconciliation, and in the reconciliation to God-in-Christ we are made ambassadors of Christ, be-
seeching others to be reconciled to him. The thought thus runs from
the past, present, and future work of Christ in reconciliation, and from
"reconciliation" to the decisive turn to "ambassadors."

Thus grounded in the work of Christ, both "mission" and
"unity" are essential to the being of the church and its function as the
Body of Christ. In this way, the wholeness of Christ's work defines the
work of the church, and the church participates in the work of Christ.

At root, the document is akin to the Toronto Statement. Perhaps for that reason, the WCC gained credibility. Not only the "church
and churches" problem, but also the "mission and unity" problem

achieved a basic resolution early in the Council's life, through a collective turn to Christ and to the Body of Christ.

In 1958, on the WCC's tenth anniversary, an editorialist wrote in *The Times* of London that "the moment is ripe for an expression of gratitude, in which many churches and Christians will share, for this lighthouse in a stormy sea."[30] To the extent that the World Council of Churches was such a beacon, it was because the covenant had been tested, confirmed, and strengthened.

---

30. *The Times,* August 30, 1958; reprinted in *Ecumenical Review,* XI (1959), 112f.

6

Interlude: My Role

I had been in Geneva[1] about a year when a letter arrived from Harold Fey proposing that I join the editorial staff of the *Christian Century* with a view to a long-range career there. I took the matter to Visser 't Hooft.

WCC offices were located at 17, Route de Malagnou, once a small estate. The gate-house accommodated inter-church aid, the finance and administration staff, and the concierge. Further on, to the right was a large square building housing the Lutheran World Federation. Behind that was a wooden barracks, purchased from World War II surplus, in which varied staff baked in the summer and froze in the winter. Straight ahead was the chalet, the main house of the old estate, scene of afternoon tea, the meeting room, and the library. Visser 't Hooft's office was up one flight of stairs on the front right of the building, mine on the same floor at the left. Another associate general secretary, Francis House, an Anglican ecumenical veteran who organized the Oslo youth conference in 1947 and specialized in Orthodox/Anglican relations, had an office close to mine, subsequently occupied by Paul Verghese of India (now Metropolitan Paulos Mar Gregorios). All these offices had once been bedrooms.

---

1. After the period 1948-54 in the WCC's New York office, I went to Geneva, immediately after the Evanston Assembly, as associate general secretary and director of the Division of Studies. (See Evanston Report, pp. 174-215.) There were four Associate General Secretaries, each to collaborate with the General Secretary in general policy and administration, and each to be the director of a program division. The Division of Studies included Faith and Order (with its own constitution and commission), Church and Society, Evangelism, and Missionary Studies (which was also the research department of the International Missionary Council and based in London).

Early offices of the WCC, 17 Route de Malagnou (WCC Photo)

Willem A. Visser 't Hooft — familiarly known as Wim (pro-nounced "Vim") — listened to Fey's suggestion carefully and replied at once: "I can't see it. It's an important job, and you could probably do it, but you're not really an editor. You're an engineer, an ecumenical en-gineer." I had never thought of it that way, but it was true that I wanted more than anything else to help make the "ecumenical" *happen.*

My work fell into three categories: engineering ecumenical events, engineering to continue the growth of an emerging ecumenical intellectual tradition, and engineering in response to trouble. This chap-ter discusses the first two; Chapters 11 and 14 the third. Not a little of the excitement of this work from 1948 to 1963 arose from my close as-sociation throughout with Visser 't Hooft.

ENGINEERING ECUMENICAL EVENTS

In response to Visser 't Hooft's invitation at Buck Hill Falls in 1947, the family and I had arrived on a Saturday in late May 1948 at the Pension Sergy in Geneva, where we spent the summer. In the midst of our un-packing, the phone rang. It was Visser 't Hooft, calling to welcome us and to ask, "Can you come tomorrow afternoon to a meeting at Bossey with a few of us concerned with Amsterdam?" It was a question in form only; but I was very glad to be included. Hendrik Kraemer—in my eyes the giant of Madras — was there, as were Nils Ehrenström, Visser 't Hooft's wartime colleague in the provisional days of the WCC, who now headed up the Study Department, in charge of the preparatory work for the First Assembly, Oliver Tomkins of Faith and Order, over from London, and Visser 't Hooft himself. In retrospect I saw the meeting as my baptism in First Assembly planning; at the time, I was more impressed with the people present than with the substance. At its end, Visser 't Hooft asked me to see him at 9:00 the next morning.

As I entered, he motioned to an ancient and excessively un-comfortable leather chair (which, with its twin, seemed endowed with immortality—they survived even the move into the new headquarters in 1964) and began at once. "I hope you don't think that all you are going to do is organize the visitors' conference at Amsterdam. We need more than that." I told him I was quite willing to do anything needed.

"Good. You have just organized a large conference [the Inter-seminary Movement conference]. I have never done that. Here is a list of people. Go see them. Ask what they are doing. I want you to tell me whether everything is being done as it should be. The Assembly con-venes on August 22. Report to me."

I asked if the people would be expecting me, and received a quick assenting nod. "When do you want a report?"

"In a week."

Had I then known Visser 't Hooft well, I would have recognized that the Saturday phone call, the Sunday meeting at Bossey, and this assignment probably signalled trouble. I was ready in a week, with no option but to be frank. "We're in trouble," I told him. "Much is behind schedule, some hasn't been started, and some hasn't even been thought of." I offered two or three examples, and said I could go on, but he didn't want that.

"Can we get ready by the time of the Assembly?"

"Yes, but just."

"Go ahead," he said, "and keep in touch with me, especially if there is any trouble."

We were ready just on time. I flew from Geneva to Amster-dam with Wim, carrying about 100 crucial stencils. Wim said not to worry about customs; he waved a diplomatic passport and we sailed through.

The mechanism of the Assembly functioned, which secured my nomination as organizer for the next two Assemblies as well — Evanston in 1954 and New Delhi in 1961.[2] In addition, it fell to me after 1954 to organize the annual "summer meetings," when the committees for some dozen departments met, nearly 200 people, followed by the Executive and Central Committees, also numbering some 200.

"Ecumenical engineering" meant something special to me. As I understood ministry, every act and word, every plan and stratagem must be carried out so as to help or enable people to respond to the ever-present Holy Spirit of God-in-Christ. The enabling measures varied endlessly, but at the bottom ecumenical engineering meant using my training to create occasions within which the Holy Spirit—who was already there—might work. The presupposition of the whole was this "already there," already searching for the human heart, already engaged with the powers of life and history, already fashioning, upholding, and renewing the Body of Christ.

Ecumenical engineering was never a task of receiving a blueprint, whether from Visser 't Hooft or the WCC Central Committee, and putting it into effect. Plans were developed, put through rigorous examination by staff and Central Committee, and subsequently followed through in organization.

The most obvious problem arose from the international, intercultural character of the WCC membership. Differing languages, cultures, and nationalities required special measures to facilitate communication, especially in Assemblies. Written translation and oral interpretation required many translators and interpreters as well as equipment. Small groups led by competent people lay at the foundation of all deliberation, and Assemblies had to be organized to provide for them. Systems of chairing, note-taking, reporting, and drafting had to be devised, explained, and used. Liaison work among groups concerned with different aspects of the work was required. The objective of all was to facilitate open, free communication.

2. *The First Six Years, Report of the Central Committee to the Second Assembly*, p. 19. For Amsterdam, I was putting into place plans already made and machinery already fashioned, in feverish haste. For the Evanston and the New Delhi Assemblies I had staff responsibility for design and organization from the beginning (*ibid.*, p. 106). Descriptions of the complex structure of the Assemblies are found in the Amsterdam, Evanston, and New Delhi reports. Assembly staff—mostly volunteers—numbered in the hundreds. At Evanston my associate William K. Du Val produced a miracle of administration, one illustration of which was that seven tons of mimeograph paper were run off, collated, and distributed to audiences at times reaching 7000 people. Walter Wagoner was the liaison with Northwestern University, where he was chaplain. At New Delhi, Jens Thomsen was my administrative associate throughout, handling the complexities of housing and bus transportation as well as a large staff. Korula Jacob, general secretary of the National Christian Council of India, undertook the initial intricate work of planning local arrangements and liaison with the government of India.

Second, balance in representation was essential. Some of the pressure points, where imbalance was disastrous, were European/US, Western/Third World, black/white, Protestant/Anglican/Orthodox, clergy/laity, men/women, theologians/non-theologians. Imbalance in the meeting as a whole or in any part of it produced resentment and closure.

Third, the WCC inherited a tradition of using major meetings to address world and church conditions, whether by resolutions, messages, or longer reports. This demanded its own processes of preparation, discussion, reporting, drafting, and liaison. It also required expertise, provided by inviting special consultants to the meetings to supplement the expertise of the official delegates. The roster of speakers was drawn up to provide the most stimulating thought on the major topics of the meeting.

Good engineering also had to take into account the public impact of a meeting. At Amsterdam, six thousand people attended a youth rally addressed by Martin Niemöller. The intensity of Dutch hatred of the German language in the postwar period could scarcely be measured. Niemöller was introduced by these words: "We will now hear a message in a language which we learned to hate from a man whom we've learned to love." The standing ovation he received was "a tribute not only to the beloved German church leader but also to the power of the Christian faith to express itself in acts of charity and forgiveness."[3]

During the Evanston Assembly, 125,000 packed Chicago's Soldier Field—with 25,000 more outside—for a pageant of massed choirs, music, and dance celebrating the themes of creation, redemption, and consummation.[4] The Assembly, which brought delegates from Eastern Europe into a heightened atmosphere of anti-Communism in the US and dared to speak of "Living Together in a Divided World," surpassed all previous religious events in attention from the US mass media.[5]

The number of journalists accredited at the Third Assembly in New Delhi was the largest, secular or religious, on record to the time.[6] Amidst the resurgent Hinduism of India, independent for less than 15

---

3. Amsterdam Report, p. 174.

4. Evanston Report, pp. 21-23. Other public events included a summer ecumenical institute, sponsored by ten Chicago seminaries, with 1785 in attendance; an outdoor concert by the Chicago Symphony Orchestra (when I asked Karl Barth what he thought should be played to mark the Assembly theme of "Christian hope," he replied instantly, "Mozart, vierzig, G Moll." So it was); and an exhibit of religious works by the Chicago Art Institute.

5. Samuel McCrae Cavert, "Evanston and the American Churches," *Ecumenical Review*, VII (1955), 112.

6. Report of the general secretary, in the Central Committee minutes, 1962, p. 2.

years, the Assembly addressed the theme "Jesus Christ — the Light of the World."

In every meeting, large or small, the engineering questions were: What public is to be addressed? What word is to be spoken? How may a situation be created in which the meeting may best witness to the presence of God-in-Christ?

Engineering also had to provide means to accomplish the WCC's business with clarity, participation, and decision in the meetings of the Assembly, Central Committee, and Executive Committee, to whom the general secretary and staff were accountable.

In the early years US churches provided some 70-80% of the WCC budget. One might have feared that they would exert undue influence on WCC policy, especially when the issues became heated. But as Bishop Oxnam in the first six years and Eugene Carson Blake in the next chaired and reported for the finance committee, invited discussion, asked for and received approval, and as one listened in the hallways and at the dining tables, there was never heard a whisper of suspicion that "dollar imperialism" was in effect.[7] I did not always like the theology I heard from US mouths, but I was proud of the way the churches of my country handled WCC finances.

AN EMERGING, ECUMENICAL INTELLECTUAL TRADITION

Organizing WCC Assemblies and "summer meetings" was absorbing for a time, but I did not want to be engaged only in that kind of engineering. And so the chance to assume major responsibility for engineering ecumenical study appealed to me.

One attraction lay in the heritage of a substantial precedent. On the basis of what the forerunners had done, study seemed to be the foundation of the whole ecumenical initiative in recent history.[8] Faith and Order, Life and Work, and the International Missionary Council had all been primarily study-oriented. Study was needed to select the most important—that is, the most pressing, most strategic, most divisive — problems. Study required cross-fertilization by writing and by conference of Christian insight and experience. Study evoked the effort to crystallize an "ecumenical mind."[9]

---

7. Visser 't Hooft, *Memoirs*, p. 344.
8. Visser 't Hooft, *Genesis and Formation*, p. 59.
9. *The World Council of Churches: Its Process of Formation* (Geneva: WCC, 1946),

Study went to the heart of things. Its task was to insure that the intellectual content of the growing ecumenical tradition did not dissipate under the pressure of increased ecumenical activity. This implied that study was instrumental to the renewal of church life, adding depth and providing direction in the midst of ferment.[10] Study also had the function of thinking ahead, seeking to anticipate and thus be prepared for trends likely to become dominant in the future.

Ecumenical study was not an "objective" pursuit in the modern academic sense. It began from commitment to God-in-Christ and proceeded to discern the meaning of that commitment for the church and the world. This involved the development of "ecumenical theology."

But ecumenical theology was not a search for a "common denominator." It did, however, stand in substantial contrast to customary church, confessional, or denominational theology. K. E. Skysgaard, a Danish theologian whom I did not know well but admired, a man whose rather dour and cramped platform personality was more than offset by a brilliant imagination, described ecumenical study in the language of "symbolics." Symbolics, he wrote, is the discipline in which the "doctrine and total ethos of every Christian body are set forth." The ecumenical situation, in which there is no monologue, but rather continuous struggle to appreciate the logic, belief, and psychological conditioning of others, produces "dramatized symbolics." The drama lies in the struggle, the constant exercise of imagination and understanding, climaxing in the acceptance of the judgment which results from finally submitting all to the "ultimate authority of the truth of God's word."[11] To "engineer" within these realms was to move very close to the spiritual nerve centers of the whole enterprise.

All the organizational units in the WCC of the time carried on studies; and there was the major Division of Studies which only carried on studies. This came about because of Visser 't Hooft's fear that if there were no division specifically charged with "study" this historic ecumenical function might be neglected. That could not happen in Faith in Order because of its constitution, but elsewhere activity might overtake reflection.

---

p. 79; see also *The First Six Years*, p. 28; Robert S. Bilheimer, "Problems of Ecumenical Action," *Ecumenical Review*, IV (1952), 355-67; *Evanston to New Delhi* (Geneva: WCC, 1951), pp. 69f.

10. Visser 't Hooft, *The Pressure of Our Common Calling*, pp. 73-75.

11. K. E. Skysgaard, "Faith and Order—Our Oneness in Christ and Our Disunity as Churches," *Ecumenical Review*, VI (1953), 10-18. For variations see Samuel McCrae Cavert, *The Road to Unity*, p. 45; Walter Freytag, "Ecumenical Study Work," in *Division of Studies Bulletin*, Vol. 1, p. 7.

Everyone in and out of the Division of Studies participated in a staff study coordinating group, which I chaired. This relieved people of the pressure of becoming either defensive or imperialistic by giving access to the overall ecumenical function. It gave me a needed way of getting a large part of my job done, namely taking initiative in proposing new areas of needed study.

The coordination was substantive as well as administrative. It seemed to grow as from within, by an inner logic. "All our work," I reported, "deals in one way or another with the Christian understanding of history and our understanding of the Church. . . . This raises questions of both ultimate goals and expectations and immediate goals. . . . We struggle for new categories realizing that the churches do not exhibit the Church."[12]

Throughout, I was conscious of a debt to my former professor, H. Richard Niebuhr. In his classic book *Christ and Culture*,[13] he made penetrating distinctions as to how Christians and churches have historically related Christ to human culture. Two of his five models seemed to me to fall outside the pale, at least in the situation in which we were working: the view that Christ is *against* culture, and its opposite, that Christ is *dominated* by culture. Three distinct but kindred views, however, defined "the church of the center": (1) that Christ provides a *synthesis* of culture; (2) that the relation of Christ to culture is a *paradox* of rejection and judgment on one side, and of salvation on the other; (3) and that Christ is the *transformer* of culture.

It seemed to me that the post-Christendom era focused attention primarily on "the church of the center." Like many in the WCC orbit, I did not respond to the idea of Christ as the center of a post-Christendom synthesis of culture, but that did not rule it out. On the other hand, our era gave credence to those who saw Christ and culture in a paradoxical relationship, to those who spoke prophetically of both the corruption of culture and the hope of Christ. At the same time, the post-Christendom era seemed to beg for the view that Christ is the transformer of culture, engaging its corrupt yet also constructive elements with the promise of transformation both within and beyond human history. Personally, I felt myself somewhere between, partly a realist with those who saw Christ and culture in a paradoxical relation, but mostly looking to transformation.

Far more important was the perspective Niebuhr's analysis gave to my work of "ecumenical engineering." Niebuhr once told me that he

12. Central Committee minutes, 1962, p. 15.
13. New York: Harper and Brothers, 1951.

had intended his work as a venture in "ecumenical theology." It was that in its basic categories of Christ, church, and world. It was that also in its comprehensive discernment of historical movements and their patterns. But, especially when combined with Skysgaard's idea of "symbolics," it also seemed to me to be normative ecumenical theology, in the sense of indicating the fundamental ingredients of the ecumenical vocation and task. As I saw it, we were all engaged in a continuous effort to discern "the church of the center" and to arrange for the "dramatized symbolics" involved in perceiving its mission and its unity amid the portent of post-Christendom world cultures.

VISSER 'T HOOFT

I was fortunate in being closely associated with Visser 't Hooft. Though a good administrator, he was no engineer at all, but unlike many administrators he saw the value of engineering, and that was the secret of our collaboration. Twice he entrusted me with highly sensitive missions, largely I think because he sensed in advance that the solution for each required ecumenical engineering. And he never interfered with my work in ecumenical study, partly because I saw to it that he was constantly involved in it, and partly because he viewed it, too, as an engineering task.

It is obvious from his achievements that Visser 't Hooft was a policy maker of genius, an administrator of high capacity, a diplomat *par excellence*, and a prophetic voice. During my years in the WCC's New York office, he insisted that I go to the winter Executive Committee meeting and the summer departmental and Central Committee meetings. There, among other things, I took the minutes. Being the author of some dozen volumes of WCC minutes does not exactly qualify one as a literary genius, but it does provide learning opportunities. I often played the game of guessing how Visser 't Hooft would respond to questions and situations, usually learning how not to respond, but always discovering much about Wim.

He revealed himself in his work. Intense energy, sometimes at rest but instantly galvanized, characterized everything from his entry into a room, to conversation, to his ultimate commitment, the latter always expressed by the words "calling" and "common calling." Energy was in his walk, his mind, his choice of words, his delivery of them, his eyes. One met him with energy, or one didn't meet him. His staff was full of energetic people. During times when he would be in the Geneva office for a long period with little happening he would seem to age: one

W. A. Visser 't Hooft (WCC Photo)

could trace fatigue in his face; his hand would shake so as to rattle the coffee cup; he would tend to shuffle papers. Then a visitor would arrive or an issue would come up which demanded attention, or a conference or a speech, and he would slough off twenty years, vibrant again.

That energy showed itself in Visser 't Hooft's capacity of discernment. He did not engage in long analyses, nor did he listen to them patiently. His mind grasped the essential point—whether of world historical developments, proposed departmental programs, or drifts in the Central Committee or the life of the member churches—with virtually immediate clarity and penetration. It was a capacity that made him unable to suffer fools gladly. When conversation dawdled, whether in the office or in the Central Committee or at 4 o'clock tea, one could almost see his mind wander, only to spring to life again when something "interesting" was said or happened.

I believe it was the intensity of his capacity of discernment that produced Wim's most unfortunate trait. He could and did hurt people, those of whom he was fond and those to whom he was a virtual stranger. I often wondered whether he had any idea how deeply these wounds struck. His acid tongue lashed out when people seemed to miss the point as he saw it, or went on and on explaining a point, or were simply obtuse in grasping it. He had little gift for putting up with what appeared to be the foolishness of others. His irritation rose, his rudeness obtruded, his anger flashed when his own discernment ran ahead of our ability to keep up with it.

Here he needed help and we all tried—mostly by simply "taking it" for the love of the job and, after we cooled off, for the love of Wim. Robert Mackie, a Scottish pastor and an associate general secretary, carried on a whole ministry of healing staff members who had been wounded by Wim. Others who were close to him helped, like Philippe Maury and Madeleine Barot. My own role was mostly preventive: I came to know Wim well enough to recognize before a speaker was finished how Wim would react. When proposals were made that seemed likely to evoke Wim's impatience or anger, I would enter the discussion quickly, reinterpreting the matter to meet his mind. In the study coordinating group and the small staff executive group, essentially the "staff cabinet," it became a habit for Wim not to react without first giving me a chance.

Sometimes irritating, sometimes hurtful to persons, this driving mental instinct of discernment was nevertheless a priceless gift. Wim was always accessible. No departmental staff had to go through the appropriate associate general secretary to consult with him, and the benefit of consultation with Wim was high. Moreover, he had a pastoral gift, for he was a good listener and helped many a person to sort out problems. And, supremely, his gift of discernment kept the WCC, always being pulled in different directions, on a near-even course.

The capacity of discernment was nowhere more evident than in Visser 't Hooft's exposition of the gospel. He was not an academic theologian (though respected by them) but an expositor of the gospel, of the place of the church in the gospel, and of the relation of churches and world to the gospel. Admittedly, that involved theology, but his series of relatively short books make their points with stabbing insight rather than lengthy disquisition. To be sure, he valued scholarship and knew it and used it. But his passion was to begin with the gospel and to expound its meaning. This is the point behind his insistence that he could not make a budget without theologizing. He was not seeking to justify administrative arrangements by doing that. Rather, he sought direction. Not an evangelist, he had evangelistic power. That lay in his capacity to discern the meaning of Christ, the meaning of a situation, and the meaning of their relationship.

Visser 't Hooft was a first-class example of a rare being. He was a genuinely prophetic church policy-maker and administrator. The prophetic quality lay in his capacity to discern and his fearlessness in laying out what he discerned. He wrote and preached a prophetic gospel. He acted a prophetic role in international affairs. He attacked ecclesiasticism in a manner worthy of Amos. He had a prophetic sense of mission. Even his insistence on tying the ecumenical movement to the churches, frequently questioned, was prophetic. He understood clearly that the churches were the carriers of the Body of Christ; and an ecumenical movement that was not tied to the churches had no relevance to anything. Given that, Visser 't Hooft could then turn the whole around, bringing "church" to bear on churches in withering analyses. Because he loved the church, he loved the churches.

Reflecting after the breathtaking changes of Vatican II, I felt that the modern ecumenical movement could be summed up by reference to three people, to whom it owed more than to anyone else. One was John R. Mott, the founder; the second was W. A. Visser 't Hooft, who put it on an enduring course; the third was Pope John XXIII, who transformed it by beginning the completion of its scope.

III

CHRIST THE LORD:
LORDSHIP, UNITY, AND
WITNESS

7

The Lordship of Christ over the Church and the World

LOYALTY WITHOUT HIERARCHY

What conditions, what faith produced the Amsterdam covenant and enabled it to develop? The people who "covenanted together" in 1948 moved warily in a new world. Christendom was no more. Europe and vast parts of Asia lay in ruins. Populations were being shunted across borders and oceans. New wars threatened, now under the spectre of nuclear weapons. The task of reconstruction in Europe was at hand. The independence of India, soon to be followed elsewhere in Asia and somewhat later in Africa, presented an enormous challenge, calling forth vision and energy.

Did the covenant mean that the churches and their representatives were huddling together for comfort in reaction to their changed status in the world?

Had the Western churches been looking only for warmth amid the cold winds of devastation, they would have used the language of "the church against culture," turning their shoulders against their fellow human beings. Had the churches in the newly independent nations perceived only their nationalistic opportunity, they would have ignored their ecumenical calling, using the language of "the church of culture." As the act of "covenanting with" one another was understood, however, it required the language, posture, and faith of "the church of the center," which sought, in various ways, the transformation of society.

What was to be transformed? Much of the remainder of this

book looks at the answers given by the ecumenical movement during this period of its life. Here we note two aspects of an intense, world-wide spiritual struggle.

The first had to do with society—the struggle of different worlds to exist, to develop, to live with one another. In the political realm, it was the "West," the US and its allies, the "East," the USSR and its allies, and the "non-aligned," whose movement would take shape in 1955 following the conference in Bandung, Indonesia, led by Nehru and Sukarno. In the economic realm, it was the North and the South, with the wealth and power of the mostly white North (albeit with substantial areas of poverty) standing in contrast to the poverty and powerlessness of the darker-skinned peoples of the South. There was also the religious world of Christianity amid other vigorous religions. And there was the world of fast-developing technology beginning to permeate non-technical cultures. These worlds were not mere abstractions; they were robust, and their varied claims and encounters spelled out the depth of an inherently spiritual situation.

Moreover, as the Amsterdam covenant developed, rival hopes were vying for human loyalty. The substance of one was democratic humanism, in which democracy devoted to humane ends appeared as a saving hope for people on many continents. Scientific humanism, which saw "science" as rescuing people from misery, spelled hope for many. Marxism offered energy-releasing hope to multitudes oppressed by poverty and powerlessness and longing for national and religious renaissance. These hopes could be neatly categorized, but they seldom appeared that way. It was more arresting to speak of "nationalism, reviving Fascism, devotion to one or another sort of economic and technological order as the way of salvation, nostalgic efforts to recapture the supposed glories of a bygone era, faith in the power of political and military force."[1]

Against this backdrop, the people of the ecumenical covenant consistently affirmed "the Lordship of Christ over the church and the world." This was not just a theological proposition or a mere expres-

---

1. For the foregoing see Amsterdam Vol. 1, pp. 13-16; Robert L. Calhoun, "The Dilemma of Humanitarian Modernism," Oxford Vol. 2, p. 81; Evanston Report, pp. 4, 28-47; Eugene Lyman, "The Kingdom of God and History," Oxford Vol. 3, pp. 102-104; Central Committee minutes, 1955, p. 15; Executive Committee minutes, February 1954, p. 2; Philip Potter, "Youth and the Evanston Assembly," Ecumenical Review, VII (1954), 105-10; "Theme and Preparatory Studies for the First Assembly of the World Council of Churches, in 1948," mimeographed, Study Department of the WCC, 1946; Visser 't Hooft, "Europe —Survival or Renewal?", in Charles Tudor Leber (ed.), World Faith in Action (Indianapolis: Bobbs-Merrill, 1951), pp. 73-96.

sion of intense, subjective religious experience. It was a confident truth claim, born of experience and tried by fire.[2] The ultimate source of the covenant was the Lordship itself.

It was not that the delegates in Amsterdam decided that they needed a theme, thought one up, worked on its phrasing, and adopted it for use henceforth. Their claim that Jesus Christ is the Lord of the church and the world arose from trials and commitment. Several moments of personal encounter made that plain to me.

In 1946, shortly after the war's end, Philippe Maury of France spent an evening at our home on Long Island. The first postwar general secretary of the WSCF, later to be a leader in the WCC, the brilliant, imposing Maury radiated energy and charm. He had fought in the Maquis during the war, a close comrade of Albert Camus. In the course of our conversation I asked him if he had ever heard "The Battle Hymn of the Republic." As an historian with a degree from the Sorbonne, he knew the meaning of the US Civil War, and he was fresh from his own freedom-fighting, but he had not heard the hymn. As a record of it played, I watched him closely. At the moment of "with a beauty in His bosom that transfigures you and me . . . as He died to make men holy let us die to make men free," Maury's warm, brown eyes deepened. He stood and began to pace the floor, enrapt. *Lordship*.

World Council meetings were being held in the English cathedral town of Chichester in the summer of 1949. As was the custom, evening prayers were at nine o'clock. The sessions had run late, and only a few were present. Anglican Bishop Stephen Neill led, speaking in his quiet, penetrating, controlled manner of Jesus' meeting with the centurion (Matt. 8:9). "I also am a man under authority." Neill had achieved one of the most brilliant records ever at Cambridge. When he announced that he intended to go to the mission field in India, his advisors in university and church said, "Not the mission field. Your talents would be wasted. It is not worth it." In India, he had learned to speak Tamil, native Tamil-speaking people told me, as it was rarely heard from even the highly educated among them. It was the beginning of a long life under authority, of evangelistic power in India and the West, in speech and in writing. *Lordship*.

A WCC study conference on "Lordship" brought theologian Barnabas Nagy from Budapest to Germany. Because he did not want to

2. See the Message of the Second Assembly, Evanston Report, pp. 1-3; Central Committee minutes, 1962, p. 124; "The Inner Life of the Church," in the Madras Report, pp. 54f.; Madras Vol. 7, pp. 20f.; D. T. Niles, "The Calling of the Church to Mission and Unity," in the Lund Report, p. 215; Visser 't Hooft, *None Other Gods*, pp. 99f.

talk where he might be overheard, we walked together in the woods. No one could meet with Eastern Europeans without feeling a great sorrow. They had fought the Nazis; they had hoped for peace and liberation and reconstruction. Instead, they got stern oppression and a life of physical drabness beyond description. "What," I asked Nagy, "keeps you going? What does the Lordship of Christ mean?" A quiet moment, and then: "It means the *hypomone,* the 'steadfast, patient endurance' of the New Testament." *Lordship.*

In a reflective moment in conversation in his office, Visser 't Hooft once told me: "My verse is in Second Corinthians [4:6]: 'For it is the God who said, "Let light shine out of darkness" who has shone in our hearts to give the light of the knowledge of the glory of God in the face of Christ.'" From that scion of the European intelligentsia had come an acknowledgment that his favorite Bible text spoke of Christ *in our hearts!* When Wim prayed spontaneously in staff meetings, a sense of reverent awe immediately communicated itself through his voice and the deliberate pace of his speech. Light out of darkness, the light of knowing the glory of God. *Lordship.*

WHY "LORDSHIP"

The ecumenical affirmation of the Lordship of Christ had its base in a theological renaissance that began in the 1920s and carried force through the first decades of the life of the WCC. This new movement was often associated with its most prominent figure, Karl Barth; and the question of how Barthian was the WCC was asked frequently. If by "Barthian" one meant the sort of disciple who could not make a theological point without prooftexting it from the writings of Barth, the answer is, Not at all. Although Visser 't Hooft was frequently associated with Barth, negatively and positively, I never heard him justify a theological point of his own by reference to Barth. Instead, he would quote Scripture. And whether one was talking with Paul Minear from the USA or Hans-Ruedi Weber from Switzerland, the point of reference was the same: not Barth but the Bible. Therein lies the clue.

The World Council both reflected and stimulated the general movement of biblical theology of the period,[3] and for good reason. On

---

3. The point is substantiated by most of the WCC literature cited in this book. Particularly pertinent are *Bulletins,* reports (including reports to the Second and Third Assemblies), and pamphlets produced by the WCC Study Department (later Division of Studies). The "Guiding Principles for the Interpretation of the Bible," accepted by the ecu-

the one hand, the movement was a broad one, existing in many forms in many churches in many countries. Barth had been a prime force with the publication of the second edition of his *Epistle to the Romans* in 1921, but something had already been going on.

One day when Visser 't Hooft's phone interrupted my conversation with him, I wandered to the bookshelf and found four volumes of P. T. Forsyth, whom I had greatly admired in divinity school.[4] After the call was over, I mentioned that. Smiling, Wim said: "You know, one day Karl Barth was standing where you are, and pointed to these books and said: 'He was Barth before Barth.'" It does not detract from Barth's influence to suggest that the rise of biblical theology in so many places and ways indicated a movement far broader than the designation "Barthian" implies.

But there was a more important reason for the WCC turn to Scripture. To put it simply, where else could it turn? When Orthodox and Protestants were locked in debate, what was the court of appeal? Protestants could go to Luther and Calvin and Wesley, but what did that mean to Orthodox or to the Anglicans, who did not turn naturally to the Reformers? The Orthodox could go to the Fathers, but it was all but impossible for Protestants to take the Fathers' reading of Scripture as the starting point.

Similarly, when Germans talked theology, they spoke in a very different idiom from even the so-called "neo-Orthodox" Americans. In 1951 Reinhold Niebuhr almost walked out on a meeting in which the most prominent European was Karl Barth. Anglicans injected varied theologies, as did those from other communions and countries. Perforce, Scripture became the companion of ecumenical discussion, whether it concerned theology as such, or theology implicit in policy.

Other forces, too, produced a concentration on the "Lordship" theme. The pressures of the times worked to concentrate life on loyalty, power, and authority.

---

menical study conference at Wadham College, Oxford, in 1949, are published in *Ecumenical Review*, II (1949), 81-86. See also *Jesus Christ, the Light of the World* (Geneva: World Council of Churches, 1962); Jaroslav Pelikan, *The Finality of Jesus Christ in an Age of Universal History: Dilemma of the Third Century* (Richmond: John Knox Press, 1966); Alan Richardson and Wolfgang Schweitzer, *Biblical Authority for Today* (Philadelphia: Westminster Press, 1951); Edwin H. Robertson, "The Place and Use of the Bible in the Life of the Churches," in the Central Committee minutes, 1959, p. 175; W. Schweitzer, "The Bible and the Church's Message to the World," *Ecumenical Review*, II (1949), 123-32; Oliver S. Tomkins, *The Wholeness of the Church*, p. 32; Olive Wyon, "Evidences of New Life in the Church Universal," in Amsterdam Vol. 1, pp. 117-19.

4. In particular, *The Principle of Authority* (1913; repr. London: Independent Press, 1952) and *The Person and Place of Christ* (London: Independent Press, 1909).

Loyalty

The struggles of the different worlds we have described put strong pressure on the loyalty of the churches within the nations and cultures. The experience and influence of the Confessing Church in Germany and elsewhere were never far in the background. Equally prominent was the steadfast witness of minority churches in Asia. The vision of US churches for peace and reconciliation amid victory was also present. Everywhere, loyalty was put to the test: Christ or Hitler; Christ or the new nationalisms.

In the summer of 1947, a large group had been convened at the Ecumenical Institute to prepare for the Amsterdam Assembly. As people were gathered on the lawn at tea-time one day, the sky a marvellous blue, Lake Geneva and Mont Blanc in the background, an interesting group drew my attention. Caught up in vigorous discussion were Emil Brunner, an early leader of the theological renaissance of the time, John Baillie, Scottish theologian and principal of New College, Edinburgh, Fr. Florovsky, and M. M. Thomas of India, more than a generation younger than the rest, destined to give major leadership to the WCC. At the moment M. M. Thomas was vociferous. As I listened, it became clear why they were so animated. From their different experiences of the gospel in Eastern and Western Europe, Great Britain and India, they discerned something held deeply in common. Better said, there was a mutual recognition of being bound by the gospel even more closely because of the differences in their experience.

Time and again as Asians, Europeans, Americans, and Africans met one another in the WCC, one could see the same electricity of mutual recognition, discovery of one another's experience, and response to the test of loyalty. This experience of recognition fired ecumenical growth and vigor for years. For all, the loyalty was to Christ who rules our lives, Christ as Lord.

Power

"Lordship" went beyond a demonstration of loyalty, however profound and personal. Power was involved. Brunner, preparing for the Amsterdam Assembly, wrote that he could not

> follow Jakob Burckhardt . . . , who opposes power to culture and makes culture, so to speak, the innocent martyr of power. . . . It is not culture; it is only respect for justice, love, and reverence for the divine law which are capable of overcoming the lust for and the misuse of power. It is only that mind

which would rather suffer injustice than do it which is willing to "overcome evil with good," which is capable of resisting the temptation even of very great power. The greater the power, the greater the temptation of being godlike. Against this temptation no education or culture can prevail. The "demonism" of power is overcome by Jesus Christ alone.[5]

This conclusion was not an insight of Brunner's alone; it was a fact of ecumenical church life. In 1936 Pastor Iwand wrote of the Confessing Church in Germany: "God's Word reassembled the people, it strengthened the confessing Christians, it gave to leaders and pastors the armour of the Spirit; the Scripture was opened to us as had not happened for a long time, for the Lord Himself was among us with His Word and His Spirit."[6]

Fourteen years later in Toronto, the Central Committee spoke in confessing tones of the ecumenical movement itself as

a deep, spiritual current in the life of the Churches. As men and women who stand themselves within the movement, we would go further and say, this rediscovery of the essential oneness of the Church of Christ which occurred in so many places at one and the same time, and this eager turning of the Churches toward each other, is the work of the Lord who gathers His children together in a marvellous way.[7]

One was driven back in memory to Christmas Eve 1938, when the international atmosphere was heavy with the portent of catastrophe, and Christians gathered from around the world at the missionary conference near Madras and heard the preacher speak of "the quiet coming of the Lord, the still advent of the power that was to shake the world."[8]

Authority

The affirmation of "Lordship" also contained the twin of "power," namely "authority." This reached beyond the test of loyalty, beyond the exercise of power, to Christ's authority to reveal humanity to humanity. "The Cross," wrote a commission preparing for the Second Assembly,

---

5. Emil Brunner, "Christian Responsibility in a World of Power," Amsterdam Vol. 4, p. 199.
6. Cited by Visser 't Hooft, *The Kingship of Christ*, pp. 46f.
7. Central Committee minutes, 1950, p. 64.
8. A. G. Hogg, "The Word Made Flesh," Madras Vol. 7, pp. 124-36.

is that place at the center of the world's history where the Lord of history has finally exposed the sin of the world and taken that sin upon Himself, the place where all men and all nations without exception stand revealed as enemies of God, lovers not of truth but of the lie, children not of light but of darkness, and yet where all stand revealed as beloved of God, precious in God's sight, children for whom the Son of God was content to die. . . . We are stripped naked of all our claims and pretensions and clothed afresh with His mercy. We are dead and made alive again.[9]

As that implied power but went beyond it, it suggested also the height of Christ's Lordship: the authority which enabled him to reveal, to forgive, and to save.

As time went on there were those who questioned the theme of "Lordship" on the grounds that it sanctified a hierarchical presentation of the gospel. Yet the criticism could not stand. The one to whom loyalty was given, the one from whom power derived, the one who had supreme authority was the Servant who suffered. The paradox of Servant-Lord and Lord-Servant, central to the Lordship theme, dissolved hierarchical connotations.

NEW REALITY: PRESENT AND FUTURE

The searing tests of loyalty, the discovery of power, and the recognition of authority suggest certain components in the ecumenical apprehension of Christ's Lordship, but its full scope is summed up in a word. The word itself, "eschatological,"[10] I found extremely difficult, although it rolled off the tongue of many a theologian.

Signifying a total way of understanding the gospel, "eschatological" pointed to spiritual vistas that reached far beyond other interpretations of Christ. If, for instance, Jesus was the supreme Teacher, "es-

---

9. Report of the Advisory Commission on the Main Theme—Christ the Hope of the World, in *The Christian Hope and the Task of the Church* (New York: Harper and Brothers, 1954), p. 2 (also in *Ecumenical Review*, VI [1954], 430-64).

10. See Georges Florovsky, "The Church: Her Nature and Task," Amsterdam Vol. 1, pp. 43-58; Hans Jochen Margull, *Hope in Action* (Philadelphia: Muhlenberg Press, 1962), pp. 27-33; Reinhold Niebuhr, "Christian Faith and the Common Life," Oxford Vol. IV, pp. 69-97; Visser 't Hooft, "The Church and the Churches," in *The Church and Its Function in Society*, ed. J. H. Oldham and Visser 't Hooft (Chicago and New York: Willett, Clark & Company, 1937), pp. 7-88; "Faith and Order and the Second Assembly of the WCC," in the Lund Report, pp. 128-38; "German Delegates Statement," in the Madras Report, p. 150.

chatological" transfigured that teaching from thoughts about God and life to guideposts leading to a new sphere of present and future reality. If Christ was present (in whatever manner) in the sacrament, "eschatological" put that presence into the context, not of a merely religious act of remembrance or worship, but of a foretaste and assurance of God's future. If Christ was the personal savior, "eschatological" rescued that salvation from the triviality of mere private spirituality.

Two interpenetrating aspects compose the "eschatological" meaning of the Lordship of Christ.

History and Cosmos

One aspect of "eschatological" brings together the sweep of human history and the range of the cosmos. The Lordship of Christ commands both. Christ is not the possession of the church or any one part of it. Christ is not merely the head of a religion whom those in the church go out and tell other people about. Christ is the figure in the form of a servant who was crucified by Roman soldiers, and Christ resurrected is the Lord of the principalities and powers which killed him and which operate in human history. Christ is the Lord of all human history, beginning, present, and end, and the church itself bears witness to this Lord of all.

Furthermore, Christ is the Lord of *all things*. "The doctrine of redemption," said US Lutheran theologian Joseph Sittler in an eloquent speech in New Delhi at the Third Assembly, "is meaningful only when it swings within the larger orbit of a doctrine of creation."[11] The Lord of "all things" is both final and ultimate: final in the sense of "the end," and ultimate in the sense of "you can't get beyond."[12]

Time: Present and Future

The second aspect of "eschatological" concerns time. As Christ is the Lord of history and the cosmos, he is also Lord of both the present and the future, the future and the present. This inescapable tension is difficult to express and has given rise to wide misunderstanding.[13] Chris-

11. Joseph A. Sittler, "Called to Unity," *Ecumenical Review*, XIV (1962), 177-87.

12. "The Finality of Jesus Christ in the Age of Universal History," in the WCC Division of Studies *Bulletin*, Vol. VII (1962), is a substantial treatment, raising questions for further study based on many references to "finality" in previous WCC documents. See also the New Delhi Report, p. 165.

13. Particularly associated with the term "realized eschatology," as developed by C. H. Dodd; see "The Kingdom of God and History," Oxford Vol. 3, pp. 15-38, and *The Coming of Christ* (Cambridge: Cambridge U.P., 1951): "God's victory was won; it was

tian hope depends not only on the knowledge of being "in Christ" now, but also on Christ's coming again in full glory at the consummation of history and the final establishment of the Kingdom of God.

Over this issue the WCC's most dramatic theological venture of the period almost failed. Already in 1950 the Central Committee decided on "Christ—the Hope of the World" as the theme of the Second Assembly, to be held in 1954. Under the leadership of Henry Van Dusen, a "Commission of Twenty-Five" was convened, meeting first in 1951. Present by virtue of my responsibilities for the Assembly, I offered to take notes, from which resulted a précis of every utterance of any substance made during the ten-day meeting. For me it was a concentrated graduate course in contemporary theology.

On the evening of the fourth day, it was clear that the commission was in major trouble. In essence, there was total disagreement about the meaning of the Second Coming of Christ at the end, the eschaton. Was that *the* Christian hope? In the background was an historic difference. When the Europeans spoke of hope as lodged in the Second Coming, the Anglo-Saxons heard them saying, "Sit down, O men of God, you cannot do a thing." When Anglo-Saxons insisted on the reality of present hopes, the Europeans heard them saying that the hope of the Second Coming is not sufficient and corrupting it with lesser human hopes.

With no resolution of the problem in view, there was serious talk of breaking up. Leaving the room at the end of the day, Edmund Schlink of the Confessing Church in Germany said to me, *"Schwierig, Schwierig"* — difficult, difficult. During a brief stroll on the lawn of the Ecumenical Institute where we met, Niebuhr fulminated against "the Europeans"; it emerged later that he had already packed his bags to go home.

Schlink had been asked to lead the worship service which opened the next day's work. Slight of stature, gentle, and professorial but strong in spirit and utterance, he stood before us as one wrestling with the Word of God, not as one defending a position. He spoke of the experience of the Confessing Church in Germany and of what they had learned.

> In this expectancy of the coming Lord the faithful are free from anxiety and sorrow, and wholly realistic in their judgment of the world, and full of zeal to serve both friends and enemies.

---

yet to win. Both things were true. So the Christian life became a tension between realisation and expectation" (pp. 8f.). Misunderstanding arose when one or the other side of the tension was emphasized. See also the discussion recorded in Central Committee minutes, 1953, pp. 12-16.

A true expectancy of the end is the strongest possible impetus to be watchful, to hurry, to lose no time, and to see that no one gets lost. The expectancy of the Lord releases the strongest possible zeal because it liberates man from worrying about himself. For the faithful knows himself to be sustained because Jesus has already led the way through sorrow to glory. He therefore lives in a state of unspeakable joy which makes him think no longer about himself, but of his neighbour.[14]

We all noted that it was in worship, not in argument, that Schlink had made the crucial point. From the experience of the German church struggle he had simply told how the hope of the End nourished the present hope and life of the Christian. Sitting in the service, one could feel the deadlock breaking. Discussion followed immediately. The report was completed and published, widely talked about, appreciated — as well as criticized — by the Second Assembly.[15] The whole showed that as regards the end-time and the present, a "both-and" response is required: the Lordship of Christ in the present and the future, held in a vital tension of faith.

In this view, the Lordship of Christ and the Kingdom of God were not separable. The Lordship pointed to, was the substance of, and provided the hope for a new realm of life, a new sphere of reality, into which one entered.[16] Christianity was no mere moralism, no vague "religion." "The Lordship of Christ" was a serious shorthand to designate a very different realm in which one could begin to live now. It was a realm not to be built, but rather entered into; and it also stood as the final end of "all things."

To understand "the Lordship of Christ over the world and the church" in these ways was to envisage the figure of Jesus as the center of human affairs past and present, as the one who introduces the Kingdom of God into human history, and as the one who consummates the transformation of the kingdoms of this world and the creation itself at

14. Edmund Schlink, "A Meditation on the Christian Hope," published in *Ecumenical Review*, IV (1951), 181-83.

15. The commission's reports were published in *Ecumenical Review*, IV (1953), 71ff.; V (1952), 73ff.; VI (1954), 430ff. (final report). Comments are found in *Ecumenical Review*, IV (1954), 161ff. and the Executive Committee minutes, February 1954. See also the "Statement on the Report of the Advisory Commission on the Main Theme," Evanston Report, pp. 70-72; "Declaration of the Eastern Orthodox Concerning the Main Theme of the Assembly," *ibid.*, 329ff.; and addresses by Edmund Schlink and Robert L. Calhoun to the Assembly, reprinted in *Ecumenical Review*, VII (1954), 127ff.

16. An "ecumenical classic" on this score is Hendrik Kraemer, *The Christian Message in a Non-Christian World* (New York: International Missionary Council, 1938) and its treatment of "biblical realism."

the end of time. "We do not know what is coming to us," said the Message of the Second Assembly, "but we know Who is coming. It is He who meets us every day and who will meet us at the end—Jesus Christ our Lord. Therefore we say to you: Rejoice in hope."[17]

CHURCH AND WORLD

Thus conceived, the Lordship of Christ produced an invigorating tension between the churches and the world. "Lordship" always contained a combination of the cosmic and the personal, the universal and the particular, the Great Design and the community of believers, the present and the future, the "already" and the "not yet." Some called this the "dialectical" element in Christian faith, shorthand for the tension of "both-and" as well as the result of that tension. The Lordship of Christ meant always *both* this *and* that: both faith and reason, both person and world, both sin and grace, both in the world and not of the world.

The Lordship of Christ placed the believing community in a special tension with the world. The essence of the matter was put by Visser 't Hooft in an early book, *The Kingship of Christ.* The New Testament, he wrote,

> demands that we let ourselves be liberated from the domination by the world and that we represent in this world the Kingdom of Christ. It is in this light that we can grasp the real difference between the Church and the world. That difference is not that the one belongs to Christ and the other is left to itself. Both belong to him, but the Church knows the King, while the world does not. In the Church his Kingship is revealed; in the world it is hidden. The Church lives as the people who know that the victory *has* been won. The world lives on as if nothing had happened. The Church realizes that the powers which militate against God's plan are under control. The world lives on as if these powers were still able to shape [our] ultimate destiny.
>
> But this is not all. The Church not only knows about the victory; it shares in the victory. It is the realm in which the new creation is already taking place. It is "in Christ," that is to say, it belongs to the new age of which he is the pioneer. . . .

But, Visser 't Hooft went on, we in the Western world live in "half-secularized churches."[18]

17. Evanston Report, p. 3.
18. Visser 't Hooft, *The Kingship of Christ,* pp. 123-25.

One saw, therefore, a tension between Christ and the world, and thus a tension between Christ and the world in the church. The Lordship—the authority and power of Christ and the loyalty they evoke, the reality inaugurated already which will come fully at the End—pertained not just to the church but to the world and the church.

Two crucial points follow. First, the Lordship addresses the worldly, corrupted communities of the churches, continually accomplishing renewal in them, evoking the church within the churches. Second, the Lordship enables Christians and the churches to discern Christ's work of inaugurating the New Creation in the world, to discern, that is, the work of God-in-Christ in the processes of human history. How this was developed in terms of unity, witness, and varied aspects of the church's social mission is the subject of the remaining chapters.

The affirmation of "the Lordship of Christ over the world and the church," emerging as the churches faced their Lord, one another, and the world of their time, was the foundation of ecumenical thought in the WCC.

This affirmation reflected a particular theology. Overall, it was a theology of "the church of the center," but it was a theology of "the church of the center" at a particular time, thus incomplete in many thrusts and accents. The Holy Spirit was only infrequently mentioned (here the Orthodox might have contributed more). Frequently, the "Lordship" theme was regarded as a unitarianism of the Second Person, too exclusively centered on Christ.

But the Lordship claim was not such a unitarianism, nor a dressed up form of "Jesus religion." Rather, ecumenical confession of the Lordship of Christ was reminiscent of the frequently embattled early Christian struggle, concluded at Nicea in 325, to understand the place of Christ in Christian faith. The modern world—and the modern world in the church—had so attacked the Second Person of the Trinity, creating such confusion in the churches, that concentration on Christ was imperative.

That is why, in the epic confrontations between church and world in this period of the twentieth century, *loyalty* was so important. Why give up everything for the sake of Christ? Why, in the age of science and power, defend the gentle Jesus? The answer was the trinitarian answer: precisely because the loving Jesus *is* the Son of God. Amid the erosions of modernity, the Lordship theme focused Christian consciousness on the Second Person of the Trinity.

8

Unity—To Search and Proclaim

The emergence of the ecumenical movement already demonstrated that Christian unity was not only a concern but also an achievement. "From the standpoint of overcoming the age-old divisiveness in the church, the last fifty years have been the richest in Christian history," Cavert wrote in 1961.[1] The manifestations of unity were varied, but largely dominated by cooperation in missions and social action. As we noted in Chapter 3, concern for unity in the churches' faith and in their order had been a major thrust in the developing ecumenical enterprise.

The covenant made at the WCC's First Assembly provided a spiritual structure of coming together and of staying together, a new context for the discovery of unity at the heights of faith and the roots of order. The post-Christendom environment increased the urgency and clarified the substance of the quest. The overall result was an intensified search for unity and a profound transformation of the approach to it.

Amsterdam did not inaugurate this approach, but stood on the brink of it. Firmly placing unity on the agenda of the new WCC, this First Assembly spoke clearly concerning "our given unity." Mindful of the lesson of the war years that "the Una Sancta was no mere luxury but an indispensable part of faith,"[2] Amsterdam made it clear that "God has given to His people in Jesus Christ a unity which is His creation and not our achievement." Church is part of the gospel, and unity belongs to the church, to the Body of Christ.

Immediately following this affirmation came a new analysis of

---

1. Samuel McCrae Cavert, *On the Road to Christian Unity*, p. 9.
2. *The World Council of Churches: Its Process of Formation*, p. 12.

"our deepest difference."[3] Traditionally, Faith and Order had focused on agreements and differences in doctrine and order. Now, however, analyses penetrated to a difference which seemed to underlie everything else. That lay in the contrast between the "catholic" and the "protestant" ways of perceiving the church. The strategy behind highlighting this "deepest difference" was to evoke an eventual response in discerning a deeper agreement. "Wherever we find ourselves thus speaking together of our unity," the Report states, "we also find ourselves faced by some stubborn problems. In dealing with them, we discover disagreements which are to be traced back into our different ways of understanding the whole and, beneath those disagreements, we find again an agreement in a unity which drew us together and will not let us go."

A dynamic element was thus discovered. The prophetic contrast between the "glory of the Church and the shame of the churches" led to the discernment of more profound differences and therefore agreement at ever deeper and more telling levels.

A REVOLUTION

Four years later, on Sunday evening, August 17, 1952, in Lund, Sweden, two people spoke to the third world conference on Faith and Order, inaugurating a revolution in the traditional ecumenical approach to church unity.

The setting in southern Sweden inevitably made me reflect. Since the Great Depression, I remembered Sweden as exemplar of the "Middle Way" between capitalism and socialism, admired in our home, though castigated in others. Neutral in World War II, Sweden was characterized by a sharply advancing secularism; but Lund's cathedral and university bespoke continuity with bygone ages, and leadership in the ecumenical age. This was the country that had provided the famed Söderblom, known for his leadership in the ecumenical response to acute church-society problems.

At the opening service of the conference in the cathedral, the well-known theologian Bishop Anders Nygren preached, and all were invited to partake of Holy Communion. No one suspected that a vast

3. Amsterdam Report, p. 55. The "deepest difference" had been foreshadowed by Anglican Leonard Hodgson, a chief figure in Faith and Order, in *The World Council of Churches: Its Process of Formation*, p. 38. See also Oliver S. Tomkins, *The Church in the Purpose of God*, p. 26; and, on the method of discerning agreements and differences, A. M. Ramsey, "Amsterdam and the Doctrine of the Church," *Ecumenical Review*, I (1949), 382-92.

change was about to take place in the ecumenical movement's approach to Christian unity.

The first speaker at the conference itself in the imposing university aula was Edmund Schlink, then nearing the height of his ecumenical influence. The year before he had turned an angry discussion about "hope" into a fruitful exploration of its meaning. Now he spoke of unity:

> The Church is on her way between the first and second Advent of Christ. She is on her pilgrimage towards her Master who is coming again. . . . But we must not forget that the Lord will come not only as our Redeemer but also as our Judge, and not merely as the Judge of the world, but also as the Judge of Christendom. . . . He will effect a separation made by man. . . . [No one] can foresee the result of the separation on the Day of Judgment. It may be that then great proud Churches, which seemed to be firmly built, will collapse like a pack of cards, and that only a small Remnant will stand firm in the time of trial and testing. . . . The first will be last and the last first. . . . We must learn to look away from the past, and to look forward steadily to the Lord who is coming again. This is the only direction which has any meaning for those who are "under the Cross." This forward movement, however, is also the tendency of the whole witness of the early Church. As we hasten forward in this direction we shall see each other with new eyes.[4]

Schlink concluded that the Faith and Order movement found itself in a true crisis concerning its method. Hitherto, that had been systematic comparison of agreements and differences in doctrine among the churches. But, he said, "we have now arrived at a limit in the use of this method." Continued comparison would demand no sacrifices and lead no further.

The second speaker was Oliver S. Tomkins, a priest of the Church of England and no stranger to the ecumenical movement. Active during university days in the SCM, he had been a member of the youth delegation at the 1937 Faith and Order conference in Edinburgh. Now he was the principal staff officer of Faith and Order. In that capacity—and later as chair of the Faith and Order Commission—he would continue as the main leader of Faith and Order for over two decades.

Tomkins began by disavowing any collusion with Schlink—a forewarning that by his own route he was going to reach the same con-

---

4. Lund Report, pp. 151-61; also in *Ecumenical Review*, V (1952), 27-36.

clusion. He had come to certain conclusions which challenged long-held assumptions.[5]

Admittedly, Tomkins said, the problem of engaging in ecumenical discourse has "a great deal that is common to any experience of foreign travel and exchange — the sheer human difficulty involved in explaining a barbecue or a chicken-fry to those raised on *smorgasbord* or *bouillabaisse*." But more was involved. The covenant relationship in the WCC spells the end of "what I would call a mere comparative ecclesiology. . . . The work is there, for us to enter into up to the limits of its validity. But let us not suppose that we shall get any further by simply explaining about bishops or baptism all over again."

Tomkins followed with another key statement: We need to "grasp more firmly the central problem of our relationship. We claim that we have a unity in Christ; we cannot show that we have unity in His Body, the Church. That is the heart of our dilemma, but it is also the ground of our hope."

Tomkins had a remarkably easy manner and style, but when he said something, it was said. His address gave evidence of long preparation and reflection. Before the Amsterdam Assembly he had written about two defective views of the church, noting that "above them both stands the One, Holy, Catholic Church, declared by God, and obscured, even while it is professed. . . . Loyalty to *that Church* corrects the errors of the lesser loyalties which are but broken parts of an intended whole."[6] Furthermore, in his work with Visser 't Hooft on the Toronto Statement, he had doubtless seen that the implications of recognizing *vestigia ecclesiae*, elements of the church, in each other applied to the work of Faith and Order as well. Bringing these to bear, Tomkins, admirably introduced by Schlink, accomplished a major turn in the work of the Faith and Order movement.[7]

When Charles Brent had set in motion the founding of Faith and Order in 1910 it was another time, another world. Tomkins, a modest man of spiritual power, was in fact a second Brent, operating in a new context, moving Faith and Order beyond earlier perspectives and lifting it from the danger of inconsequence into permanent leadership of the WCC commitment to churchly unity.

5. Lund Report, pp. 161-73; also in *Ecumenical Review*, V (1952), 15-26. Foreshadowings are to be seen in Oliver S. Tomkins, "Regional and Confessional Loyalties in the Universal Church," Amsterdam Vol. 1, p. 145; Georges Florovsky, "The Church—Her Nature and Task," *ibid.*, p. 47; and the Amsterdam Report, p. 34; see also Tomkins, *The Wholeness of the Church* (London: SCM Press, 1949), p. 65.

6. Amsterdam Vol. 1, *loc. cit.*

7. Lukas Vischer, *A Documentary History of the Faith and Order Movement 1927-1963* (St. Louis: The Bethany Press, 1963), pp. 13f.

THE SOURCE AND SUBSTANCE OF UNITY

The day before, Lutheran Archbishop Brilioth of Sweden, in his presidential address, had quoted Brent's opening words at Lausanne in 1927: "We are here at the urgent behest of Jesus Christ. We have come with willing feet."[8] In his address Schlink had harked back to the trial by fire of the confessing churches, using the language of eschatological expectation, judgment and hope, faithfulness and obedience. Tomkins, drawing on the Anglican tradition, had used the language of catholicity, of the church and its marks of unity, holiness, universality, and faithfulness in witness. Different as they were, the respective languages enriched each other. They signified varied aspects of the same reality. With an inherent logic of spirit and mind, all testified to the source of unity.

"Jesus Christ," says the Report from Lund, "is the King of the new People of God."

> Christ is never without His Church; the Church is never without Christ. Both belong inseparably together, the King and His people, the keystone and the temple, the Head and the Body. . . .
> As members of His Body we are made one with Him in the fellowship of His life, death and resurrection, of His suffering and His glory. For what concerns Christ concerns His Body also. What has happened to Christ uniquely in His once-for-all death and resurrection on our behalf, happens also to the Church in its way as His Body. As the Church is made a partaker in the crucified Body of Christ, so also it is given to be partaker in the risen Body of the same Lord. This means that the Church is called to continue the mission of Jesus Christ to the world, so that the way of Christ is the way of His Church.[9]

This expression of "the Lordship of Christ" does not suggest that the source and substance of churchly unity is something static. On the contrary, it signifies a divine process taking place between the first and the second coming of Christ. Three phases describe this process.

(1) The church continues to be a pilgrim people of God, a community of forgiven sinners who patiently await the final consummation of their redemption. Again, that does not imply a passive stance; for in the strange land of pilgrimage ungodly powers are rampant, seeking to confuse the church and defeat its mission. On its pilgrimage the church lives and works, not by institutional efficiency, might, and grandeur, but "by the power of Jesus Christ."

8. Lund Report, p. 98.
9. *Ibid.*, pp. 17f.

(2) The second phase of the divine process has to do with finality, with the end. "At the end of its pilgrimage Jesus Christ, the Crucified and Risen, will come again to meet His Church in order to complete His work of redemption and judgment, . . . to gather his own." This vision of the cosmic End does not suggest beleaguered pilgrims behind a barricade warding off outside attack, but a community beyond the barricades on a journey. The community is a Body. It has a structure and is in motion, participating in the movement of God-in-Christ toward human history and of human history toward its final end and consummation in Christ.

(3) The energy which makes the difference between beholding an ideal and being on a journey derives from the Holy Spirit. "Through the indwelling of the Holy Spirit the new age of the future is already present, and through union with the risen Jesus Christ the Church on earth is already given to participate in the power of the resurrection." Brokenness, estrangement, and divisions continue in the church, for the new age has not yet come. Nevertheless, *essentially* the church belongs to the new creation, and is thus summoned to perpetual renewal.

The process thus evoked enables people in the churches, and sometimes the churches themselves, to "penetrate behind the divisions of the church on earth to our common faith in the one Lord." That means there is no use in seeking clever stratagems to fit together the divided inheritances of the churches.

> We can grow together towards the fullness and unity in Christ only by being conformed to Him who is the Head of the Body and Lord of His people. . . . Those who are ever looking backward and have accumulated much precious ecclesiastical baggage will perhaps be shown that pilgrims must travel light and that, if we are to share at last in the great Supper, we must let go much that we treasure.[10]

---

10. *Ibid.*, pp. 20f.; see also the Lund "A Word to the Churches," pp. 15f. Both this and the report on "Christ and the Church" are also in *Ecumenical Review*, V (1952), 64-69. The Lund Report on "Christ and the Church" dominated Faith and Order work and WCC thought concerning unity for the remainder of the period with which we are concerned. See for example the following, arranged in chronological order: Report of the general secretary, Central Committee minutes, 1952, p. 73; K. E. Skydsgaard, "Faith and Order — Our Oneness in Christ and our Disunity as Churches," *Ecumenical Review*, VI (1953), 10-18; Wilhelm Menn, "Roman Catholic Voices on the Lund Conference," *ibid.*, 294-98; Evanston Report, pp. 82-91; Visser 't Hooft, "Various Meanings of Unity and the Unity Which the World Council of Churches Seeks to Promote," Central Committee minutes, 1955, Appendix I, also in *Ecumenical Review*, VIII (1955), 60-64; Gabriel Hebert, "The Church Which is His Body," *ibid.*, IX (1957); Thomas F. Torrance, "What is the Church?", *ibid.*, XI (1958), 6-21; Visser 't Hooft, *The Pressure of our Common Calling* (1959);

NONTHEOLOGICAL FACTORS, TRADITION, AND THE LUND PRINCIPLE

When Faith and Order turned from "comparative ecclesiology" to Christ and his church as the source and substance of churchly unity, derivative themes immediately appeared. One of these concerned the "nontheological factors" in church disunity; the other was the existence of various traditions.

"Nontheological factors." In an informal conference in late 1948 or early 1949, Tomkins had heard the renowned biblical scholar C. H. Dodd turn his skills as an interpreter to the phenomenon of ecumenical discussion. Suspecting that Dodd's point might be important for Faith and Order, he sought him out at Cambridge and extracted from him a letter dated June 1949. This letter was made available to the Lund meeting.[11]

In the letter Dodd referred to what had been known since the Edinburgh Conference of 1937 as "nontheological factors" in the achievement of church unity. Consideration of these had been largely initiated by church leaders from the US, and the issue was regarded as mainly sociological in nature.[12]

But Dodd suspected something else. Unconscious or unavowed motives apparently prevent ecumenical discussion from "following the argument whithersoever it leads." On the one hand, such hidden motives take the form of confessional or denominational loyalties which constrain people in the ecumenical discussion to be true to "sacred traditions" or to "historic principles."

On the other hand, Dodd felt, the unconscious constraints operate where separate and differing traditions are implicated in social and political traditions. His first illustration of this was the Cavalier and Roundhead conflicts in England, which Anglicans and Nonconformists have "in their bones." But he also brought the point up to date. "This whole question, indeed, is (it appears) becoming one of the really outstanding questions we have to face, largely through the pressure of the

---

Report of the Central Committee to the Third Assembly, pp. 37-44. Two other Lund reports — on "Ways of Worship" (Lund Report, pp. 39ff.) and "Intercommunion" (*ibid.,* pp. 49ff.) — followed the "comparative ecclesiology" method and carried little weight.

11. *Commission on Faith and Order of the WCC* (London: Commission on Faith and Order, 1949), pp. 25-28. See also *Ecumenical Review,* II (1949), 52f.; C. H. Dodd, G. R. Cragg, and Jacques Ellul, *More than Doctrine Divides the Churches: Social and Cultural Factors in Church Divisions* (New York: World Council of Churches, 1952).

12. W. A. Visser 't Hooft, *Genesis and Formation,* p. 37. The sociological interest continued up through the Fourth World Conference on Faith and Order in 1963.

East Europeans; and there will almost certainly be the same pressure from further East."

Speaking to the subject at Lund was Josef Hromadka of Czechoslovakia. Hromadka, whose rugged appearance was complemented by a kindly face and demeanor, had impressed me strongly at a Student Volunteeer Movement conference in Toronto in 1941, and I admired his return to Czechoslovakia after teaching at Princeton Seminary. He combined a biblical theology centered in the Lordship of Christ with a radical politics of the left. At Lund he spoke powerfully and frankly, acknowledging that although his theological views stirred little debate in ecumenical discussion, his Christian loyalty had been questioned on account of his political and social point of view and his decision to support, yet dialogue with, the Czech regime.

> Somewhere at the bottom of our inward life, of our theological thought, may be a hidden ulterior driving force. Our struggle for an adequate understanding of the Word of God, of the Prophets, of the Gospel, of the Church, of its functions, may be, in a perilous way, coloured and transformed by our unconscious, or almost unconscious, social, political, cultural fears, anxieties and desires.

Hromadka acknowledged that he was speaking at a time of big problems: Communism, the Korean War, the new China, discussions of the unification and neutralization of Germany, NATO, European federation, the peace movement.

> The more vigorously we identify ourselves with a given social structure, political regime and cultural tradition, the more uneasy and irritated we get if anybody questions the purity and integrity of our actions, of our theology and faith.[13]

Dodd and Hromadka had put their fingers on a veritable plague. It afflicted the churches which had been persecuted, but especially those churches which had not. Analyzed already in 1929 by H. Richard Niebuhr in his enduring study, *The Social Sources of Denominationalism,*[14] it was a plague for which there was no cure, endemic to the life of the Body of Christ within human history. There was, however, an antidote, namely the self-revealing effect of the ecumenical encounter itself.

Traditions. For me, the word "tradition" in the context of achieving unity was an eye-opener. "Tradition" had seemed on the whole something that weighed one down, "excess baggage" that one needed

13. Lund Report, p. 196.
14. Cleveland and New York: Meridian Books, The World Publishing Company, 13th printing, 1970.

Josef Hromadka (WCC Photo)

to get rid of, or at least minimize. But when the discussion went beyond
the merely institutional aspect of a church denomination, and "our
church tradition" was in view, something of more weight and substance
was at hand. A real discovery was in the making.

Lund spoke primarily of the church's continuity down through
the ages and the need to seek unity within varied views of that continuity. "Continuity" thus pointed to something essential for Christian life.
Though concerned with the problems of ministry, schism, and apostasy,
Lund was conscious of going beyond that.

The conference marked the seed ground for appreciating the
positive function of tradition in the quest for unity. Tradition pointed
to a dynamic element in the search for unity. The matter became clearer
in Lund's proposal for a sustained effort "to explore more deeply the

resources for further ecumenical discussion to be found in that common history which we have as Christians and which we have discovered to be longer, larger and richer than any of our separate histories in our divided Churches."[15]

In a notable article after Lund, US Methodist Albert Outler pressed for an exploration of what it means to have a history common to all, a common Tradition with a capital "T", and the various traditions — with a small "t" — of the respective churches.[16] As discussion continued, a great deal would come to hang on the distinction between "T" and "t's" and the relation among them.

There were substantial reasons for pursuing the matter. For one thing, the far-reaching meaning of the Toronto Statement had begun to sink in. The affirmation of a fundamental community and of *vestigia ecclesiae* in all the churches suggested inquiry into what the coexistence of traditions and the Tradition really means. This was augmented by the Orthodox presence, and the patience of the Orthodox in explaining their presence. It was *the* church of tradition, and the church which recognized that wider *koinonia*. Furthermore, the scholarship *(Traditionsgeschichte)* which underlay much biblical theology was based on a study of biblical traditions and their unity and relation to one another within Scripture. Thus "tradition" was biblical — that is, in the Bible — and (to the benefit of everyone) the simplistic Bible *vs.* tradition controversy was undercut. Jaroslav Pelikan, whose Protestant credentials were impeccable, showed in a blistering article that the hallowed *sola scriptura* of the Reformation could not stand. Theological history, he wrote, has proved that Scripture is never "alone"![17]

"Tradition" is derived from an active verb meaning "to hand down." What was handed down? Whether one had the Bible in mind or the various churches, the core of what was handed down was Christ. The very content of Christian tradition is the life, death, and resurrection of Christ. Christ, fulfilling the Old Testament, begins the tradition and constitutes the tradition.

At the same time, Christ breaks with all traditions, especially lesser church traditions ("but we *always* do it this way!") which may be-

---

15. Lund Report, p. 27.

16. Albert Outler, "A Way Forward From Lund," *Ecumenical Review*, V (1952), 59-63.

17. Jaroslav Pelikan, "Overcoming History by History," in *The Old and New in the Church* (London: SCM Press, 1961), p. 38. See also the preface to Alan Richardson and W. Schweitzer, *Biblical Authority for Today* (Philadelphia: Westminster, 1951) and, in the same publication, Panayotis I. Bratsiotis, "Greek Orthodox" (pp. 17ff.) and Regin Prenter, "Lutheran" (pp. 98ff.).

come idols. But identifying the idols in ecclesiastical traditions does not mean hostility to tradition or traditions. Doing so requires progress in understanding the revelation of God, and in perceiving the relation between the handing down of the revelation ("T") and the interpretations ("t's") which accompany that handing down.[18]

The revelation contained in the apostolic tradition, the core, must be handed down and

> not simply repeated; else it becomes lifeless. The traditions must be criticized and reformed, and not simply maintained; else they become archaic or even decadent. But this demands that the Christian community assumes the responsibility of correlating its multiple forms of interpretation with its essential form of revelation. This is one of the most crucial tasks of the ecumenical movement.[19]

Thus launched, the "Tradition and traditions" discussion was both weighty and exciting. It gave a context for the new identity of church and churches which the ecumenical movement was trying to work out. If the tension did not find resolution (and perhaps it never would), it created a new perspective and gave new impetus to the quest for unity. Skydsgaard was right: "The ecumenical movement, while seeking unity, is at the same time a great disturber of the peace, putting aggressive questions to the churches."[20]

Something else was stirring in Oliver Tomkins' mind when he gave his address at Lund. He had shifted the total approach of Faith and Order from "comparative ecclesiology" to the constructive, highly charged dynamism of the meaning of Christ and the church for unity among the churches. Beyond that he had a genuinely activist principle in mind.

> I believe that if we took seriously our "given unity in Christ," it would, in course of time, completely reverse our normal structure of church organization. The implication of our confessed unity in Christ, beneath and above our divisions, is that we should do together everything except what irreconcilable difference of sincere conviction compels us to do separately.[21]

This came to be formulated as the "Lund Principle."

---

18. K. E. Skydsgaard, in *Tradition and Traditions*. Faith and Order Paper No. 40 (Geneva: WCC, 1963), pp. 47f.

19. Albert Outler, "Traditions in Transit," in *The Old and the New in the Church*, p. 50.

20. *Op. cit.,* p. 27.

21. Lund Report, p. 170.

Hearing Tomkins' words, D. T. Niles insisted that it be in the Lund "Word to the Churches," where it was phrased this way:

> The measure of unity which it has been given to the Churches to experience together must now find clearer manifestation. . . . Should not our Churches ask themselves whether they are showing sufficient eagerness to enter into conversation with other Churches, and whether they should not act together in all matters except those in which deep differences of conviction compel them to act separately?[22]

The WCC was no super-church, but one of the "functions" listed in the constitution of Faith and Order was "to proclaim the essential oneness of the Church of Christ and to keep prominently before the World Council and the Churches the obligation to manifest that unity and its urgency for the work of evangelism." The essential oneness and the obligation to manifest it were put succinctly and creatively in the Lund Principle.

The genius of the Lund Principle was to connect overriding loyalty to Christ with action in "all matters"—not just unity—except where "deep differences of conviction" prevented it. That gave a wide scope to imaginative Christians, especially at the local level, where they could take the Lund Principle very far in the manifestation of the unity of Christ.

To pursue the Lund Principle, whether locally or elsewhere, would provide a fine exercise of spirit and imagination, of loyalty and flexibility. How else could people distinguish commitment, near commitment, and mere opinion? What were the really deep "differences of conviction" which would prevent common action?

"ALL IN EACH PLACE"

In the nine years between Lund and the WCC's Third Assembly in New Delhi, a general impatience was growing. It came from a younger ecumenical generation, mostly from Asia and Africa. They wanted progress towards unity visible, local, and *now*.

The Kenyan economist G. Kiano put it vividly:

> We have in the same village Catholics, Seventh Day Adventists, Church of England; and some of the "saved" people doing their work in a vehement and intolerant way, feeling that if you are

22. *Ibid.*, p. 16.

not of them, you must be against them. And in these same villages it is very difficult to believe that we all belong to the same clan, because the louder the Catholics sing on their side, the louder the saved people on the other side sing, and the more and harder the Adventists work to get a few more people to close their shops on Saturday and open them on Sunday. Thus in a small village the Christian Church becomes, I think, wrongly a divisive force.[23]

The 1960 Faith and Order Commission meeting in historic (for golfers especially!) St. Andrews in Scotland was insistent. If Faith and Order is to "proclaim" the essential oneness of the Church of Christ, this "involves facing the question 'what kind of unity does God demand of His Church?'" Generalities would not do; a specific definition was needed.

Behind the insistence of the international group there lay, for the first time in Faith and Order history, national conferences — New Zealand (1955), India, Indonesia, Philippines, Japan (1957), and the North American Faith and Order Conference at Oberlin in 1957. As Paul Minear wrote, there was a telescoping of the distance between the global and local, a telescoping that worked both ways, all the time.[24]

Overall, the currents in both history and faith which had brought the Amsterdam covenant into being and had accentuated faith in the Lordship of Christ also produced revolution at Lund. By the will of the Triune God, a renewed vision of Christ and the church was surging through ecumenical consciousness, enhancing a sense of urgency and arousing people's imagination as to cogent lines of work to be done.

By the time of the New Delhi Assembly, the presence of the Orthodox churches and of those from Asia, Africa, and Latin America had increased beyond all early expectations. From seven churches in 1948, Orthodox membership increased to 17 in 1961; in 1948 there were 30 churches from Asia, Africa, and Latin America, in 1961 there were 70. Furthermore, as succeeding chapters will show, a substantial part of the WCC program and intellectual energy engaged and was engaged

---

23. G. Kiano, "At What Points Can Christianity Make a Difference to Political and Economic Development in Africa?" Address at the WCC study conference on "Christian Action in Rapid Social Change," Thessalonica, Greece, July 1959, published in *Background Information for Church and Society*, No. 23 (Nov. 1959).

24. Paul Minear, "The Significance of the Oberlin Conference," *Ecumenical Review*, X (1957), 123; see also *The Nature of the Unity We Seek* (St. Louis: Bethany Press, 1958).

by the churches in these continents. From the whole, pressure rose up to require more specificity in the quest for churchly unity.[25]

"We believe," the New Delhi Report reads (in one of the longest ecumenical sentences ever written), "that the unity which is both God's will and his gift to his Church is being made visible as all in each place who are baptized into Jesus Christ and confess him as Lord and Saviour are brought by the Holy Spirit into one fully committed fellowship, holding the one apostolic faith, preaching the one Gospel, breaking the one bread, joining in common prayer, and having a corporate life reaching out in witness and service to all and who at the same time are united with the whole Christian fellowship in all places and all ages in such wise that ministry and members are accepted by all, and that all can act and speak together as occasion requires for the tasks to which God calls his people. It is for such unity that we believe we must pray and work."[26]

Oliver Tomkins said later that this New Delhi description of the nature of the unity we seek was a landmark in the history of the modern ecumenical movement.[27]

What made it so? One thing was the fact that it was produced by the same Assembly which accomplished the final ecumenical integration. "Life and Work" had been united with "Faith and Order" at the Amsterdam Assembly in 1948. It took nearly fifteen years of seemingly interminable negotiations to accomplish the integration of the International Missionary Council—begun as a result of the Edinburgh world missionary conference of 1910—with the WCC. That happened also at New Delhi. This was far more than an administrative accomplishment; the integration of IMC and WCC had a fundamental conceptual significance for the meaning of churchly unity.

The New Delhi description of churchly unity weaves mission and unity together. In it, unity involves witness and service, and these entail unity. Unity is not static, but dynamic, moving towards the world. The Central Committee in 1951 had spoken of unity and mission; now the concept was fully developed: the church exists, the Report explains, by the power of the Holy Spirit "who effects in [the Church's] life all the elements that belong to her unity, witness and service."[28]

25. *Evanston to New Delhi,* pp. 42-44; see also the report of the general secretary, Central Committee minutes, 1962, p. 80.
26. Each of the key points or words or phrases was spelled out in the full report, *New Delhi Report,* pp. 117-22.
27. Oliver S. Tomkins, *A Time For Unity,* p. 11.
28. *New Delhi Report,* p. 119.

ROMAN CATHOLICS

This is not the place to retell the history of relationships between the ecumenical movement and the Roman Catholic Church. That has been well done elsewhere.[29]

It is germane, however, to note the temper of those relations. One might have expected a vigorous anti-Catholicism. Even the gentle Norman Goodall, coming from England, where there was a fair amount of Catholic-Anglican-Protestant cooperation, spoke of the "fifty year 'No'" from Rome to ecumenical overtures,[30] governed by the encyclical *Mortalium Animos.*There was regret, of course, but underneath it lay a sense of longing and realism.

In 1904 Marc Boegner was in his twenties. He had been asked to set in order the papers of an esteemed relative who had just died. This man, Pastor Thomas Fallot, had been a saintly evangelical of the Reformed Church of France. Among the papers was a packet of letters addressed to the Roman Catholic philosopher Ernest Naville in Geneva and Abbé Birot, Vicar General to the Archbishop of Albi.

In a letter written by Fallot to Abbé Birot on November 3, 1894, the young Boegner read: "When the time comes that Protestants understand all they can gain by contact with Catholics, and when Catholics, inspired by feelings such as yours, understand that Protestantism is more than a denial of Catholic faith, then heart will search out heart, and the angels will get ready to sing the hymn that welcomes the coming of peace in charity and regained unity."

Some sixty years later, on the eve of the Second Vatican Council, Boegner wrote:

> No wonder [these words] came to me as a shock. Who at that time, in the French Protestant Churches, would have dared to write such words? What Protestants were sustaining soul and mind with these ambitions, these visions and prophecies? . . . When, for the first time, their long echoes reverberated in the

29. For example, by G. K. A. Bell, *The Kingship of Christ*, p. 73; Samuel McCrae Cavert, *On the Road to Christian Unity*, pp. 114-34; Norman Goodall, *The Ecumenical Movement*, pp. 160-65; James Hastings Nichols, *Evanston: An Interpretation* (New York: Harper and Brothers, 1954), pp. 15-19; Thomas F. Stransky, "A Basis Beyond the Basis: Roman Catholic/World Council of Churches Collaboration," *Ecumenical Review*, XXXVII (1985), 213-22; "The Foundation of the Secretariat for Christian Unity," in *Vatican II Revisited*, ed. Albric Stacpoole (Minneapolis: Winston Press, 1986), pp. 62-87; Oliver S. Tomkins, *A Time for Unity*, pp. 120ff.; Lukas Vischer, "The Ecumenical Movement and the Roman Catholic Church," in *A History of the Ecumenical Movement*, II, ed. Harold E. Fey (Philadelphia: Westminster Press, 1970), pp. 311-52; Visser 't Hooft, *Memoirs*, pp. 319-39.

30. Norman Goodall, *op. cit.*, pp. 163f.

depths of my interior life, it seemed to me as though a thick mist that surrounded me was being torn aside, that glorious peaks were emerging on the horizon, to be gained at the end of a magnificent and perilous adventure.[31]

Longing and hope dominated the repeated overtures the ecumenical pioneers made to Rome, continued by the WCC after 1948. WCC membership for the Roman Catholic Church was out of the question, as the WCC leaders knew. At the same time, anxious to demonstrate openness, they did so on the occasion of every major ecumenical event. In particular, WCC leaders sought and cultivated direct relationships with some Roman Catholics, particularly in France. Fresh from struggles with their own churches, the WCC pioneers recognized the promise of the Roman Catholic pioneers and the difficulties with which they were beset. Throughout the whole period, Visser 't Hooft's role was crucial.

On at least one occasion Roman Catholics helped the WCC substantially and perhaps decisively. In 1949, a year before the Toronto Statement was worked out, ten Roman Catholics and ten WCC people met at the Istina Center in Paris. Father Yves Congar, whom Visser 't Hooft called "the father of Roman Catholic ecumenism," strongly suggested that the concept of *vestigia ecclesiae* yielded a sound starting point for ecumenical ecclesiology; and Father Jean Daniélou urged that a dynamic understanding of *vestigia ecclesiae* be worked out.[32] That concept was indeed to play a major role at Toronto. Visser 't Hooft obviously felt himself bound to secrecy concerning this germinal meeting until well after Vatican II. Closely as we discussed matters, he never mentioned it, nor did rumor of it come from the other nine. All had clearly agreed to keep silence for the sake of the Roman Catholic pioneers.

James Nichols begins his interpretation of the Second Assembly at Evanston in 1954 with an account of "Those Who Were Not There."[33] The Roman Catholics, who had not been at Amsterdam, were not at Evanston either; indeed, they had been forbidden to enter the city. In 1960, on the initiative of Cardinal Augustin Bea, first President of the Vatican Secretariat for Promoting Christian Unity, Monsignor (later Cardinal) Jan Willebrands, Visser 't Hooft, and Bea held a super-secret meeting.[34] One item on the agenda was the possibility of Roman Catholic observers at the WCC's Third Assembly in New Delhi; another was the

---

31. Marc Boegner, *The Long Road to Unity*, pp. 30f.
32. Visser 't Hooft, *Memoirs*, pp. 319-21; *Genesis and Formation*, pp. 74-76.
33. *Op. cit.*, pp. 31-44.
34. Visser 't Hooft, *Memoirs*, pp. 328f.

possibility of WCC observers at the forthcoming Second Vatican Council in 1962.

In both cases, the observers were present. The Holy Spirit of God had been in motion among a few to accomplish a far-reaching work.

9

Witness

For reasons that were never quite clear to me, Visser 't Hooft wanted me to be not only on the Assembly staff at Amsterdam in 1948, but one of the "consultants" as well. I liked that not only because it gave me a voice in the Assembly, but also because it gave me a chance to work with my favorite subject. Of the four Assembly "Sections"—Unity, Witness, Church and Society, and International Affairs—I chose "Witness."

What I understood by witness had been part and parcel of my SCM undergraduate experience and my theological training. Whether from the vantage point of a very small group on the secularized Yale campus, or from the perspective of the history of the church and its worldwide expansion, the essence of witness was testimony to God's truth and God's purpose. Christian life had within it the pressure of an outward thrust, a movement towards others. Christian faith was not what one did in private, but what one did in relation to truth and the neighbor.

I worked during divinity school days in the Student Volunteer Movement for Foreign Missions, then near the end of its life. The old watchword, preached with immense effect by Mott and others, "The Evangelization of the World in This Generation," was under fire. I could dispense with the last three words as reflecting too much nineteenth-century optimism. But I did not want to let the first part of it go, and proposed as an alternative "The Student Volunteer Movement for World Mission." There were times, I believed, when witness meant not only mission but evangelism in the direct sense conveyed by the "Great Commission" of Matthew 28:29-30.

In March 1946, John Currie, a pastor friend, asked me to conduct a communion service and to preach at a small new church in the New York City borough of Queens—an invitation which in fact began a part-time ministry lasting eight years. I knew that this was a church composed of black people, who met in a building that "belonged" to a disintegrating white congregation. The white congregation had refused to merge with the black congregation, so the blacks paid rent to worship at noon, immediately after the white congregation's 11:00 service.

Arriving some fifteen minutes early, I was surprised to find the black congregation waiting on the sidewalk. The whites, I was told, had not finished. It came to be 12:00 and, not a little impatient, I said I would go in and see why they were late. "You can't do that," my black friends said, "the door is locked." Thus witness for me came to be related indissolubly to community and unity.

Some three or four years later, the black congregation was firmly ensconced in the church building. We were in the basement on a Wednesday evening for a meeting of the governing session. Suddenly, the front doors of the church were loudly shaken. I started to run up to see what was going on, but two elders held me back. "No, no, Reverend; we're going."

We could hear talk, and soon they came back. "It's a young man, running from the police, and we have told him he can stay in the church. We think he hasn't done anything."

"Why not let the police take him, if they come," I asked. "They'll let him go if he's innocent."

One of the elders, a deputy district attorney of the city of New York, said, "Reverend, don't you know about the rubber hose? The cops will take him to the station and beat him till he confesses anything. We won't let them do it."

I looked around. Every man and woman there agreed. He stayed. After the meeting, one member took him to his home. I had had a burning lesson in the connection between witness and justice, "sanctuary" and community.

Witness can mean everything the church does and all that Christians do. In the emerging ecumenical tradition, however, its meaning was somewhat sharper. "Witness in word and deed," reads one of the most carefully prepared documents of the WCC, "is the essential mission and responsibility of every Christian and of every church. All disciples stand under the Great Commission of the one Lord."[1]

Witness has two components. One is testimony to the truth—

---

1. "Christian Witness, Proselytism and Religious Liberty in the Setting of the World Council of Churches," in Central Committee minutes, 1960, Appendix XXVII.

as in the case of a person on the witness stand in court. The other is the conscious, outward thrust of Christians and the church into the surrounding world of disbelief. Sometimes "evangelism" was used to designate the outward thrust of mission, and sometimes "mission" or "world mission" was employed; but these usages depended more on the context at hand than on theological distinctions among the terms.

In the sense of the outward thrust, witness includes a reference to society, increasingly important in the post-Christendom era. The various concerns of Chapters 10-13 therefore complete the present chapter, which deals with the narrower meaning. In a distinctive fashion, ecumenical thought moved back and forth between "evangelism" and "social action" because of its conscious calling to witness. The nature of the covenant prevented the WCC from doing evangelism directly. No super-church, the Council deliberately had no mechanism for organizing and carrying out evangelistic campaigns. Its function was, rather, to help focus the churches' intellectual energy in their own pursuit of the Great Commission.

We shall speak first of perspectives, the background of concerns that animated ecumenical thought concerning witness; second, of the emerging certainties of faith and insight; third, of a new pattern and strategy of mission; fourth, of evangelism, revival, renewal, and church structures; and finally of the laity, the cutting edge of the church's witness.

PERSPECTIVES

In an article prepared for the Amsterdam Assembly Paul Tillich argued that the creative forces in an integrated society are held in balance by an embracing, determining principle. When this principle loses its force, a vacuum erodes community life or other disrupting principles destroy it; and the individual falls prey to the mass.[2]

The center had been lost in most Western countries with the disappearance of Christendom. The power of rapid social change would soon illustrate the same fundamental truth in the traditional societies of Asia, Africa, and Latin America.

As the postwar atmosphere gave way to the 1950s, the "mass" character of modern society was prominent in all considerations of Christian witness. The desperation of mass poverty, whether in East

---

2. Paul Tillich, "The Disintegration of Society in Christian Countries," in Amsterdam Vol. 2; see also, in the same volume, Wilhelm Pauck, "Rival Secular Faiths."

Harlem or Glasgow or Calcutta; the mechanization, organization, and corporate decision-making that characterized industrialization; the profound changes driven by scientific and technological development; the growth of wealth, accompanied by a deepening materialism; the move among whole populations from "inner directed" and more personal to "other directed," which indicated conformity to the mass — all these pressed on people everywhere and on the churches.

Ecumenical concern about society was not judgmental, and its descriptions showed a fine discrimination among the goods and evils. Nor was reform the main concern, although everyone hoped for constructive changes. The point of stressing the "mass" character of much of modern society was to help churches and their evangelists to connect the gospel with the spiritual situation of people. Social analysis helped to define the target.[3]

At the same time, ideologies and religions offered hope or challenge or oppression. Some were promoting the quasi-religion of "scientism," an uncritically high confidence in the possibilities of science for curing human ills. Totalitarianism, chiefly Stalinism, threatened. Communism in other forms appeared to millions as salvation, or seemed to. Alternatively, in the nontechnical societies, the humane aspects of Western civilization offered hope, gave meaning, and spurred many leaders in the task of nation-building to action. Hinduism, Buddhism, and Islam were resurgent, sometimes in fundamentalist forms and sometimes in forms that welcomed and appropriated the democratic, scientific humanism of the West.

Frequently, tendencies contradicted one another. Ancient religions were resurgent, but strong syncretistic and relativistic tendencies appeared in all continents, encouraged as "one world" pressed on minds and spirits, shaping how people apprehended truth itself. Early optimism concerning the benefits of scientific technology gave way in some measure to disillusionment, for none could escape the shadow of the atomic bomb.

Clearly there was no "center." Pluralism provided a large part of the spiritual context for the witness of the church. Yet, there was another component of the world scene. "Those who stand on the watchtowers of the Church can tell us that our rejoicing over the spread of Christianity throughout the world is often still premature. Scores of mil-

---

3. Cf. Oxford Report, p. 57; Amsterdam Vol. 2 (unsigned survey); report of the general secretary in Central Committee minutes, 1962, p. 80; H. H. Ulrich, *Evangelism in Germany* (London: Lutterworth Press, 1958); George Sweazey, *Evangelism in the United States* (London: Lutterworth Press, 1958); George Webber, *God's Colony in Man's World* (Nashville: Abingdon Press, 1960).

lions, in Asia and Africa and elsewhere—in Muslim lands, to cite conspicuous examples — have as yet never even heard the Gospel. The Church of Christ is still today, at home and abroad, 'on mission sent.'"[4]

Perspectives on evangelism and mission arose out of a highly varied church situation. In Eastern Europe generally, it was true that "to serve the church has once again become dangerous";[5] while in West Germany's "economic miracle" the churches were again prosperous, responding generously to human need.

Workers and intellectuals in France were severely estranged from the church, while in the USA there was so much regard for the American religion of "Protestant, Catholic, and Jew" that it was considered to be in the national interest, a kind of American Shinto. Except in places where renewal was being brought forth, a "suburban captivity of the churches" seemed to reign.[6] The church in Asian lands, although surrounded by the multitudes of those who had not heard of Christ, "is a reality. It has taken root. And everywhere there are signs of deepening life, increasing influence, widening boundaries . . . and signs of weakness."[7] What was said of Asia was true of the phenomenal growth in Africa.

The worldwide variations and contradictions in church life could be multiplied. But in the face of the pluralism all around, the covenant at Amsterdam expressed not only the intent to stay together, but also faith's knowledge that "there is a Word of God for our world."[8]

"Yet no nation or people has been discovered," wrote Stephen Neill, "from the Eskimos to the Balinese, in which the Gospel cannot take root, and there is no church which God has not been pleased to use to bring men to Himself, from sedate Anglicanism to fiery Fundamentalism."[9]

---

4. Amsterdam Vol. 2, "The Gospel at Work in the World," pp. 114-67; cf. the Evanston surveys of "Evangelism" and "The Laity"; the Message of the Third Assembly, New Delhi Report, pp. 320-21; *The Evangelisation of Man in Modern Mass Society* (Geneva: WCC Study Department, 1949); Paul Devanandan, *Christian Concern in Hinduism* (Bangalore: Christian Institute for the Study of Religion and Society, 1961); Visser 't Hooft, *None Other Name*.

5. Martin Fischer, "The Witness of the Prisoners," *Ecumenical Review*, V (1953), 394ff.; cf. Johannes Hamel, *A Christian in East Germany* (New York: Association Press, 1960).

6. Will Herberg, *Protestant-Catholic-Jew* (Garden City, NY: Doubleday Anchor Books, 1960); Gibson Winter, *The Suburban Captivity of the Churches* (Garden City: Doubleday & Co., 1961).

7. "The Church's Call to Mission and Unity," *Ecumenical Review*, V (1953), 287-91.

8. Amsterdam Report, p. 10.

9. Amsterdam Report, p. 35.

"To become engaged in the mission to the non-Christian world, whether in the West or in the East," wrote Visser 't Hooft, "is to receive a new sense of proportion. The great essential truths become greater and the secondary issues become smaller. But that means, at the same time, that we are thrown back on those elements of the witness which constitute the faith once delivered to the saints."[10]

CERTAINTIES

These perspectives on the varied societies of the world and the churches within them were accompanied by the affirmation of two certainties of the faith: that the Christian faith is a missionary faith; and that the church is a missionary body.

The Christian Faith Is Missionary

In responding to the post-Christendom world, ecumenical thought had a clear starting point. The gospel speaks of an act of God for the salvation of the whole world. In this act God has done something unique, and in this unique act God reaches to the final depth of human need. With God the verbs are active: God acts and God works even when the powers of evil rebel. Whether one thinks of secular history or of sacred history, the entire process is controlled by the purposive will of God. "The Christian life cannot be lived," wrote missiologist Walter Freytag of the German Confessing Church, who chaired the WCC Division of Studies, "without the wide horizon, the view of the world which God has in mind, the world which God loves. There God's mission is going on."[11] Faith in God does not mean the act of taking God to people among whom God is not present. It means, rather, that witness, evangelism, mission are testimony to the God who is already there, at work everywhere.[12]

---

10. W. A. Visser 't Hooft, *The Pressure of Our Common Calling*, p. 39. On perspectives in general, see also Kenneth Scott Latourette and W. Richey Hogg, *Tomorrow is Here: The Mission and Work of the Church as Seen From the Meeting of the International Missionary Council at Whitby, Ontario, July 5-24, 1947* (New York: Friendship Press, 1948); and the New Delhi Report, pp. 77-90.

11. Walter Freytag, "Changes in the Patterns of Western Missions," *International Review of Mission*, XLVII (1958).

12. *Ibid.*; cf. "The Gospel at Work in the World," Amsterdam Vol. 2, pp. 115f.; Walter Horton, "The Gospel in its Relevance to the Present Time," *ibid.*, pp. 88-97; New Delhi Report, pp. 320ff.; Paul Devanandan, *Preparation for Dialogue*, "Witness Called to Witness," and "The Renaissance of Hinduism in India," *Ecumenical Review*, XI (1958).

"The purpose of God," said Amsterdam, "is to reconcile all men to Himself and to one another in Jesus Christ His Son."

> That purpose was made manifest in Jesus Christ—His incarnation, His ministry of service, His death on the Cross, His resurrection and ascension. It continues in the gift of the Holy Spirit, in the command to make disciples of all nations, and in the abiding presence of Christ with His Church. It looks forward to its consummation in the gathering together of all things in Christ.[13]

The gospel itself, thus set forth in historic trinitarian terms, was the anchor of the missionary character of Christian faith. The reach of the mission was the reconciliation of all people to God.

This gospel did not merely inaugurate a new and different religion. Rather, it produced a new situation for humanity, bringing it into a decisive relationship with God:

> The gospel of God's kingdom is a Gospel for the nations. This King has willed to rule as Saviour. . . . The end of this saving concern is the gift of peace, the establishment of *shalom*. To receive God's shalom is to enter into an inheritance where many things belong together — mercy and truth, righteousness and peace, goodness and plenty, man's salvation and God's glory. . . . This shalom is in Jesus Christ in whom God has proclaimed His gospel.[14]

In other words, a new situation was created because the End, the eschaton, was introduced into history, and because history therefore moved toward the End and the End toward history. The gospel announced an eschatological reality. It was missionary.

That knowledge provided the answer to the question of the authority by which the church lives and preaches. The authority to preach the gospel resides in Christ, the author and finisher of the Kingdom, the New Reality of God.

I had first encountered the question of authority during undergraduate days in the SCM. Then, if there was interest in religion at all, it was a complete relativism: "You go to your church and I'll go to mine"; in other words, "Mind your own business." In a stumbling way, I soon found that the bedrock issue was not whether the evangelist had sufficient enthusiasm, persuasiveness, or ability to communicate, but whether the evangelist could point to a final, intrinsic authority.

13. Amsterdam Report, p. 64.
14. "A Theological Reflection on the Work of Evangelism," *Bulletin* of the Division of Studies, Vol. V, Nos. 1 and 2 (Geneva: WCC, 1959), pp. 6ff.

On the world scene, the issue of "authority" stood vividly to the fore. Often unintentionally, earlier missionaries had been heard to preach Christ on the authority of Western Christian civilization, which was in the process of "exploring," subduing, and ruling millions of people. With the passing of Christendom, that authority was gone, not only in Asia and Africa but also in the territory which had for so many centuries been the home base of world missions. Worldwide there had to be a different answer to the question "By what authority?"

In 1959 the Central Committee received and recommended to the churches "A Theological Reflection on the Work of Evangelism," long in preparation under the leadership of D. T. Niles and US Episcopalian Theodore O. Wedel. This study said that "the coming of Jesus Christ in the flesh and in the power of the Spirit is a 'secular' event. It is an event in the world and for the world."[15] Thus the missionary or evangelist did not have a warrant to meddle in someone else's religion. Rather, the witnessing person had the authority of his or her faith to announce a world fact. The gospel of Christ was the "proclamation of the mighty acts of God. These stand over against all human beliefs and pretensions."[16] Therein lay the authority of the gospel and of the evangelist.

At times, the missionary faith was stated too starkly. In 1938 Hendrik Kraemer of the Netherlands, a professor of world religions with phenomenal erudition and a man of all but overpowering personal presence, published *The Christian Message in a Non-Christian World*. Written by request for the world missionary conference at Madras, it created an uproar.[17] Kraemer expounded what he called "biblical realism," vigorously proclaiming the Kingdom, the new reality, the reign of Christ in such terms that it led him to deny any "point of contact" between the gospel and the human condition and person to whom it was addressed. Many could not agree, and the debate it sparked off lasted into the 1950s.

Reading the book in 1939, my last undergraduate year, I was stunned by the description of "biblical realism" — the idea that Scripture spoke not of a religion but of a new realm of reality, different from anything the world had to offer. I had studied the Bible, but had scarcely encountered the "biblical theology" of the time. The concentrated introduction via Kraemer opened a new world. Later I recognized that Kraemer's presentation was too harsh, and was relieved when he him-

15. *Ibid.*
16. *Ibid.*, p. 14.
17. Madras Vol. 1 is entirely concerned with the "Kraemer thesis"; there is an excellent summary of Kraemer's point and the ensuing debate in W. Richey Hogg, *Ecumenical Foundations*, pp. 295ff.

Hendrik Kraemer (WCC Photo)

self reformulated his position,[18] thus bringing to a close the long and finally fruitless debate about the "point of contact" between Christianity and the non-Christian religions.

At other times, the eschatological vision was presented in terms too glorious. Hans Hoekendijk set forth the *shalom* of the Lord who promised "peace, my peace," in such brilliant ultimacy as virtually to eliminate any need for the church.[19] Yet the eschatological reality which in different ways had seized Kraemer and Hoekendijk gave clarity to

18. Hendrik Kraemer, *Religion and the Christian Faith* (London: Lutterworth Press, 1956).

19. J. C. Hoekendijk, "The Call to Evangelism," *International Review of Mission,* XXXIX (1950); "The Church in Missionary Thinking," *ibid.,* XLI (1952).

the witness. Theirs was a contribution of needed shock. After absorbing what they said, one did not speak lightly of the "image of God" as something needing only to be refurbished or of the church as a body to be somewhat improved.

Still, the missionary faith as understood ecumenically retained its basic eschatological character. Two conclusions stood out. One was that God had "not left himself without witnesses," whether in the midst of ideologies or religions or no religion. The second, preached by D. T. Niles for a generation, was the "previousness of Jesus, Jesus being ahead of us, making his appointment with us unknown to us."[20] Such reference to Jesus the Lord, the Second Person of the Trinity, was frequently expressed in other language. Especially prominent was "God is at work in human history." This note of "already" — quite independently of whether I might be there—also had the connotation of engaging powers, principalities, and "all sorts and conditions" of people.[21]

The Church Is a Missionary Body

The second affirmation was that the missionary faith produced a missionary church. Florovsky put it vividly: The Church "is a missionary body indeed, and its mission-field is the whole world. But the aim of its missionary activity is not merely to convey to people certain convictions or ideas, not even to impose on them a definite discipline or a rule of life, but first of all to introduce them into the New Reality, to *convert* them, to bring them through their faith and repentance to Christ Himself."[22] In similar vein, the 1952 world missionary conference at Willingen, Germany, affirmed: "The missionary obligation of the Church arises from the triune God. God sends forth the Church to carry out His work to the ends of the earth, to all nations, and to the end of time."[23]

20. D. T. Niles, *Upon the Earth* (London: Lutterworth Press, 1962), which grew out from a study sponsored by the WCC Department of Missionary Studies.

21. Besides Assembly statements on evangelism, mission, and witness, see "A Theological Reflection on the Work of Evangelism" and "Theological Reflections on the Missionary Task of the Church," both in the *Bulletin* of the WCC Division of Studies, Vol. VII, 1961; Walter Freytag, "The Meaning and Purpose of the Christian Mission," *International Review of Mission*, XXXIX (1950); Norman Goodall, "Towards Willingen," *ibid.*, XLI (1952); Stephen Neill, *The Unfinished Task* (London: Lutterworth Press, 1957); Lesslie Newbigin, "One Body, One Gospel, One World," *Ecumenical Review*, XI (1959); *The Relevance of Trinitarian Doctrine for Today's Mission* (London: Edinburgh House Press, 1963); Niles, *op. cit.*, p. 172.

22. Georges Florovsky, "The Church—Her Nature and Task," Amsterdam Vol. 1, p. 55.

23. "A Statement on the Calling of the Church to Mission and Unity," *Ecumenical Review*, V (1952); cf. Johannes Blauw, *The Missionary Nature of the Church* (New York: McGraw-Hill, 1962).

The accent fell not on obedience to the commandment to go into all the world, but on participation in Christ. The commandment required obedience, but also served to indicate how the person and the community would live were they truly "in Christ." That required personal (though not individualistic) experience — personal knowledge of the Father, of Christ's servant death for all, of his triumph over the powers, and of the establishment of the Kingdom of God. Participation in these provided the substance of the mission and gave power to it.

The source of unity and the source of mission were thus the same. As the divided churches confessed Christ, they perceived the source of unity. As churches captive to the world or their own interests confessed Christ, they perceived the source of mission. The church, therefore, was seen as a vibrant *koinonia,* a people, the Body in the world for the purpose of witness, evangelism, mission.

The church's most basic way of communicating the gospel was through the quality of its communal life. The love of Christ became knowable and visible through its power to draw people out of isolation and sinful separation, out of pride of race, language, authority or sex, into a community where "all are made equal with the humblest that all may share the glory of the Son."[24] From such a community, communication about God-in-Christ could go forth with authority.

A NEW PATTERN AND STRATEGY OF WORLD MISSION

Besides affirming the missionary character of the faith and the missionary character of the church, those who made the covenant at Amsterdam and those who joined in subsequent years developed a new pattern of conducting world mission. Particular strategies appeared for Asia, Africa, and Latin America on the one hand, and the West on the other.

The embryo of this new pattern had appeared in 1910 in Edinburgh and evolved further in 1938 at Madras. At the first postwar world missionary conference in Whitby, Ontario, in 1947 it was endorsed. The new pattern was called, "partnership in obedience."[25]

This meant a radical shift in missionary relationships. The dominant mode had been the sending of missionaries from the West to the

---

24. Amsterdam Survey, "The Mission of the Church to Those Outside Her Life," p. 165; cf. the New Delhi Report on "Witness."
25. See Norman Goodall, *The Ecumenical Movement,* pp. 35ff.; W. R. Hogg, *Ecumenical Foundations,* pp. 339-42; Kenneth Scott Latourette and W. Richey Hogg, *Tomorrow Is Here.*

"non-Christian" countries. Their work had yielded breathtaking results, churches were now established, and the dominance of the Western missionary societies and personnel was rapidly drawing to a close. In the eyes of many Western missionaries and of most church leaders in Asia, Africa, and Latin America, the sooner this happened, the better.[26]

With every church throughout the world as the base of operations for a universal mission, the calling to be a "foreign missionary" not only remained but was extended. It was answered by Westerners who went to the countries of Asia and Africa, as well as to other countries in the West. Especially after the formation of the East Asian Christian Conference (now Christian Conference of Asia) and the All Africa Conference of Churches, it was felt by Asian and African Christians who went to different countries in those continents and in the West. The new pattern produced a different kind of missionary—one dedicated to help in the shared task of mission under the authority of the church in the foreign country. Sometimes that produced severe strains, but it was also liberating. With the "home base everywhere" and missionaries going from one home base to another to help in the vast work, there was the sense of organism, a vibrant Body in the service of its Head.[27]

As the missionary faith and the missionary church required a new pattern of relations, they required also a new strategy. This also had been long a-borning in the ecumenical enterprise. It was described by a word which in its literary awkwardness stood on a par with "eschatology," namely "indigenization."

The new pattern of missions affected churches everywhere; "indigenization" referred primarily to the "younger churches." What did it mean?

In 1960, as freedom and independence gathered force in Africa, the outspoken Edmund Ilogu of Nigeria answered clearly. He spoke against the background of the "younger churches" of Asia and Africa, which now, generally self-determining, independent, and autonomous in their governance, were nevertheless largely "in their structure and style of expression, spiritual colonies of the West, copies of something, but not grown up." In contrast, indigenization meant "to make native,"

---

26. See references in note 22; also, "The Calling of the Church to Mission and to Unity," Central Committee minutes, 1951, Appendix VI.
27. Samuel McCrae Cavert, *On the Road to Christian Unity*, p. 65; Paul Devanandan, "The Ecumenical Movement and the Younger Churches," in Amsterdam Vol. 1; Norman Goodall, *op. cit.*, pp. 99-100; "The Unfinished Evangelistic Task," Madras Report, Section III, p. 28; Rajah B. Manikam, "The Calling of the Church to Mission and Unity," Lund Report, pp. 209ff.; Lesslie Newbigin, "The Work of the Holy Spirit in the Life of the Asian Churches," in *A Decisive Hour for the Christian Mission* (London: SCM Press, 1960).

to "adapt to a given area," to "acclimatize or habituate to a new climate."[28] To maintain Christ's Lordship in indigenous ways was the universal strategy of witness, from Korea clear around to the Nigerian coast.

If, however, indigenization was the main strategy for pursuing the church's world mission, how was the process of indigenization to be set forward? Partnership in personnel and money helped, usually, but did not reach the basic problem.

At root, there were two answers.

The first was to witness to the truth in Christ. From war-torn Holland in 1948, as from Evanston on Chicago's North Shore in 1954 and the Vigyan Bhavan in New Delhi in the new India of 1963, a truth claim rang out. It affirmed the uniqueness and finality of God's revelation in Christ and of the act of Christ in the redemption of the world. There was little or no support for entering into a debate concerning religions as such, and particularly as to whether Christianity was superior to the other religions. Arguments about systems of religions had scant, if any, place. Rather, all concerned fought for freedom of expression (Ch. 11) so that dialogue and cooperation with people of all faiths and no faith could transpire. Testimony from churches everywhere registered the basic standpoint of indigenization: accepting the mission of God-in-Christ, and affirming the triune God within the accustomed culture.

A second part of the basic strategy of indigenization was identifying with people, "being with," not "apart from," as a fundamental stance. Moreover, it meant identification with people seen as human beings, not as "Hindus" or "Muslims" or "Buddhists." It meant also not speaking and dressing and living and building churches and worshiping in Western ways, but in ways drawn from the common culture. In particular, it meant serving, bearing burdens, healing, expressing the love of which they spoke. This latter, of course, had strong precedents in the great missionary expansion, which expressed identification with the people in the form of schools and hospitals and agricultural production and the role of women and village development.[29] This form of witness broadened, especially as national aspirations were expressed and political, economic, and social change took place. In much of Asia and Africa, Christian witness became indigenous through involvement in the processes of nation-building.

Thus understood, the basic strategies of witness encountered the

28. Edmund Ilogu, "The Problem of Indigenization in Nigeria," *International Review of Mission*, XLIX (1960), 173; see also *The Calling of the Church to Mission and to Unity*, pp. 67f.

29. Kenneth Scott Latourette, "Distinctive Features of the Protestant Missionary Methods of the Nineteenth and Twentieth Centuries," Madras Vol. 3.

historic problem of the church everywhere. In becoming indigenous to culture and in identifying with the people, how should the City of God relate to the city of the world? Too close a relationship vitiated the witness; too remote a relationship reduced its relevance. Again, ecumenical thought maintained the position of "the church of the center," emphasizing critical participation in society and culture and the transformation of personal and social life by the reconciling power of God-in-Christ.[30]

REVIVAL, RENEWAL AND CHURCH STRUCTURES

In the West, however, the witness of the church turned attention to other issues. Most prominent was the debate between the radicals, who sought deep renewal in the life of the churches and hence a more compelling witness, and the traditionalists, who sought revival of individual commitment within the churches. Both claimed evangelism as their objective.

In 1958 there was a ten-day consultation at the Ecumenical Institute on "A Theology of Evangelism." The fifty participants included people from industrial missions in Great Britain, Germany, and the US, church leaders in evangelism from Europe and North America, and Billy Graham.

I anticipated the conference with some trepidation. Visiting Geneva before it began, Tom Allen, a pastor in Glasgow who had been

---

30. In addition to WCC and IMC reports cited above, see further James P. Alter and Herbert Jai Singh, *The Church in Delhi* (Bangalore: NCC of India, 1961), and "Christianity, British Rule and the Challenge of Indian Nationalism," *Reflection*, No. 3 (Rajpur: Christian Retreat and Study Centre, 1971); K. A. Busia, "Has the Christian Faith Been Adequately Presented?", *International Review of Mission*, L (1961); Ernest Y. Campbell, *The Church in the Punjab* (Bangalore: NCC of India, 1961); Paul D. Devanandan, *Our Task Today* (Bangalore: Christian Institute for the Study of Religion and Society, 1958), and "Christian and non-Christian Faith," *Indian Journal of Theology*, VI (1957); Edmund Ilogu, "The Problem of Indigenization in Nigeria," *International Review of Mission*, XLIX (1960); Philippe Maury, *Politics and Evangelism* (Garden City: Doubleday, 1959); David Moses, "Christianity and the Non-Christian Religions," *International Review of Mission*, XLIII (1954); Lesslie Newbigin, *The Work of the Holy Spirit in the Life of the Asian Churches*; D. T. Niles, *The Preacher's Calling to be Servant* (London: Lutterworth Press, 1959) and *The Preacher's Task and the Stone of Stumbling* (London: Lutterworth Press, 1958); John V. Taylor, *Processes of Growth in an African Church* (London: SCM Press, 1958), *The Growth of the Church in Buganda* (London: SCM Press, 1958), and *The Growth of the Church in the Copperbelt* (London: SCM Press, 1960); U Kyaw Than, "The Christian Mission in Asia Today," *International Review of Mission*, XLVII (1958); M. M. Thomas, *The Acknowledged Christ of the Indian Renaissance* (London: SCM Press, 1969); K. H. Ting, "The Life of the Churches in China," *Ecumenical Review*, IX (1956); Oliver S. Tomkins, *The Church in the Purpose of God*, p. 54; Visser 't Hooft, "The Asian Churches in the Ecumenical Movement," in *A Decisive Hour for the Christian Mission*; E. R. Wickham, *Church and People in an Industrial City* (London: Lutterworth Press, 1957), and "The Encounter of the Christian Faith and Modern Technological Society," *Ecumenical Review*, XI (1959).

asked to chair the sessions, had come to my office. "Bob," he said, "do ye know what George McCleod [the radical pioneer of evangelism who founded Scotland's Iona Community] said to me t'other day? He said, 'Tom, my boy, do ye know what the matter with ye is?' 'No, George,' I said, 'I don't.' 'The matter with ye is, Tom, that ye've got one foot in the camp of the World Council and the other foot in the camp of Billy Graham, and ye've got a permanent pain in the groin!'"

In fact, the conference did not break down under the stress of the deep differences among participants. The reason was Billy Graham himself. Although often a minority of one, Graham held his own in discussion with a stature that took everyone by surprise. He might have conducted himself as the golden haired idol that much of the public saw. Around the world, he was probably the best-known Christian figure of the day. His access to the political leaders was unequalled by any other Christian leader, and he could attract masses on a scale unheard-of, not only in his native country but abroad as well. None of that was evident at Bossey, even when he spoke of it in private. Decades to come would confirm what was so impressive about Graham at this meeting —the steadfastness of his central convictions, his effectiveness in mass evangelism, his statesmanlike attitude toward the ecumenical movement, and his ability to change his opinions and outlook. We owed a debt to Tom Allen for enabling Graham to be present at the Bossey meeting. He conversed, he was modest, he stayed the full ten days, and with him we got to the bottom of things.

The "radicals" were represented by those who worked in poor, alienated industrial areas— Sheffield, Glasgow, the Ruhr, East Harlem —and by people at "centers" like Iona in Scotland, Taizé in France, the Evangelical Academies in Germany, the College of Preachers in the US. They knew first-hand of the enormous alienation from the church of the poor, the hopeless, the sophisticated, and the empty. They wanted a renewal in the church that could reach "those outside its life." They could not deny that Billy Graham's revivalism was also renewal, but it was of a different sort, and there was a gulf between the two.

In that sense the 1958 conference was a microcosm of the churches. Is it the function of the church to transform society or to be a part of society? Graham, too, said "to transform"; but the terms of his transformation did not carry weight with the others. Marshall Frady later pointed to the essential problem in the subtitle of his biography of Graham: "A Parable of American Righteousness."[31]

---

31. Marshall Frady, *Billy Graham: A Parable of American Righteousness* (Boston: Little, Brown, 1979).

Graham of course was not alone in using the terms of his own culture to interpret the gospel, rather than vice versa. Germans interpreted the gospel in German terms, British in British terms, and so on. Here the church/world problem became acute. Does the particular society or culture interpret the gospel, or does the gospel transform the world? The answer is never clear-cut, but which predominates? On evangelism, it was not simply a case of Graham *vs.* the ecumenical movement; it was—and is—the *fundamental* problem of Christian witness.

Evangelists also had to consider the need for church structures to support their task. If alienated workers in Europe were to be won back to the church, it was argued, they would need a convincing demonstration that the church cared for them and was not simply looking for their support. But did the churches have the structures to convey Christian compassion and care for the alienated? Did US denominationalism, for example, convey the impression of mere competition for the membership of mobile populations?

Much of the structure of churches arose from church tradition —and ultimately from the nature of the gospel. That was not at issue. What was significant for evangelism, however, was that the structure of the church had legitimately arisen in the past from the nature of society, and should do so in the present. That was the problem. A sociological concept was embedded in church life.

A first step seemed to be careful analysis of society in order to make church structures relevant to the evangelistic obligations which modern populations place on the church. In practice, flexibility could be achieved by creating new structures to supplement the basic structure of church. Some of these provided experience and hope in the endeavor to reach people outside the life of the churches. They did not compete with church structures, but they did supply a healthy tension.

Other than supplemental organizations and movements, what experience lay behind the demand for structural change? Was it really possible? Did renewal of Christian living come about in this way? Ecumenical people were absolutely certain that the answer to all these questions was Yes. The Confessing Church of Germany was a supplemental structure; the evangelical movement for foreign missions was another; the SCM still another; and in Eastern Europe, perhaps especially in East Germany, heavy pressure on the church produced new life in varied forms, including church structures. Too rigid ecclesiastical structures hindered the living and the presentation of the gospel. The hope for breakthrough was not a mere wish; it was testimony to God's action.[32]

32. Cf. "The Mission of the Church to Those Outside Her Life" (Evanston Sur-

THE LAITY

In my view, the most original aspect of ecumenical thought concerning the church's witness was its stress on the laity.[33] The processes of indigenization in the younger churches and the tension between radicals and traditionalists in the older churches reflected different views of the relationship between Christ and culture, church and society, church and world. In this realm, thought concerning the laity made a particular contribution.

The starting point was in another form of supplemental church structures—the European lay institutes. They arose after the war, wrote Kathleen Bliss of England,

> because Western culture and institutions are deeply secularized and alienated from Christian roots. The Church in its institutional form is remote and irrelevant to society. The purpose of the institutes is to stimulate and instruct the laity to perform their own inalienable duty as people of God in the world of daily life. . . . Their new work means that we should ask, not what should the church be doing, but what is the church.[34]

There were pioneers: Kerk en Wereld in Holland; Glay and Villemetrie in France; Agape in Italy; Boldern and Castel Mainau in Switzerland; Bad Boll and other Evangelical Academies in Germany; Sigtuna in Sweden; Lay Training Institutes in Finland; the Iona Community in Scotland; YMCA colleges in England; and the WCC's own Ecumenical Institute at the Château de Bossey in Switzerland.

The "laity movement" grew because of an increasing awareness of a split personality. Hans-Ruedi Weber, who headed WCC work on the laity, put the fact in the form of questions:

> Is it not . . . true that laymen and laywomen become gradually absorbed by the world because they conform to the spirit, the

veys); "A Theological Reflection on the Work of Evangelism"; *Evanston to New Delhi*, pp. 55f.; "Theological Reflections on the Missionary Task of the Church"; H. J. Margull, "Structures for Missionary Congregations," *International Review of Mission*, LII (1963); Charles C. West and David M. Paton, *The Missionary Church in East and West* (London: SCM Press, 1959).

33. "The Significance of Laity in the Church," Amsterdam Report, pp. 153-55; *The First Six Years*, pp. 40, 60ff.; "The Laity—the Christian in His Vocation," Evanston Report; *Evanston to New Delhi*, pp. 77ff.; "Witness," New Delhi Report, especially the section on "Reshaping the Witnessing Community"; Hans-Ruedi Weber, "The Laity and the Third Assembly," *Ecumenical Review*, XIII (1961); Central Committee minutes, 1962 ("The Tent-Making Ministry") and 1963 ("Statement on Study and Lay Training Centres"); Hendrik Kraemer, *A Theology of the Laity* (Philadelphia: Westminster Press, 1958).

34. In Hans-Ruedi Weber (ed.), *Signs of Renewal: The Life of the Lay Institutes in Europe* (Geneva: WCC Department on the Laity, 1956), pp. 4-6.

criteria and the hopes of this world? Do not most of the church-members live a schizophrenic life, having two different sets of ethics, one for their private Sunday life and the other for their behaviour in the work-a-day world? Does the Christian remnant really live in the world to function there as the salt of the earth? or does it not rather stand aloof from the battlefield?[35]

The implication was clear: change that split personality and the churches' witness would be transformed.

The power of the laity was not unknown in church history. In the apostolic age laity were prominent; the monastic movement rested on lay women and men; the power of the laity helped drive the Reformation, the Great Awakening, pietism, and modern missions. During World War II, not only had laypeople taken responsibility as the ranks of the clergy were depleted, but they had discovered "a new vision of their responsibility for expressing the true nature and task of the Church, not only within its own fellowship, but in the world in which the Church has been set and their own lives are lived."[36]

At the center was the relationship of church and world. Amsterdam stressed the point: "Only by the witness of a spiritually intelligent and active laity can the Church *meet* the modern world in its actual perplexities and life situations."[37] Christian faith and the pressure of the world meet in the layperson.

> Therefore in daily living and work the laity are not mere fragments of the Church who are scattered about in the world. . . . They are the Church's representatives, no matter where they are. It is the laity who draw together work and worship; it is they who bridge the gulf between the Church and the world, and it is they who manifest in word and action the lordship of Christ over that world which claims so much of their time and energy and labour.[38]

This view led back to the faith and the church. It opened up the great phrases: the royal priesthood, the holy nation, the peculiar people; the Body of Christ, with its varied members, one of another. Thus the *ministry* of the laity was recognized. The church abandoned its merely Sunday aspect and took on the special character of being gathered and scattered.

An aspect of lay ministry which especially interested me was

---

35. *Ibid.,* p. 59.
36. *The First Six Years,* p. 40.
37. Amsterdam Report, p. 154.
38. Evanston Report, p. 161.

the issue of work, since I had collaborated with Robert Calhoun on a condensation of his *God and the Common Life* as it bore upon human work.[39] The basic point was that work itself is a channel of God's ordering of the world and life. As such, a person's work in the world was regarded and performed as a calling or vocation from God. On this view, human work is a necessary ordering of daily life to meet human needs; honest work is a service rendered to society; and work is an expression of creativity.

This "work" aspect of the ministry of the laity was put forth by the Second Assembly, but did not withstand the criticism that work itself needed to be restructured if such worthy criteria as these were even to be approximated "on the job." The whole thing, I felt in retrospect, was abandoned too soon, without enough attention given to the point that changing the structures of work would accomplish change in society.

There were other aspects of the ministry of the laity. One was the "incognito" situation of Christian laypeople who, without recognition of their faith as Christians, joined others to perform costly service. Here one heard echoes of the Suffering Servant of Isaiah, who "opened not his mouth." Allied to this was a concern for the multitudes of people, Christians among them, who were or could be "non-professional missionaries." The point was frequently made in WCC circles that people who travel whether on business or leisure might well be missionaries, and suggestions were made as to how this could be done.

Whether conceptually or practically, two biblical images, both pertaining to the church's witness, animated ecumenical thought on the function of the laity: "the salt of the earth" and "the city set on a hill." Both gave body to the church's witness.

*   *   *

Those engaged in the witness of the church in the emerging ecumenical world received a mandate and a vision from their faith in Christ. At times, the Christ to whom witness was born was presented in such ultimate terms as to seem harsh and finally irrelevant to the life of the churches. At other times, Christ seemed to be so domesticated in society as to have lost the power to transform. Overall, however, witness in and

---

39. Robert L. Calhoun, *God and the Common Life* (New York: Charles Scribner's Sons, 1935); *God and the Day's Work* (New York: Association Press, 1944).

to the world was understood to derive from the missionary faith and the missionary church. Therefore, Christian witness stood at the cutting edge. Witness to God-in-Christ put one at the edge defined by truth. The correlates of witness, mission, and evangelism put one at the edge defined by action.

IV

A PEOPLE AMID THE PEOPLES

10

Service: From the Rich to the Devastated, with Dignity

In front of the churches who covenanted together in 1948 stood Christ; all around them was the agony of devastated neighbors—hungry, thirsty, estranged, naked, sick, and imprisoned.

THE HOMELESS

Most staggering of all was the vast number of homeless people and refugees. The hostilities of World War II had ended, leaving 15 million people in Europe without homes; and the factors creating refugees continued elsewhere in the world. By 1959 the world had some 40,000,000 refugees. "Many of them," wrote Edgar Chandler, head of the WCC Refugee Service, "are herded into dingy and primitive camps, or sardine-packed into already overcrowded and dirty cities without work or, even at this very moment are trudging wearily, hungrily and almost without hope along the roads of Europe and of Asia, seeking what is surely everyone's right — a home, and the freedom and security that home should mean."[1] At the time when Henry Luce of *Time* and *Life* proclaimed "the American Century," Chandler's colleague Elfan Rees spoke of "the century of the Homeless Man."[2] The churches and the WCC responded with homes literally for multitudes.

1. Edgar H. S. Chandler, *The High Tower of Refuge* (London: Odhams Press Limited, 1959), pp. 20f.
2. Elfan Reese, *The Century of the Homeless Man* (pamphlet) (The Carnegie Endowment, 1951).

Except for representing the WCC at board meetings of Church World Service in the US between 1948 and 1954 I was a spectator of this work. In Geneva from 1954 onward, I remained a spectator, but at closer range. Chandler, a US Congregationalist, had been a pastor in Boston, fleet chaplain in the US Navy during the war, and director of the Congregationalist effort to help Palestinian refugees before joining the WCC to head its Refugee Service. In formal reports at staff meetings and memoranda sent to our desks, as well as in informal conversations at tea each day or in our homes, Chandler and his colleagues stretched our imaginations and sympathies as the "refugee situation" unfolded.

The United Nations Relief and Works Agency for Palestine Refugees was created in 1950; the next year the WCC held the first Beirut Conference on Arab Refugees.

There Alford Carleton, a US Congregationalist and president of Aleppo College, spoke a telling word:

> The important question is not whether Jews or Arabs attacked first. The fact is that the answer to that question would vary widely from place to place. In reality, it is we, the people of the West, who should be called the true aggressors in Palestine. It is we, through our Governments, who permitted the setting up of such a situation that people would inevitably fly at one another's throats. I wish that every Christian community in England and America would bear this well in mind.[3]

Aware that the WCC's presence in Beirut at this moment would attract attention, Visser 't Hooft was clear as to the basic purpose:

> Christians are concerned with human need, not only with the need of fellow Christians. We do not dream of restricting our help to those of our own religion. . . . This is not a political conference, although in the last resort the problem can only be solved in the realm of politics. Politics have often done more harm than good and it may be that a certain naive approach from the human angle may help.[4]

A second Beirut Conference was held in 1956. During the intervening five years, the Near East Christian Council—with WCC support — had carried on a substantial ministry in the framework of UNRWA, but the "unhappy condition of over 900,000 Arab refugees was fundamentally unchanged." The conference statement stressed ac-

3. Alfred Carleton, "The Background of the Refugee Problem," in *A Report of a Conference on Arab Refugee Problems, 1951* (Geneva: International Missionary Council and the Department of Inter-Church Aid and Service to Refugees of the World Council of Churches, 1951), pp. 11-18.
4. W. A. Visser 't Hooft, *ibid.*, p. 10.

Edgar H. S. Chandler (WCC Photo)

tion to alleviate "the agony of this great company of people, half of whom are children."[5]

On Sunday, November 4, 1956, the first refugees from the Hungarian revolt crossed the frontier into Austria. Within 36 hours, the Refugee Service had given sanctuary to 10,000, and continued with as many as 5000 per night—those who "had waded through the slime of muddy forests in a cruel winter . . . and whose loved ones had been shot, raped and tortured by the frontier guards."[6] Of the total of 180,000, some 165,000 were provided homes outside Austria.

5. "Conference Statement," in *A Report of a Conference on the Problem of Arab Refugees From Palestine, 1956* (Geneva: IMC and WCC, 1956), p. 10.
6. Chandler, *op. cit.*, pp. 39ff.

From 1951 the WCC had a refugee office in Greece to help ethnic refugees make a new life: Rumanians, Albanians, Bulgarians, Yugoslavs, Armenians, White Russians. "The trickle of refugees into Greece never ceases," Chandler wrote, "and to the credit of the Greek government, no genuine refugee is ever turned back." Here as elsewhere the work was "a constant struggle against disbelief, depression and stupid heartless obstruction. Self-respect, and confidence and belief in the world has to be restored."[7] The means were housing, vocational training, and emergency relief.

A "Greek team" sought agricultural rehabilitation of impoverished villages in Greece. Working with the welcome and participation of the Orthodox Church of Greece, this famous team had an extraordinary ecumenical composition, including representatives of Baptist, Brethren, Disciples, Lutheran, Presbyterian, and Mennonite churches, as well as ecumenical agencies from Europe, North America, and Australia.

In the early cold war, refugees had three ways out of the ring around Vienna, all used by the WCC: "over," by airplane; "under," the "greenway" through woods, mines, and miles of barbed wire left; and "through," by railway. Everything involved false papers, which were expensive; plane and train fares made the "over" and the "through" methods even more expensive. Often it was necessary to break the law to help refugees; but, as Chandler wrote, "in this Christian job of freeing the refugees we have to argue the ethics on a rather higher plane than man-made laws."[8]

Funds, goods, food, and medical supplies were required in Korea beginning in 1950. Even before his plane landed in Pusan on his first visit to Korea, Chandler wrote, he

> noticed from aloft that radiating from the city perimeter were ridges that could be deep tank-traps, trough roads or gulleys. Within the hour I discovered that these were trenches that led to rat-holes, in which entire families live — while overhead roared military jet aircraft, this century's latest weapons of destruction. . . . And I was to discover, too, that these rat-hole families were only the advance guard of the awful total of 22 million uprooted Asians, Koreans included, who are making our refugee problems in the Far East so difficult to ease.[9]

Church World Service, Korean Church World Service, and the WCC provided funds and ton after ton of food, medical supplies, and other relief needs.

7. *Ibid.*, p. 78.
8. *Ibid.*, p. 31.
9. *Ibid.*, p. 154.

The story unfolded: Europeans streaming out of the People's Republic of China into Hong Kong; the Old Believers of Russia transported, unbelievably, to Brazil; expatriates from many countries living in Turkey. By 1961 about 325,000 people had been resettled overseas, and if one adds the 350,000 brought directly by Church World Service from Europe prior to 1950, the total is 675,000—not including the substantial numbers resettled by the Lutheran World Federation.[10]

The numbers are impressive—all the more so when one considers a point made by my colleague Norman Goodall in 1961. At the time, the WCC figures broke down to about 1000 refugees every month, thirty every day.

> I remember turning over the pages of a large day-book or journal in an office where some part of this operation was being administered. This was not just a series of numerical items adding up to a grand total. Each page was headed by a name and there followed notes about the history of the person. There were blanks in most of these histories, blanks between the different countries or camps in which the "case" had stayed for a time. There were intermittent references to escapes and deportation. There was information about the nearest relative (so often "none"), about illness, employment, and (especially) unemployment. Here were references to children, to hospitals, to physical defects. And each page was a moving story of some *one*. Twelve thousand a year, about one thousand a month, thirty a day: thirty tomorrow, thirty today; one of the thirty, this minute in my office or home. Today, no passport, no citizenship, no means of livelihood, no home. Tomorrow, or later today—*now*, before the "case" says goodbye and the "caseload" is reduced by one, this *one* has touched me.[11]

Why did Goodall underline the word *one?* Because he introduced the paragraph with these words: "'Master, the multitudes throng thee and press thee; how sayest thou 'Who touched me?' And Jesus said, 'Some *one* hath touched me'. . . .'" The operation embodied dignity.

INTERCHURCH AID

Interchurch aid meant sharing among Christians, "a recognition that when one member suffers, all suffer. It is a strengthening of the weak by the strong. It is an expression of the whole Church in mission. . . .

10. *The First Six Years*, pp. 71f.; *Evanston to New Delhi*, p. 117.
11. Norman Goodall, *The Ecumenical Movement*, p. 86.

The concept is not of Asian churches, African churches, Latin American churches, European or North American churches, but of the one Church, the one community of Christ's people. . . . In such a fellowship to give aid is not to merit honour, to receive it is not to suffer indignity."[12]

Interchurch aid traced its beginnings to an initiative of the European churches in 1919, after the end of World War I. During World War II the Provisional Committee for the WCC set up an Ecumenical Commission for Chaplaincy Service to Prisoners of War. The goal was to provide a regular service, on an international basis, to chaplains among the prisoners of war. In addition to providing Bibles, service books, church equipment, and the like, it carried out the necessary—and often maddening—negotiations involved to ensure that prisoners could be served by clergy of their own confession and language. In some camps theological students could continue their training with an imprisoned "faculty." Although prohibited in many camps, the program showed that "a Church in Captivity is a reality. One of its characteristic features is its real and conscious feeling of belonging to a community which goes beyond its own."[13]

A dramatic development of interchurch aid took place within the missionary enterprise during World War II. When the German invasion of Poland threatened the highly creative German missions at work in Sumatra, Indonesia, Dutch missionary societies sprang to an emergency rescue. As the war intensified in Europe and spread through Asia, more and more missions and missionaries were cut off from their home base. Through the energy and imagination of the International Missionary Council a fund was set up, from which a large number of "orphaned missions" were supported, often ecumenically. "Christians around the world assumed responsibility for the welfare of unknown and sometimes 'enemy' missionaries. Those of other nations and churches safeguarded their property and, often at great sacrifice, maintained their work. Unity born of love was manifesting itself. Here was prime evidence of the inner meaning of the word 'ecumenical'."[14]

At the end of World War II, interchurch aid became a major ecumenical program, established in the WCC even before the Amster-

12. Leslie E. Cooke, *Bread and Laughter* (Geneva: World Council of Churches, 1968), p. 50.

13. Norman Goodall, *op. cit.,* p. 79; cf. *The World Council of Churches: Its Process of Formation,* pp. 164-71.

14. Kenneth Scott Latourette and W. Richey Hogg, *World Christian Community in Action: The Story of World War II and Orphaned Missions* (New York: International Missionary Council, 1949), p. 33.

dam Assembly. The focus was first Europe; and as needs were met there, basic principles were established for work that soon came to be seen as a permanent ecumenical obligation. The need in Europe was to help disabled churches take their place in the urgent spiritual struggles of the time. There was a transition from "a period when an effort was made in a spirit of compassion to restore what had been destroyed to a period of seeking to make the Church more effective for the task laid upon it. The necessity for the churches in Europe to fill the vacuum caused by the disillusion following the war was constantly emphasized."[15]

The needs were both physical and spiritual, if such a distinction can be made. The material needs, especially for food, were substantial. From 1955 to 1960, 49,000 tons of supplies, valued at $51,000,000, were distributed from church sources; and in addition, through the Surplus Commodities Programme of the US government, administered by Church World Service, more than 1,000,000 tons of food, worth $195,000,000, was distributed in 45 different countries.[16] In Germany, *Notkirchen*, churches built from the rubble, had to be constructed. Other priorities were the health and training of pastors, development of the witness of the laity, new experiments in evangelism, and aid to minority churches in France, Belgium, Austria, Italy, Spain, and Portugal. Scholarship money was sought to enable theological students from impoverished churches to study abroad.

We noted earlier how meaningful interchurch aid had been for the Church of Greece. During the dark decade of 1949 to 1958, when peoples and churches of Eastern Europe were cut off from the rest of the world, "a thin red line maintained contact between churches of east and west. In the World Council of Churches' Health Programme parcels of rare drugs were sent regularly to sick priests and pastors and church workers. As far as Rumania and Bulgaria were concerned it was the only open line of communication. It became the symbol of an unbroken fellowship."[17] Thus the postwar years saw "a new understanding and confidence growing up between Protestant and Orthodox Christians within the general pattern of Interchurch Aid."[18]

Beginning in 1946 some 6000 young people participated in ecumenical work camps in 30 countries in Latin America, the Middle East, Europe, and Africa. From their original concern with postwar reconstruction and relief, the work camps evolved. The practice was to select a situation in which church relations were tense, perhaps because of is-

15. *The First Six Years*, p. 64.
16. *Evanston to New Delhi*, pp. 120f.
17. Leslie E. Cooke, *op. cit.*, p. 63.
18. *The First Six Years*, p. 68.

sues of faith and order, or of Christian social action, or of the cooperation of men and women. For the young people in the camps, these problems ceased being merely theoretical. They learned about the growing
pains of ecumenism while helping the church situation in which they
were working.

Moved by hearing the reports of my colleagues and seeing them
work to the limit of endurance and then be refreshed by the demands
of the next day, the next emergency, and the next appeal for help, I
sometimes wondered whether all the study work, the theological reflection, the endless discussion of sometimes fine points were worth it in
view of the commanding need of fellow human beings. At such moments, Visser 't Hooft came to the rescue, albeit unconsciously. In conversation and meetings, his sense of balance and proportion was a kind
of saving grace. Whether responding to the daily or yearly round of
concerns, or to the latest international crisis, or to our reports, he had
a way of making us see the essential point: how it all fitted, in his typical phrase, into "our common calling."

Early on, the administration of interchurch aid and service to
refugees made a fundamental decision not to try to become an agency
which, by annual appeal or endowment raising, would amass vast sums
of money to spend. Nor would it become a huge worldwide agency
doing relief work itself. That would have been the expression of a "super-
church" in the field of meeting human need, a way of using human
need for ecumenical self-aggrandizement.

Indeed, one of my first acts of trouble-shooting in the WCC was
precisely at this point. It occurred in the summer of 1948, while I was
at work on the organization of the Amsterdam Assembly. I suppose because I had access to Visser 't Hooft, people began informally, sometimes confidentially, to complain to me about the administration of interchurch aid, then in the hands of James Hutchinson Cockburn, a Scot
of such regal bearing that he had earned the name of "King James"
(especially among those who disliked the way he worked). He appeared
to want all the money given for interchurch aid to be unearmarked, so
that he could decide how to dispense it. That did not sit well with representatives of other churches—among them Benjamin Bush of my own
church — who were responsible for seeing that substantial sums of
money were well spent on interchurch aid. Complaints became so
frequent and strident that it became clear that I must do something.

But what? I could not intervene, and instinct told me that to
take the matter to Visser 't Hooft would only earn me a "mind your own
business" from him. Then I learned that Samuel Cavert was coming to
Geneva. Before his bags were unpacked, I was having tea with him on

the veranda of his hotel and acquainting him — in confidence — of the situation, urging him to take action as he deemed fit. Cavert, seeing the danger of a financial super-church operating in interchurch aid, acted discreetly, wisely, and decisively. I never heard further about the matter until, some two months later, it was announced that Robert Mackie would replace Cockburn.

From this point on, interchurch aid leaders in the churches and the WCC made a distinction. On the one side were needs, such as refugee service, which demanded a relatively large staff, mostly in regional or country offices; on the other side were services such as health assistance to pastors, scholarships, work camps, and aid to minority churches in Europe, which required a minimal headquarters staff and relatively small facilitating funds, and could be directly administered from headquarters.

The innovative side of the distinction was the "Project List," at first a thick document, later a good-sized book which listed specific projects proposed by churches or groups of churches to meet certain needs. Projects originated in the country, and required clearance from a council of churches or other ecumenical committee there before being sent to Geneva for discussion and then to a world consultation of interchurch aid people from various countries, convened every year by the WCC's Division of Interchurch Aid. Approved projects became a part of the list, which was forwarded to the churches as a request for help. Response came from around the world, directly from giver to receiver, with the Division of Interchurch Aid being kept informed.

This method of churches helping churches had immense ecclesiological importance. As far as the WCC was concerned, it kept the Council in its proper place as helper of the member churches. For member churches, the Project List was a means of "conversation." One part of that conversation concerned the urgency — and hence the priority — of the project itself. But another part of the conversation went deeper. Did the project aim to meet a need sufficiently urgent to take precedence over differences in faith and order between "giving" and "receiving" churches? Indeed, to what degree did differences of doctrine and tradition among the churches matter when it came to supporting these projects?

On the whole, churches supported one another. Even when they responded along confessional lines, they did so within the larger framework. The *need* presented by one member of the Body of Christ and the response by another member to it transcended the specific doctrinal positions of both, as both stood in relationship to Christ and the need within his fellowship.

Robert C. Mackie and Robert S. Bilheimer (WCC Photo)

It was this dimension of aid inspired by need within the ecumenical fellowship which led Visser 't Hooft to comment that "only with regard to interchurch aid is our record perhaps somewhat comparable to that of the early church."[19]

THE POOR

It was not long before the range of vision expanded dramatically. By the time of the Second Assembly, economic recovery in Europe meant that the immediate concerns of the postwar period had receded. It was decided to break new ground. Henceforth, Evanston directed, WCC Interchurch Aid would operate outside Europe as well.[20] By the time the Third Assembly met in 1961, the pressing and longer range needs of the churches in Asia and Africa stood at the forefront.

In 1955, during the Central Committee meeting in Davos, Switzerland, Robert Mackie rose to make a scheduled address on "Interchurch

19. W. A. Visser 't Hooft, *The Pressure of Our Common Calling*, p. 24.
20. Evanston Report, pp. 233ff.

Aid."[21] A clergyman of the Church of Scotland, he had been general secretary of the British SCM and then of the WSCF. Experienced, gentle but firm, always a pastor, instantly and sincerely a friend, a man of unerring theological instinct if not a theologian, Mackie was addressing the Central Committee no longer as director but as chair of the Division of Interchurch Aid. He spoke of the new turn of interchurch aid towards being a world agency.

Mackie began by quoting the Lebanese ambassador to the US, Charles Malik, a devout Orthodox and delegate to the Second Assembly, concerning "the great stirring for social justice, for the elimination of discrimination and misery, for the liberation of the eternally depressed and dispossessed, for conferring some dignity upon millions of human beings who are only human by name. All this certainly reflects the will of Christ. Whoever misses the bus with respect to fundamental social change is certainly going to be left by the wayside."

Governments, Mackie recognized, would respond, but so should the churches. Governments would operate from natural self-interest, from political and commercial motives; and behind governmental action there would always be "the shadow of the balance of power." Moreover, governments would be unable to touch the moral and spiritual consequence of the Asian and African social revolutions.

In these countries, Mackie went on, the churches were minority churches in non-Christian and sometimes anti-Christian environments. Recently independent themselves, these churches had the further burden of a wholly new political and social situation. If aid to them were bilateral from the West, it was an open question how far the presence of the West might help or hinder them.

"We have," he said, "a fellowship represented in this room in which there are no 'older' and 'younger' churches, in which there can be no hint of patronage due to size or history. In all our churches there is the same story of human weakness and divine strength. We all stand under the judgment and mercy of the Cross of our Lord Jesus Christ. And in our World Council there has grown up a will to bear one another's burdens. That is a new factor in Christian history."

Stressing that the primary response to human need is the gospel of Jesus Christ, Mackie outlined another form of response appearing now in a new guise: "We must see whether God is calling us to . . . work out again the nature of the service of Christians to one another and to their fellow human beings."

21. Robert C. Mackie, "The Responsibility of the Churches in the World Council Towards the Needs of the Churches and of the Peoples of Asia and Africa," in Central Committee minutes, 1955, pp. 79-84.

The Central Committee was composed of august church officials, all of them exceptionally hard-nosed when it came to speeches, of which they had heard many. But when Mackie finished, it was evident that he had gotten through. The Central Committee put its full backing into a historic turn of the Division of Interchurch Aid. The new director, Leslie E. Cooke, would guide and superbly interpret the new dimensions of work through and past the Third Assembly. Much of the customary work would go forward, but the pioneering ecumenical thought and energy in Interchurch Aid would be consumed with helping the churches in the revolutionary continents of the poor.

Of the interchurch aid enterprise, Stephen Neill wrote in 1960, "In the whole history of the Christian Churches, there has never been so great, so sustained, and so simply generous a manifestation of Christian charity."[22] To this it should be added that the understanding of *diakonia*, service, behind this manifestation contributed powerfully to the content of the growing ecumenical tradition. This understanding of *diakonia* contained three elements.

First, from the ecumenical aid to earliest refugees in Europe to its extension to Asia, Africa, and Latin America, "service" recognized the primacy of the poor, the powerless, and the outcast. Energy and substance flowed toward them as toward nothing else within the sphere of ecumenical church interest. Millions of dollars were contributed ecumenically for helping them even before the WCC was constituted; and this continued. The first WCC "General Budget"—which included everything but interchurch aid — was authorized at $363,000; and the ratio between that and the millions for interchurch aid was maintained. The particular credit for this does not go to the WCC managers, but to the awakening of the churches to the absolute primacy given to "the poor" by the gospel.

Second, there was a growing recognition of the relation of "service" to governmental structures and power. In practice, ecumenical work for refugees proceeded hand-in-glove with intergovernmental agencies. Other interchurch aid work took full account of governmental reconstruction in Europe, as well as intergovernmental and bilateral efforts of "foreign aid." Theologically, this translated into an earthy perception of both the constructive and the corrupting role of what the New Testament called "principalities and powers."

Third, "service" or *diakonia* as expressed in relation to the poor and outcast made a giant contribution to the understanding of "fellow-

---

22. Stephen Neill, *Brothers of the Faith* (Nashville: Abingdon Press, 1960), p. 147; quoted in Cavert, *On the Road to Christian Unity*, p. 41.

ship" or *koinonia*. This went far beyond the old slogan of the Life and Work movement that "service unites." From one point of view, the service was generous; from another, it was partial. No church was completely self-sacrificing. In this respect every church possessed only the *vestigia ecclesiae*. That in turn meant that this concept of the "traces of the church" applied not only to the problem of unity, but to the essence of the life of the church. The work of interchurch aid accomplished a deepening in the comprehension of the *vestigia ecclesiae,* so that the work signified an undeniable quality of churchliness. In this quality, the church was perceived to live within the churches, to be brought to expression whenever homes were found for the homeless and true service done for the poor.

11

Peace and the World of Nations

The world of the WCC's first decade-and-a-half was filled with international tensions, dangers, and sometimes eruptions. The Cold War was severe. Strong and expectant nationalism animated the newly independent peoples in Asia and Africa and expanded the world of nations. To those great wellsprings of mutual suspicion, the "East" and "West" blocs, was added the "non-aligned" of Afro-Asian countries. There and elsewhere, awakened aspirations and the urgency of justice stood behind the desire of nations and peoples for development. Still a tower of economic and military strength, the US was beginning to lose its immediate postwar moral leadership, as people elsewhere became more and more fearful of its intense anti-Communism. Wars broke out in Korea, Suez, Hungary, and Indochina. Everywhere promoting and securing human rights became increasingly urgent. And the dreaded prospect of nuclear holocaust overshadowed all.[1]

By 1952 four worlds — North America, Western Europe, the USSR with Eastern Europe, and Asia — pressed on international consciousness. "They live," said Visser 't Hooft, "in different stages of history. It is not for us or perhaps for anyone to say which or any of them represents the future. It is, however, the great task of the World Council to keep ourselves aware and to make the Churches conscious of the relativity of each of these worlds. None of their ideologies and concerns can claim to have absolute value and all need, therefore, to be kept in

---

1. On the world situation, see Amsterdam Report, p. 88; Evanston Survey, "The World Crisis and Christian Responsibility," pp. 3-5; Evanston Report, p. 131; New Delhi Report, pp. 106f.

living contact with each other."[2] Soon, there would be the fifth world of independent Africa. "One world," which inspired hope during three or four postwar years, became only a distant dream, except for those who saw that under the fragmentations wrought by history "the world is in God's hands."[3]

Those who covenanted with one another at the First Assembly in 1948 were guided thereafter by their first affirmation concerning international disorder. "We are one in proclaiming to all," they said, that "war is contrary to the will of God."[4] Immediately it was necessary to recognize three positions taken by Christians concerning their participation in war: (1) because of the mass destruction of modern warfare, Christians should not participate; (2) because there are no supranational institutions of law and order, force remains the sanction of law, and Christians must defend the law by force if necessary; (3) Christians are called to an absolute witness against war and for peace and may never accept military service.

Those holding these positions were united in the conviction that justice must be upheld in international as well as national life, and that in war or peace the state may not use Christian spiritual or moral principles to propagate an ideology. "Churches must teach the duty of love and prayer for the enemy in time of war and of reconciliation between victor and vanquished after the war."[5]

Some people raised questions about following an absolute statement that war is against the will of God by an acknowledgment that there are three Christian positions concerning participation in war, without expressing any judgment among them. Yet in spite of the differing positions, all felt that the stark confession should be made.

In a way, of course, the critics were right. But who could deny that both Christians and churches fell far short of the gospel? There was an analogy between the basic affirmation about war and different views about participating in it, and the affirmation that the church of Christ is one and the sin of divided churches. At neither point did the ecumenical tradition shrink from the claims of the gospel or the facts of the situation. The affirmation that the church of Christ is one was followed with strenuous efforts to achieve unity. The affirmation that war is contrary to the will of God was followed by strong effort and witness for peace.

This witness consisted broadly of two parts: the delineation of

2. Report of the general secretary, Executive Committee meeting, December 1951, pp. 3f.
3. Amsterdam Report, p. 88.
4. *Ibid.*, p. 89.
5. *Ibid.*, p. 90.

substantial lines of thought offered to the member churches, and the effort to make an ecumenical impact on international disorder.

THE WORLD OF NATIONS

Living Together in a Divided World

Already in 1948 it was clear that a positive attempt was needed to insure that Communism, Socialism, and free enterprise could live together without war.[6] By 1954, the gulf between the Communist and non-Communist world was at its deepest. If the McCarthy hysteria in the US was subsiding, anti-Communism remained strong. The defense perimeter was drawn around the USSR, but in official circles there was talk of coexistence.

Meeting in the US, with delegates from behind the Iron Curtain present and voting, the Second Assembly spoke forthrightly:

> The clash of national interests, social systems and ideologies tends to dominate every phase of international life. Hostile propaganda, border incidents and a suicidal competition in arms more deadly than any hitherto used, characterize a situation which is unfit to be described as peace. Over all there moves the spectre of total war.[7]

"Coexistence" seemed to settle for something Christians could not abide. Its static connotations covered up

> the vast difference which lies between the search for an international order based on belief in Christ and His reconciling work, and the pursuit of aims which repudiate the Christian revelation. . . . We stand against submission to, engulfment by, or appeasement of totalitarian tyranny and aggression. We also stand against the exploitation of any people by economic monopoly or political imperialism. In the world community we must stand for the freedom of all people to know the truth which makes men free and for the basic civil liberties of all people to struggle for a higher freedom.[8]

The alternative to coexistence was "living together in a divided world." In a climate of coexistence, this called for a "willingness not to

6. *Ibid.,* p. 91.
7. Evanston Report, p. 135.
8. *Ibid.*

use force beyond existing frontiers," a provision which did not mean freezing present injustices or wrong divisions, but did mean giving up coercion as a means of correcting them; a strong effort to correct injustices that might lead to conflict, and willingness to submit all issues of conflict to an impartial international organization and to abide by its decisions.

Two incidents gave me a personal view of what was involved in such "living together." It had been necessary to secure a guarantee from the US government that church representatives from Eastern Europe could attend the Assembly in Evanston freely. Methodist Bishop G. Bromley Oxnam, one of the WCC presidents, who had just trounced Senator McCarthy on television in one of the famous hearings, Franklin Clark Fry, moderator of the Central Committee, O. Frederick Nolde, director of the WCC's Commission of the Churches on International Affairs (CCIA), and I had a few minutes with President Eisenhower to secure his guarantee. We were introduced to the president by John Foster Dulles, who had been prominent ecumenically but whose "cold warrior" stance as secretary of state denied any vestige of ecumenical breadth. Within three or four minutes, the president said that he would certainly admit the church representatives, provided that he was assured they were not members of the Communist Party. Dulles agreed.

Beyond the president's consent, what was important in this short interview was that the most powerful leader in the world and his influential Secretary had for a moment seen beyond the Cold War. They saw something of "living together" and the dynamics which that required. I was of course glad; if they had refused, we would have moved the Assembly out of the US.

The second incident occurred the day before the Assembly convened. I drove two Hungarian and two Czech delegates, one of them Josef Hromadka, from Chicago Theological Seminary on the south side of the city to Evanston. No one had told them how far it was, and after a half hour they asked, "How long?" I told them. Even so, they asked again about every ten minutes. Excited talk in Hungarian, Czech, and German conveyed rising tension and fear. Hromadka could not calm them, and he whispered to me that the others thought they were in the hands of the FBI. When the "Evanston" sign appeared, I slowed down to make sure they could read it. Their spirits revived. If Eisenhower had symbolized something of breadth amid the problems of power, these men had showed me the depth of the fear involved in "living together."

The United Nations

A major aspect of WCC efforts to promote peace was representations to governments through the United Nations. Opinion about the UN varied. In the US churches expectation ran high; elsewhere, there was less enthusiasm. Even so, there was a case to be made for making the UN a major arena of Christian witness.

The first consideration was the UN's capacity for peacemaking. A survey in preparation for the Evanston Assembly noted that

> The United Nations, as well as related agencies, including the International Court of Justice, provides the nations with an instrument for the development of international law, the just regulation of common interests of nations as well as for the peaceful settlement of disputes, and the discouragement of threats to peace. It also provides a world forum for the interchange of thought between diverse cultures and viewpoints. Through such cooperation these institutions offer now an effective means of developing conditions essential to the rule of law in the world.[9]

Secondly, the UN offered a substantial means for promoting human welfare. Its related organizations were rendering valuable service in combating ignorance, want, and disease. The UN was providing many essential services for refugees and migrants and helping to create a common mind as to human rights.

The Commission of the Churches on International Affairs was a registered nongovernmental organization (NGO) at the UN. Nolde, who had been a professor at Mt. Airy Seminary of the United Lutheran Church, maintained a full-time presence there. Each year, he and his staff compiled, from a carefully selected worldwide roster of correspondents, a list of what churches or interchurch agencies had said or done about items on the UN agenda. To these were added the actions of the CCIA committee and the WCC governing bodies.

Besides showing, item by item, year by year, the positions of responsible churches and agencies, this document identified ethical problems involved in each agenda item. As time went on, the document reached formidable proportions and was widely used at the UN both by government delegations and other NGOs.

From the WCC viewpoint, the document was a vehicle for Christian presence; and much of the effort of Nolde and his colleagues went into discussing agenda points of major concern with the delegates. Their diplomatic skill enhanced the WCC presence at the UN.

9. Evanston Survey, p. 10.

Three of the CCIA officers: Kenneth Grubb (top l.), O. Frederick Nolde (top r.), and Richard M. Fagley (WCC Photos)

Even so, many were uneasy. The agenda was the UN's, with the WCC and churches reacting to it. Moreover, far more thought needed to be given to the relationship between specific proposals and the basic principles of world order. Theological thought in these dimensions was at a minimum. As the CCIA officers admitted, "the difficulty of retaining a balance between Christian action for peace and justice and Christian judgment on the predicament of man and society has hardly been grappled with."[10] There was an acknowledged need for thought, for sound education concerning worldwide community, and particularly for more national commissions to serve the CCIA. Regrettably, very little was accomplished toward the achievement of these objectives.

On two occasions, the CCIA made notable contributions to the UN itself. One was to conceive the idea and then assist in securing the adoption of UN Observer Commissions, to be sent to areas of special tension, and to make such teams available to any government that feared aggression. An original idea, it represented a lasting addition to the UN apparatus for peacekeeping.[11] The other concerned religious liberty.

Human Rights and Religious Liberty

The ecumenical contribution in the area of religious liberty began in 1945, two years before CCIA was founded and three years before the Amsterdam Assembly. Nolde was present at the founding of the UN in San Francisco under US church auspices. The effort culminated with the adoption of the Universal Declaration of Human Rights by the UN General Assembly in Paris in December 1948. By then Nolde was armed with "A Declaration on Religious Liberty," a fundamental document that had been formally adopted (not merely "received") by the First Assembly.[12]

The particular ecumenical contribution to the Universal Declaration of Human Rights was Article 18 on religious liberty, of which Nolde was virtually the author. It was closely watched, and, because of its fundamental importance, the battle for its adoption was intense. Charles Malik of Lebanon, who chaired the crucial committee in the Paris Assembly, wrote later:

> What constitutes the humanity of man more than anything else is this inward freedom, which should therefore be absolutely

10. *Ibid.*, pp. 45f.
11. *Ibid.*, p. 20. The main elements were incorporated in the "Uniting for Peace" resolution approved by the UN General Assembly, Nov. 3, 1950. This was supported by the WCC Executive Committee in February 1951.
12. Amsterdam Report, pp. 97-99.

inviolable. Hence, though I cared for every word in the Declaration, I felt that, if we should lose on this Article on freedom of conscience and religion, namely, if man's absolute freedom were to be derogated from in any way, even by the subtlest indirection, my interest in the remainder of the Declaration would considerably flag. . . . And so I determined quite early that, of all battles—and we had no end of them!—we would not lose *this battle*, especially . . . that engagement which affirms *the right to change* one's religion or belief. The very essence of freedom is *the right to become,* not the right to be.[13]

The WCC's commitment to religious liberty in 1948 carried into its own life and development. A full-time Secretariat on Religious Liberty watched for abridgments of religious liberty, and, equally important, produced major studies concerning varied dimensions of religious liberty.[14]

The commitment to religious liberty on the one hand and to evangelism on the other led to the troublesome problem of proselytism, understood as a corruption of witness.

Witness is corrrupted when cajolery, bribery, undue pressure or intimidation is used—subtly or openly—to bring about seeming conversion; when we put the success of our church before the honour of Christ; when we commit the dishonesty of comparing the ideal of our own church with the actual achievement of another; when we seek to advance our own cause by bearing false witness against another church; when personal or corporate self-seeking replaces love for every individual soul with whom we are concerned. Such corruption of the Christian witness indicates lack of confidence in the power of the Holy Spirit.[15]

Even if all the corruption were eliminated—a utopian hope—the problem was inescapable. People would want to change their religion, and people would want to persuade others to change their religion. And religious liberty rested on the freedom of a person or group to do so. Among the measures suggested to alleviate the problem one seemed fundamental: where a church's witness to Christ appeared to be highly inadequate, "the first effort of other churches should be patiently to help that church towards its renewal."[16] That meant inter-

---

13. Charles Habib Malik, introduction to O. Frederick Nolde, *Free and Equal* (Geneva: World Council of Churches, 1968), pp. 10f.
14. A. F. Carrillo de Albornoz, *The Basis of Religious Liberty* (London: SCM Press, 1963); Carrillo was the staff member for the WCC Secretariat for Religious Liberty.
15. *Evanston to New Delhi,* p. 241.
16. *Ibid.,* p. 245.

church aid, and one reason for the profound welcome afforded to the WCC's interchurch aid programs lay in their purpose of renewal and their disavowal of proselytism.

Atomic Weapons and Disarmament

Efforts to overcome the threat of nuclear war began at once. The World Council and the CCIA saw no solution but the reduction and eventual elimination of atomic weaponry. But that encountered the intractable problem of reliable verification.

Given the climate of the Cold War period, however, the first problem was to secure agreement to stop testing new weapons. By preventing atomic weapons tests, the status quo could be preserved and the stage set for nuclear disarmament. The WCC made repeated statements supporting the cessation of tests, but refused to join the nuclear pacifists (who first gained prominence in the Stockholm Appeal, backed by Gunnar Myrdal) because it seemed simplistic. Nor was it able to make common cause with the Prague-based Christian Peace Conference, which seemed too closely tied to the policies of the Eastern bloc. The WCC was criticized on both accounts, but not in sufficient strength by its member churches to change its stance.

There was one variation in the succession of ecumenical statements on atomic weapons: a three-year inquiry on "Christians and the Prevention of War in the Atomic Age—a Theological Study." It aroused widespread and intense debate, and its basic conceptions found a substantial place in the Third Assembly.

In 1955, the Central Committee named a commission of recognized authorities in the scientific, political, historical, military, and theological fields. They reported to the Central Committee in 1958.[17] The commission focussed on two concepts: the "indiscriminate" character of atomic warfare and "discipline."

Describing modern warfare and especially atomic weapons as "indiscriminate" was not new. Since the Allied fire-bombing of German cities, so eloquently protested by Bishop Bell in the House of Lords, this had been a serious element in the fear of future war.[18] The possibility of an all-out atomic war raised "indiscriminateness" to such absolute proportions as to deny Christian faith. The reconciliation accomplished

17. The report in 1958 was entitled *A Provisional Study Document on "Christians and the Prevention of War in an Atomic Age—A Theological Discussion"* (mimeographed). References are from Sir Thomas Taylor and Robert S. Bilheimer, *Christians and the Prevention of War in an Atomic Age* (London: SCM Press, 1961).
18. Amsterdam Report, p. 89.

by God in Christ was personal and communal, culminating in the transformation or consummation of human history, but it was based on the
infinite precision of the self-emptying love of God, not on an indiscriminate principle.

The indiscriminate character of atomic war appeared in different aspects. All physical objectives in the portion of the world involved
in the war are destroyed indiscriminately. Political objectives are destroyed indiscriminately. "What do order or freedom or justice mean in
the wasteland resulting from a nuclear holocaust?" And atomic war is
uncontrollable to the degree that dirty bombs pollute the atmosphere.

At this point, "discipline" entered the argument, gathering force
from an analysis of science and the scientific method by the extraordinary mind of C. F. von Weizsäcker, atomic physicist, philosopher, and
theologian. A known opponent of Hitler, he had after the war, for reasons of Christian faith, refused any participation in the construction of
atomic weapons.

Von Weizsäcker maintained that the scientific method involves
a unique combination of subjective and objective. It depends on human
minds, but not on any one or group. It has an objective quality, consisting of its own inner logic, and a certain independent existence.
Moreover, the scientific method is irreversible — one cannot turn the
clock back—and public—the results of the scientific method cannot be
held privately.

On this analysis, the method on which contemporary scientific
and technological culture is based leads to a situation of "deep moral
challenge."

> A *process*, which is ambiguous and which contains its own dy-
> namic, which is irreversible and produces unpredictable results,
> which already has greatly benefited mankind and promises to
> produce greater welfare, is at present regarded idolatrously as
> the principal source of plenty, security and well being. This
> means that deep within technological society, indeed in one
> sense as its mainspring, there is a powerful, impersonal ele-
> ment.[19]

That analysis gave point to the concept of "discipline." "We
believe," the commission said, "that a new orientation, a new attitude,
is required, which we would call a new spiritual discipline, capable of
using technological achievements in a responsible and ethical fashion."[20]
This was an attack on "scientism," a pervasive idolatry of most of West-

19. Taylor and Bilheimer, *op. cit.,* p. 23.
20. *Ibid.,* p. 24.

ern society, which placed undue confidence in science for human betterment. Positively, it addressed the ambiguity — the use for good or bad — which attends the scientific method, process, and results.

The theological critique was clear. All that is involved in the Lordship of Christ denies this or any other form of idolatry.

Applied to atomic war, this analysis meant two things. First, atomic energy, and hence atomic weapons, cannot be gotten rid of absolutely. The method and knowledge which produced them are permanent and irreversible. At root, the only means of control are moral and political. Second, a limit to the policy of increasing reliance on atomic weapons "must be set somewhere. *Since this limit is not now set by the limits of technological knowledge, it must be set by a decision of mind and will.*"[21] This was the connecting concept between the reconciliation of God-in-Christ and the possibility of nuclear holocaust; it was the fundamental argument of the whole report.

Various limits were suggested. At the time, two were eye-openers. The first was:

> Christians have no alternative but openly to declare that the all-out use of these [atomic] weapons should never be resorted to. Moreover, we believe that Christians must oppose all policies which give evidence of leading to all-out war. Finally (although we would answer "No") we ask: if all-out war should occur, does a Christian have any alternative but to accept a cease fire, if necessary on the enemy's terms, and resort to non-violent resistance? We purposely refrain from defining the stage at which all-out war may be reached.[22]

The second limitation was "no first-strike":

> So long as megaton weapons are in the possession of different nations and until there is disarmament, we are all agreed in the declaration of the principle that at least it is not permissible to use them before the other party has done so, or to take any advantage from their possession, except to deter other parties from using them.[23]

When I showed the document to Visser 't Hooft after the final meeting of the commission, he took it home to read. The next morning I asked his opinion. "My word, Bob, if I have understood that document, it means that there must simply be no war and really that Christians cannot support a war." I assured him he had not missed the point

21. *Ibid.,* p. 36.
22. *Ibid.,* p. 37.
23. *Ibid.,* p. 44.

and asked him what our colleagues in the CCIA would think. Typically, he rolled his eyes upward and wrinkled his forehead, indicating that the roof would come off. But he encouraged me to put it to the Central Committee.

He was right: the roof nearly came off. The ground was prepared by strong presentations by von Weizsäcker and C. L. Patijn of Holland, a layman who knew his Bible and his theology, who had a distinguished career in the Dutch parliament and foreign office, and who was a veteran leader in the WCC. Nolde, stung particularly by "no first strike" but not liking the main point which Visser 't Hooft had unerringly discerned, vigorously opposed the whole.

The Central Committee, stressing that the document represented a study and not a policy, authorized its publication, as I had hoped, and it was widely discussed. Its influence was extended through the work of Alan Booth, who injected needed theological perception into the work of the CCIA and was instrumental in ensuring that the Third Assembly, two years later, stressed "indiscriminate," "no first strike," and the need for discipline in attitudes toward science and its results.[24]

"TRANSCENDENCE" AND THE WORLD OF NATIONS

At the First Assembly, Philip Potter, who would later become WCC general secretary, presented a remarkable report on behalf of the youth delegation. It claimed that the churches' basic task in regard to international order is to give evidence of unity, to rise above the voice of the nation in matters of both justice and peace, and to demonstrate a community that includes races without discrimination. Furthermore, the youth report stressed the need to return to the Bible for a basic understanding of international order.

> A core of international problems is the contradiction between the biblical concept of the nation and the concept which the modern nation holds about itself. According to the Bible, the nation fulfils its function only when it is obedient to God and accepts His moral law and authority. . . . Through frank ecumenical discussions the Christian should be helped to distinguish between the claims of his nation, which can be considered as just and those claims which conflict with the sovereignty of God.[25]

24. *New Delhi Report,* pp. 97, 108.
25. Amsterdam Report, p. 196.

The youth delegation had put clearly a question that would continue to challenge the Council: Could the WCC help the churches to transcend their nationalisms, both cultural and political, and thus contribute to international order?

Different ideas about what action concerning peace and international affairs was appropriate for the WCC always lay just below the surface.

On the one side was the heavy reliance on making representations to governments at the UN. I sometimes found myself asking why so much time and energy were spent in this way. One reason was undoubtedly the enthusiasm of the US churches for the UN, an enthusiasm that churches elsewhere acquiesced in, though they did not share it. Another reason lay in an article Nolde had written for the preparatory volume for Amsterdam, in which he argued for a "juridical approach" to human rights. By that he meant the development of international law concerning human rights and the adoption of it by governments and the UN.[26] Over time it became clear that this was his approach to all international issues—and it became a main approach of the WCC as well. This meant that the Council would need to have a "position" formulated by one of its organs—the CCIA executive committee or a WCC governing body—which could then be the basis of representations to governments.

The advantages of this approach were that it required the WCC to think about what position it would take on major international issues and it provided for contact with governments represented at the UN. On the liability side, it tended to restrict the WCC to the UN agenda plus such international crises as arose, keeping the Council in a situation of responding, with too little time left for thinking of initiatives. Thus proscribed in its UN operation, the CCIA could not avoid a certain captivity to diplomacy, accompanied by wariness of prophetic voices.

On the other side was a divergent concept of action for peace. The CCIA not only had an office in New York, but also one in London. Here the chief figure was Sir Kenneth Grubb, the chair of CCIA, ably assisted later by Alan Booth. A prominent laymen in the Church of England, Grubb had had a distinguished career in government during World War II. Booth was a Methodist minister and had been general secretary of the British SCM. Their approach did not contradict that of Nolde and his New York-based colleagues, but it was significantly different.

---

26. O. Frederick Nolde, "Freedom of Religion and Related Human Rights," Amsterdam Vol. 4, pp. 143-89.

In essence, the London-based operation was pragmatic. Grubb and Booth felt that conversation and dialogue with people of substantial responsibility in government, especially those with Christian convictions, was more important than presenting them with positions worked out by WCC committees. The objective was not to preach at government officials, but to secure their thought and initiative on pragmatic solutions to acute problems of peace and international affairs.

Accordingly, time was spent in seeking out responsive and responsible persons, and creating opportunities to explore politically workable and acceptable solutions. This approach produced networks of sympathetic people to whom appeals were made in times of need.

This line of work had its obvious advantages: creativity, imagination, access to influence, wide participation. It also had a built-in disadvantage: because of the people involved, these processes were (or at least were thought to be) effective in inverse proportion to the amount of publicity given them. Thus very little appears in the official WCC documentation concerning this work. On the other side, however, this approach later had the extraordinary result of an initiative by Grubb and Booth which produced the present-day Institute of Strategic Studies in London.

At the time I wished that the considerable tension between these two emphases of CCIA could have been brought into the open and given some resolution, for even then it seemed crippling—though that does not imply that it was "ineffective." On the contrary, a substantial contribution was made overall in establishing the fundamental point. Whether at the UN or with individual governments and politicians, all considered it imperative for the ecumenical movement to transcend the threats to peace and contribute to a better international order.

The specific programs were augmented by demonstrations of this transcendence. Within two years of the founding of the WCC, the question was sharply asked: "How Western is the WCC?" The Central Committee at Toronto in 1950 received worldwide press coverage for its support of the United Nations action in Korea. Referring to evidence that North Korean troops had secretly launched a calculated attack, the Committee said: "Armed attack as an instrument of national policy is wrong. We therefore commend the United Nations, an instrument of world order, for its prompt decision to meet this aggression and for authorizing a police measure which every member nation should support."[27]

Within six months, the general secretary told the Executive Committee the next February, the statement had produced more reac-

27. Central Committee minutes, 1950, pp. 91f.

tion than any other WCC document. Much was favorable, but strong negative reactions came from convinced pacifists and—for different reasons—from Hungary, Czechoslovakia, France, and some Asian countries. Within a year, T. C. Chao, the Chinese president of the WCC, resigned and Bishop Bereczky of Hungary threatened to do the same.

Could the WCC transcend the East-West divide? A large portion of the membership, mostly in the West, believed it imperative to support the United Nations in Korea. Others, interpreting the conflict as one between two power blocs which were seeking to use the UN, believed that the WCC should have nothing to do with it. The Eastern Europeans and Chinese agreed. And many believed the "police action" to be war and therefore not to be supported at all.[28]

The immediate response, in early 1951, was a letter from the Executive Committee to the member churches, pastoral in nature, but firm in speaking of the basic problems: "Uppermost in our minds were . . . the totalitarian doctrine of man in society, the menace to peace, and the denial of social justice."[29]

Looking back years later, Visser 't Hooft wrote that in the resolution on Korea "we had failed to show, in line with the whole tradition of the ecumenical movement, that we wanted to continue what Emanuel Mounier of France had called 'the struggle against the easy conscience of the West.'"[30] Failing to transcend the situation, there was a momentary lapse into the fray. The letter in early 1951 helped; the meeting of the Central Committee in Rolle that summer helped further. A lesson had been learned.

Five years later the Central Committee met in Hungary, invited by the churches there, who had been among the most vociferous concerning Korea. I had something of a role in the holding of that meeting.

In March of 1956, during a staff meeting in Visser 't Hooft's office, the phone rang. It was the Hungarians, who wanted "Bilheimer" to come at once to help make arrangements for the Central Committee meeting in the summer. To my amazement, because I had had no experience behind the Iron Curtain, Visser 't Hooft agreed to send me. I knew it was a serious mission, but I didn't realize how serious until I saw Wim at the airport to see me off. He almost never did that. He asked if I was nervous, and I replied "Very." He smiled and simply said, "Best wishes," with a handshake.

After arrival formalities, I was told that the first meeting would

28. Visser 't Hooft, *Memoirs*, p. 322.
29. "A Letter From the Executive Committee of the World Council of Churches to the Member Churches," *Ecumenical Review*, IV (1951).
30. *Op. cit.*, pp. 221f.

be the next day, and in the meantime I would be shown the theological seminary if that were agreeable. It was, especially because a highly respected ecumenical leader, Lazlo Pap, would accompany me, and I wanted to talk with him. A third man accompanied us on the visit. Pap said nothing about that, but consistently kept his distance from me, preventing any conversation that could not be heard by the other man.

At the seminary, I was told that everyone was away because of some holiday, and that I would be shown the buildings. Going through the vacant halls, Pap led the way, I came second a few feet behind, and the third man followed. To test my suspicions, I quickened my pace slightly to catch up with Pap. Immediately the man to my rear quickened his—the click, click of his heels on the stone floors resounding in the empty halls. I slackened off; he followed. After three attempts, all identical, I concluded that this was real, and that I was not to talk to Pap alone. I never did throughout the visit.

All went well for the day and a half, and I began to wonder what the visit was all about. Routine questions and routine receptions had not given me a clue. At noon on the third day, however, I was taken back to the hotel in a taxi by a man whom I knew to be with the government's ministry of religion. I could converse with him only in my halting German. Suddenly I heard him saying that we could not go ahead with the plan, long a key part of our program for the meeting, of having Committee members preach in churches throughout Hungary.

The reason for my visit was suddenly clear. Angry, I turned on him with a fluency in German that I have never equalled since, saying he should inform Bishop Bereczky that if this were so I would return to Geneva on the next plane and recommend to the general secretary that he announce to the international press that the Hungarian churches were unable to allow us to celebrate Sunday as agreed, and thus unable to entertain the Central Committee as agreed, and that therefore the WCC would meet in another country to be determined. He knew that I meant it.

By that time we were at the hotel. I left him, not knowing what to expect. He came for me at 2:00 P.M., took me to a full dress meeting of church and government officials as scheduled, and the matter was never mentioned again.

My visit concluded with a dinner reception after which I was taken to the train for Vienna. I still had one item on my own agenda— getting some word to Pap. I had been wholly with church and government officials, and did not want to give him the impression that I had been coopted. Fortunately, he was one of the party which took me to the railroad station. Suddenly my opportunity appeared. We were proceeding up a long, wide ramp. Pap was on my right, ten to fifteen feet away, no one in between. In a loud voice, so that all could hear, I called across to him in English: "Professor Pap."

"Yes," he quickly replied.

"I have been criticized by Kraemer in the *Ecumenical Review*," I said. Pap smiled expectantly, "Kraemer says that I can't see the forest for the trees," I went on, pausing to make sure that he understood the idiom. He nodded. "But I want you to know that is not always the case." Pap's blue eyes responded with a brilliant fire.

The Central Committee met, and its members and WCC staff preached in churches all over Hungary that summer.

The meeting itself was strained. Anglican Bishop K. H. Ting came from China, and gave a searching, critical speech about missions, the West, and the WCC. Western opinion in the meeting ranged from outrage to puzzlement, but the *koinonia* in Christ held.

A few months later, the Hungarian revolt was brutally crushed. Amid that tragedy, our gratitude ran higher that we had had a normal meeting in Eastern Europe, keeping our integrity, and had thus demonstrated that the ecumenical movement could transcend the deepest division among the nations.

The climactic demonstration, however, came at the Third Assembly. First, the meeting was held in Asia. That was important. To my regret, the CCIA, and thus the WCC, had ignored the Bandung conference of 1955. Did it take Asia and Africa seriously? The fact of holding the Third Assembly in Asia rather than going back to Europe or North America carried strong symbolic power.[31] The churches in India dreaded the organizational and financial problems connected with the meeting, but—along with churches throughout Asia—deeply wanted it as a demonstration of support and concern.

Beyond this, however, was the fact of the entrance of the Orthodox Church of Russia into membership. From an organizational perspective, this had taken a long time. From the perspective of church history, it happened in the blink of an eye. From the perspective of the world of nations, it was a decisive moment in the Christian ability to transcend the great division.[32] The genuine rejoicing among the Russian delegation and the Assembly as a whole was unmistakable: a rejoicing in Christ who had brought us all together.

---

31. There were not yet enough member churches in Africa to justify a meeting of the Assembly there. The big influx of African churches came in the 1960s and 1970s; and the Fifth Assembly was held in Nairobi in 1975.

32. *New Delhi Report,* p. 108.

A few months later, I was a member of the first WCC delegation to visit the Russian Orthodox Church after it had joined the WCC. There I saw something further, namely the striving of church leaders to take their place in the fellowship and make their contribution, albeit under difficult conditions.

To these demonstrations of transcendence, at New Delhi the Assembly added a conceptual aspect:

> The churches are involved with all men in a common historical destiny. As servants of their Servant Lord Jesus Christ they bring to the nations their obedience to Christ who is the Lord of the nations. They form a society that by its nature transcends political and ideological barriers; but through its members it is also deeply rooted in the life of nations with their political and ideological conflicts.[33]

Clearly, "transcendence" did not imply an empyrean existence, but rather, a wrenching struggle, personal and collective, to live with vision beyond the profound ties of race, clan, and modern nation state.

A decade earlier, at the height of the Cold War, Visser 't Hooft had put it this way:

> We need not be ashamed if we fail to find common answers and solutions. For it may well be that this is the very lesson which God desires us to learn in this hour of history, that we are not the lords of history and that we must patiently and expectantly wait for the moment when He shall give us a clear word to speak together. But we fail in our duty when we do not make desperate efforts—even in the midst of the impasse —to *be* the Church of Christ together. . . . *The greatest contribution we can make to world peace is perhaps not in the realm of statements but in the maintenance of a fellowship which transcends manmade divisions.*[34]

---

33. *Ibid.,* p. 105.
34. Report of the general secretary, Central Committee minutes, 1951-52 (Lucknow). Italics added.

12

Church, Society, and Rapid Social Change

Two memorable events of 1947 had a special symbolism. One was the beginning of the Marshall Plan for rebuilding Europe, a constructive response to the need of allies. The other was the independence of India, a victorious end to a long struggle for freedom. Together, they carried a further meaning: because of them, the world was different. Each in its own way symbolized profound, rapid, cumulative social change. Ecumenical Christian social analysis understood this as the dominant characteristic of society in the decade and a half that followed.

As the world scene had changed, so had the position of the churches in it. They no longer occupied their snug position within the *corpus Christianum* of the West, nor the position of accompanying, whether in criticism or acquiescence or both, its colonialism of the rest of the world. Weak or strong, the churches were on their own.

The end of Christendom did not mean the end of Christian and church concern for society or the end of action to make society better by Christian standards. Rather, it signified the end of a certain solution to the problem of the church's relation to and mission in society. The task at hand was to discern and elucidate this social mission.

Moreover, a new world history was in the making. As M. M. Thomas of India wrote in 1947, it was not a simple history. Thomas was a layman of the Mar Thoma Church, which had strong continuity with the Orthodox tradition in India but had become independent in the nineteenth century. Though influenced by Protestantism, it retained the Orthodox liturgy and much of its ethos. It was thus not a result of

162

nineteenth-century Protestant missions. This heritage gave Thomas a unique ecumenical vantage point.

The West, according to Thomas, had been "the bearer of world history in the modern period; and the meeting between East and West is the history of modern Asia. . . . [This latter history] arose out of the nature, and within the development of Western society, and must be considered an integral part of it."[1] Within a few years that could be said of Africa and Latin America as well.

During the depth of war, the confessing churches of Europe had responded clearly:

> Today, the voice of the Church is not an echo of the voice of the world. The Church knows that it is responsible for the world, but responsible before God. At the very moment when the world proclaims that it is autonomous and need render account to no one, another voice is raised saying that neither the state nor society, nor the world, nor man, belong to themselves but that they are all under the sovereignty of God, who already reigns through his Son.[2]

That affirmation of faith was made when the battle lines were clear-cut. There was little doubt that the churches would respond to the new situation of rapid change. But would the churches echo the world or bear a clear witness?

We shall look at that ecumenical response under two headings, in the historical sequence in which they were developed: "The Responsible Society" and "Our Common Christian Responsibility Toward Areas of Rapid Social Change."

THE RESPONSIBLE SOCIETY

The Fundamental Approach

"The Christian Church," said Amsterdam, "approaches the disorder of our society with faith in the Lordship of Jesus Christ. In Him God has established His Kingdom and its gates stand open for all who will enter. Their lives belong to God with a certainty that no disorder can destroy, and on them is laid the duty to seek God's Kingdom and His righteousness."[3]

1. M. M. Thomas, "The Situation in Asia—II," Amsterdam Vol. 3, p. 71.
2. *The Church Speaks to the World, Abridged Document in Oecumenical Study Program Series 'Ecclesia Militans'* (Geneva: WCC, 1942), p. 2.
3. Amsterdam Report, pp. 74ff., for this and quotations in the following paragraphs.

That brief paragraph contained three fundamentals. The first is the Lordship of Christ over church and world, not just confessed as a cultic affirmation but acknowledged as an affirmation about human history. The second is the establishment of the Kingdom of God, open to all. This was not an appeal to build something but a testimony to an accomplished fact: the Kingdom *is*. The third is the calling of the Christian church, here somewhat unusually stated in terms of a duty laid on those who respond.

This had a driving power. In Amsterdam's words, the judgment and mercy of the Kingdom awakened consciousness of "the sins which corrupt human communities and institutions in every age"; yet at the same time the light of the Kingdom assured Christians "of the final victory over all sin and death." More specifically, the power which gives a foretaste of this final victory lies in prayer, in response to Christ's bidding us to pray "that God's Kingdom may come and that His will may be done on earth as it is in heaven." Praying so requires that "we seek in every age to overcome the specific disorders which aggravate the perennial evil in human society, and that we search out the means of securing their elimination and control."

The power of this faith provided hope, unlike society itself, which often brought disillusionment, as changes in various systems produced fresh evils rather than the promised good. The underlying sin of the human heart operated in all systems. Nevertheless, hope lived. Faith gave no "room for . . . despair, being based on the fact that the Kingdom of God is firmly established in Christ and will come by God's act despite all human failure."

The Analysis

Having stated the essence of the faith, ecumenical social thought turned to the needs of the time, beginning with the vast concentrations of power. Under capitalism, these were mainly economic; under Communism, both political and economic. In each, social evil became manifest in greed, pride, and cruelty. At a more subtle but devastating level, these evils were exacerbated by the momentum or inertia of huge organizations which diminished the ability of individuals to act as moral and accountable beings. The need to augment personal responsibility for collective action was urgent.

A second key factor was the domination of society by technics. A growing concern, this was seen by the First Assembly as providing society with a momentum of its own. Yet technical development had relieved people of much drudgery and poverty and could do more. The appeal was not to turn away from it, but to note the independent momentum it gave society and to insist that there "is no inescapable necessity for society to succumb to undirected developments of technology."

As the First Assembly saw it, economic activity in the Industrial Revolution had burst previous social controls and had created a vast network of financial, commercial, and industrial relations known as the capitalist order. It was now clear that there were economic necessities that no political system could afford to deny—among them "the need for stability in the value of money, for creation of capital and for incentives in production. . . . Justice, however, demands that economic activities be subordinated to social ends. It is intolerable that vast millions of people be exposed to insecurity, hunger and frustration by periodic inflation or depression."

This of course bore on the debate between the advocates of capitalism and the advocates of socialism. Although the church obviously could not resolve this issue, the Assembly addressed both sides: "In the light of the Christian understanding of man we must say to the advocates of socialization that the institution of property is not the root of the corruption of human nature. We must equally say to the defenders of existing property relations that ownership is not an unconditional right; it must therefore be preserved, curtailed or distributed in accordance with the requirements of justice." That was considerably more than the impartial attempt at balance which it sounds like on the surface; in those terms, the Assembly sought to get the debate down to essentials, stripped of ideological trappings.

Many in the US, preoccupied with ideology, thought the WCC was "too easy on socialism," if not actually "socialistic." *A propos* of this, prior to the Assembly, Visser 't Hooft had told me of a dinner party he and his wife had attended in New York in the spring of 1945. Among those present were Mr. and Mrs. John D. Rockefeller, Jr. Midway through the meal, Rockefeller asked Visser 't Hooft about "European socialism." Amid utter silence around the table, Visser 't Hooft replied: "Mr. Rockefeller, suppose that you were the father of a large family, say ten or a dozen children, and for the evening meal you had only a small meat-pie. Would you let the children go at it pell mell, or would you divide it up and give each a piece?"

Rockefeller replied that of course he would divide it.

"That," said Visser 't Hooft, "is what 'European socialism' is all about." The next day, at Rockefeller's suggestion, he and Visser 't Hooft had a further conversation in his office, which resulted in a gift of one million dollars to the WCC.[4]

The Assembly insisted that "coherent and purposeful ordering of society has now become a major necessity," with government responsibility and many checks on centralized power. "By such means it is possible to prevent an undue centralization of power in modern technically organized communities, and thus escape the perils of tyranny while avoiding the dangers of anarchy."[5]

The Concept

This analysis was rooted in the experience of worldwide depression and war, causing the Assembly to take seriously the requirement of both freedom and responsibility. Human beings were called to be free and in that freedom to be responsible to God and neighbor. Amsterdam set forth an absolute: "Any tendencies in State and society depriving man of the possibility of acting responsibly are a denial of God's intention for man and His work of salvation."

That led to the fundamental concept: "A responsible society is one where freedom is the freedom of men who acknowledge responsibility to justice and public order, and where those who hold political authority or economic power are responsible for its exercise to God and the people whose welfare is affected by it."

The term "Responsible Society" — widely used in subsequent years — had been coined by J. H. Oldham, a layman of the Church of England and an ecumenical pioneer.[6] In 1928 Oldham's perception had led the world missionary conference in Jerusalem to describe secularism as a challenge to Christian faith on the scale of the traditional religions.

What the Amsterdam Assembly meant by the Responsible Society is further illuminated by its forthright condemnations of:

1. Any attempt to limit the freedom of the Church to witness to its Lord and His design for mankind and any attempt to impair the freedom of men to obey God and to act according to conscience, for those freedoms are implied in man's responsibility before God;

4. In his *Memoirs* (p. 187) Visser 't Hooft reports the dinner party but not this exchange about socialism.

5. Amsterdam Report, p. 77, for this and quotations in the following paragraphs.

6. Visser 't Hooft, *op. cit.*, pp. 205, 213. For Oldham's thought, see J. H. Oldham, "Technics and Civilization" and "A Responsible Society," in Amsterdam Vol. 3.

2. Any denial to man of an opportunity to participate in the shaping of society, for this is a duty implied in man's responsibility towards his neighbor;

3. Any attempt to prevent men from learning and spreading the truth.[7]

Positively, the concept of the Responsible Society contained a basic instrumentalism: society was an instrument to serve human beings. People must never be made a mere means for political or economic ends. Human beings are not made for the state or for production; the state and production are made for them.

> For a society to be responsible under modern conditions it is required that the people have freedom to control, to criticize and to change their governments, that power be made responsible by law and tradition, and be distributed as widely as possible through the whole community. It is required that economic justice and the provision of equality of opportunity be established for all the members of society.

Communism and the West

In 1948 Communism was strong. Its challenge arose not only from the USSR as a world power but also from its ideology. Focused in the West, its appeal extended also to Asia.

Ecumenical thought recognized this attraction. The First Assembly specifically stated that "Christians should ask why Communism in its modern totalitarian form makes so strong an appeal to great masses of people in many parts of the world." In reply, the Assembly continued with a remarkable sentence: Christians "should recognize the hand of God in the revolt of multitudes against injustice that gives Communism much of its strength."[8] Behind its appeal, especially to young men and women, lay "a vision of human equality and universal brotherhood for which they were prepared by Christian influences."

Christians who benefited from capitalism were enjoined to engage in an act of imagination. They were asked to understand how the multitudes who did not share these benefits would view the world differently, seeing deliverance from oppression in the Communist promise of a classless society. In sum, "it is a great human tragedy that so much that is good in the motives and aspirations of many Communists and of those whose sympathies they win has been transformed into a

7. *Ibid.*, pp. 77f., for this and quotations in the following paragraphs.
8. *Ibid.*, p. 78.

force that engenders new forms of injustice and oppression, and that what is true in Communist criticism should be used to give convincing power to untrustworthy propaganda."

The debate to which this analysis responded took vivid form at Amsterdam in an encounter between John Foster Dulles and Josef Hromadka.[9] Dulles espoused a clear Western Christian viewpoint, expressed in the idiom of his own culture, against Communism. Hromadka approached the gospel as a theologian who saw a profound tension between the ruling ideology and Christianity, in which the church was called to witness, but not to uncompromising resistance. Ten years later, in his definitive study of Communism and Christian theologians, Charles West concluded that Hromadka and Dulles were very much alike because both were dominated not by Christ's calling in the world, but by "the world of Communist power and pretension itself."[10] In fact, it seemed to me, there was far more true Christian transcendence of Communist claims in Hromadka the man than in his written theology.

Ecumenical thought did not need to develop the concept of the Responsible Society in order to do battle with Communism. Amsterdam cited five cogent points at which Christianity itself was in conflict with the atheistic Marxism of the time:

(1) The Communist promise of what amounts to a complete redemption of man in history;
(2) the belief that a particular class by virtue of its role as the bearer of a new order is free from the sins and ambiguities that Christians believe to be characteristic of all human existence;
(3) the materialistic and deterministic teachings, however they may be qualified, that are incompatible with belief in God and with the Christian view of man as a person, made in God's image and responsible to him;
(4) the ruthless methods of Communists in dealing with their opponents; and
(5) the demand of the party on its members for an exclusive and unqualified loyalty which belongs only to God, and the coercive policies of Communist dictatorship in controlling every aspect of life.[11]

This last point was made more explicit, in terms that applied to dictators of the right as well. Christians should resist the extension of any system "that not only includes oppressive elements but fails to pro-

9. *Ibid.*, pp. 38f.
10. Charles C. West, *Communism and the Theologians: Study of an Encounter* (Philadelphia: The Westminster Press, 1958), p. 60.
11. Amsterdam Report, p. 79.

vide any means by which the victims of oppression may criticize or act to correct it," especially in respect of terror, arbitrary arrest, torture, and cruel punishments to intimidate.[12]

The Responsible Society also had a strong bearing on the West, whose great concentrations of power scarcely manifested a society guided by ecumenical concepts of Christian responsibility. That millions should suffer deprivation from periodic economic upheavals was intolerable, as were the special privileges of dominant classes, races, and political groups.

Moreover, the Responsible Society implied church renewal. Many in the West, especially young people, workers, and intellectuals, were alienated from the church because of its complicity in the special privileges granted those of a certain class or race. Such a church could have little to say about "the art of social living," an art that began with the small or larger groups within church and family, extending itself to factory, marketplace, and the state itself.[13] Not a few, particularly in Europe, had turned to Communism for this reason.

Why was the concept of the Responsible Society so durable? As we worked with it more and more, it became clear that its mild language had strength. It clearly stood against totalitarianism of any sort. It spoke to both the West and the East, but not in the hyper-ideological terms one heard from governments and the press. It put one on the road to specific social evils, and it gave a basis of approach to the major secular faiths of scientism and materialism.[14]

Even more, it provided flexible guidance. One might say that it was the guidance of the "middle axiom," a concept introduced by Oldham in 1937 and debated by John Bennett of the US and C. L. Patijn of Holland in the Amsterdam preparatory volumes.[15] Clearly, it had helped to bring about the remarkable consensus Reinhold Niebuhr described in saying that the ecumenical movement "has, in effect, overcome the chasm between a Christian conservatism on the one hand, based upon an undue pessimism, and on the other hand a Christian perfectionism, which approached perilously close to the utopian illusions of a secular culture."[16]

I myself preferred the somewhat more esoteric language of Bonhoeffer, who before his martyrdom had written of the "penultimate."[17]

---

12. *Ibid.,* pp. 78-80.

13. Evanston Report, p. 114.

14. Cf. Wilhelm Pauck, "Rival Secular Faiths," Amsterdam Vol. 2, pp. 37-52.

15. John C. Bennett, "The Involvement of the Church," Amsterdam Vol. 3, pp. 91-120; C. L. Patijn, "The Strategy of the Church," *ibid.,* pp. 155-74.

16. Cited by James Hastings Nichols, *Evanston — an Interpretation,* p. 127.

17. Dietrich Bonhoeffer, *Ethics,* ed. Eberhard Bethge (London: SCM Press, 1955), pp. 84ff.

When it criticized both the West and the East, the Responsible Society offered a *penultimate* witness to the transcendence of God-in-Christ; when it gave guidance to action for freedom and justice, it offered a *penultimate* witness to the immanence of God-in-Christ. In it the voice of the church did not echo the voice of the world.

The Responsible Society offered a conceptual basis for significant work. Much of this concerned the struggle to keep the WCC relevant to the Communist/non-Communist conflict in the world of nations, without identifying wholly with either side. But the Responsible Society was also a focus for the informal, influential Ecumenical Commission on European Unity, instigated by WCC personnel and served by its Church and Society department. Meeting twice a year from 1951 on, this commission was made up of laypeople with considerable expertise and experience in the movement for European unity. As Paul Abrecht, who gave constant staff service to the group, would write, it "was an explicit case where Christians from political life used the Responsible Society concept in struggling to overcome Europe's divisions."[18] Its brief, cogent semi-annual statements were widely read.

Moreover, the WCC itself inaugurated a study on "Christian Responsibility for Economic Life" in 1950. An extensive study in the US, under the auspices of the Federal Council of Churches, and substantial WCC discussions were reflected in a volume by Oxford economist Denys Munby, a leader in the development of ecumenical social thought. How often, I wondered, would an economist start a book as Munby had?—"I begin with a short survey of the main doctrines of the Christian faith, with some reference to their implications for society and our daily life."[19]

RAPID SOCIAL CHANGE[20]

There had been a certain awareness in ecumenical circles before the Evanston Assembly of 1954 of rapid change in Asia and its significance. The Whitby meeting of missionary leaders in 1947 had spoken in

18. Letter to the author, July 8, 1987.
19. D. L. Munby, *Christianity and Economic Problems* (London: Macmillan and Co., 1956), p. 3.
20. The proposal for this study is found in *The Common Christian Responsibility Toward Areas of Rapid Social Change* (Geneva: World Council of Churches, 1956). In the years following there were numerous international, regional, and country studies. The study as a whole was summarized in two volumes: Paul Abrecht, *The Churches and Rapid Social Change* (Garden City, NY: Doubleday, 1961), and Egbert de Vries, *Man in Rapid Social Change* (Garden City, NY: Doubleday, 1961), both with bibliographies.

moving language of the "revolutionary world," by which it meant the rise of new nations on the world scene—what M. M. Thomas had called a new phase of world history.

Thomas himself, the only participant from outside the West in the written preparations for Amsterdam, made this more specific. He saw clearly that Christians of Asia must be closely related to Christians of the West, but that they must oppose the nations of the West as well. "In certain countries like Indonesia and Indo-China it means active participation in armed conflict against the Western European power; in the rest of Asia the war is no less real though not so open." Asia, wrote Thomas, had largely become the "'agricultural farm' of the West, producing raw materials for the machines in the West, and absorbing their finished goods."[21]

These early analyses grew by the early 1950s into a recognition of a fundamental shift in world responsibility. The background of a new sense of ecumenical Christian responsibility was a vast world upheaval, in which the East-West struggle was all but superseded by the shake-up of ancient patterns of life in Asia, Africa, and Latin America and the increasing interdependence of many nations in varied situations of change.[22]

The social commentary of the Second Assembly was relatively cursory. But the fact that this Assembly, responding explicitly to a small Asian study conference held in Lucknow in 1953, made social change in the "economically underdeveloped regions" a major concern testified to both an expanding awareness of "the nations" and the rapidity of social change.[23]

The major preoccupation of the WCC in "church and society" for the ensuing period lay in this area, focused in a study process under the heading "Our Common Christian Responsibility Toward Areas of Rapid Social Change." The substance of the work was in two broad areas: analysis of society and the simultaneously developing response.

The Developing Focus of Concern

As it was driven into the new situation, ecumenical thought followed a certain sequence. Whether the terminology was economic ("developed" and "underdeveloped"), geographical ("Asia, Africa, and Latin America"), or cultural ("traditional societies" and "modernity"), a common

21. M. M. Thomas, *op. cit.*, pp. 73, 78.
22. "Social Questions—The Responsible Society in a World Perspective," Evanston Survey, pp. 3-13.
23. Evanston Report, pp. 123-26.

theme ran throughout. This theme began with science and technology, proceeded to the awakening of peoples in nationalism, and moved to the formation of a new sense of identity in modernity.

Science

One day in 1957, in southern India, I stood on the brink of an enormous excavation being made for the construction of a new dam. I was in the midst of an extensive study tour in West Pakistan, India, Ceylon (Sri Lanka), and Indonesia, to explore the major ethical problems involved in the recently inaugurated technical assistance programs. The dam under construction was a project of the (Canadian) Colombo Plan. Two things struck me.

First, very little earth-moving equipment was visible. Instead, long lines of women walked up and down the sides of the excavation on trails with horseshoe curves. On their heads were baskets filled with the dirt to be moved. Technically, it was a labor-intensive operation. These women were not slaves, bent over and driven by heavy-handed overseers. Their bearing was erect (it has to be if you want to carry a heavy load on your head). They were dusty, but well dressed, with bangles. Nearby, their children were well supervised in good lodgings. They were women from surrounding villages who had sought work and got it, and had their own income. Obviously, here was already a major force of change in this part of India. Old enough to recollect the force of Roosevelt's Rural Electrification Act in the US, I realized that once the dam began to generate electricity the results would be even more far-reaching. Technology was at work, transforming women, villages, and family life, with the promise of much more to come.

The attraction of science and technology lay in its promise of release: technology "provides the fundamental hope for the liberation of mankind from poverty and disease."[24] It opened up social mobility and provided dignity, freedom, and health. It broke down old values and gave a setting for new in the family, in relation to nature, work, community, and social structures. And science and technology provided the only visible hope for people in the great population increase evident everywhere.[25] The grinding background of poverty turned both leaders and people to science and technology.

That same year I was working with von Weizsäcker on the prob-

24. *Dilemmas and Opportunities: Christian Action in Rapid Social Change* (Geneva: WCC, 1959), pp. 2-20.
25. Richard M. Fagley, *The Population Explosion and Christian Responsibility* (New York: Oxford U.P., 1960); Fagley was a staff member of CCIA.

lem of Christian response to atomic weapons and war. His thesis about the nature of the scientific method found confirmation in Asia, as it would elsewhere. The words "irreversible" and "ambiguous" came to mind again and again.

The problem with the great hope that stirred the nations of the South lay in the ambiguity of the scientific-technological solution. Besides hope, it also produced great anxiety in the breakdown of traditional institutions and in the moral confusion of people caught in the shift from a pre-technical village community to the industrial town or city. Peter Dagadu of Ghana, in a memorable speech at the Second Assembly, said: "Africa cannot escape the devastating effects of the atomic and hydrogen warfare any more than people in New York, London or Hiroshima. So Africa asks herself, 'Are these material things we see in Western civilization for the good of mankind or for human destruction?'" That did not mean that there was a mood of trying to turn back. There was, however, clear discernment of the universal problem of control, whether of atomic weapons or in the use of technology to achieve the eradication of poverty.

Nationalism

The second strong impression, as I looked at the new dam being built in India, was made by the manager of the project, who was showing me around. He and everyone else expressed a worthy pride. He was Indian and he was in charge. There, as everywhere, nationalism was joining with science.

If poverty stood behind the pursuit of science, indignity explained the espousal of nationalism—the indignity of colonial rule and the indignity of racism. Meanwhile, the West, which had embraced nationalism to its own detriment and that of other peoples, now seemed to want to downplay nationalism in favor of internationalism—or rather wistfully hoped the new nations would learn from Europe's nationalistic mistakes. The leading figures of enlightened Europe followed Monnet in seeking European unity. Opinion ran high in the US for an effective UN.

In Asia and Africa nationalism had an undreamed-of potency. It was the avenue of the future, the driving force behind the achievement of independence. John Karefa-Smart, who held high office in both his native Sierra Leone and in the World Health Organization, wrote:

> As Africans rose to responsible positions in the government, and later occupied the policy-making executive roles, for the first time Europeans found themselves receiving and not always

giving orders. It is difficult to assess accurately the psychological effects of such a reversal of roles. Certainly on the side of the Africans it brought with it a sense of confidence, of attainment, and of self-realization.[26]

I could seldom hear of "nationalism" in this sense without thinking of M. M. Thomas. Of medium physical stature, with deep-set, penetrating eyes and a high forehead, he always reminded me of Nehru, although the similarity was not striking and he did not share Nehru's controlled, English reserve. M. M. was excitable in mind, demeanor, and voice. Travelling together in his native Kerala one day in the late 1950s, we had to wait for a ferry across a large river. The captain sat in the pilot's cabin reading a book. "Look at him," M. M. said. "Do you see anything unusual?" I tried my best but could not. "He is reading," said M. M. "Only in Kerala would a man at that job level be able to read." It was one of M. M.'s passions and a part of his genius to relate India's growing nationalism to Christian faith and vice versa.

Between World War II and 1960, one-and-a-quarter billion people changed their form of government, and 800 million achieved independence. Among Christians in those lands there were some anti-nationalists, to be sure (mostly Westerners), but the majority were either radical Christian nationalists, who took a revolutionary position against all forms of Western political and economic influence, or "constructive nationalists," who viewed nationalism positively as evidence of God's continuing concern for justice and freedom.[27]

A New Identity within Modernity

"Modern" contrasted with "traditional," whether in Asia, Africa, or Latin America; and the new identity was expressed by the goals and processes of "nation building." In that sense "nationalism" was a large word. "The main motive force of nationalism," said an ecumenical study conference in 1959, "is the desire of a group of people to come together in order to create their own independent government, to take their place as a recognized unity among the nations, to express their own group individuality and to make what they consider to be their special contribution to the world."[28] Most of the time that group identity had to be formed out of a number of varied tribal or group identities, which frequently used different languages.

26. *Africa in Transition* (Geneva: WCC, 1962), p. 14.
27. Paul Abrecht, *op. cit.,* pp. 95-112.
28. *Dilemmas and Opportunities: Christian Action in Rapid Social Change,* p. 55.

To understand what this meant in the modern world required a backward look at Western history. The religious renewal of the Reformation, the intellectual upheavals of the Enlightenment, and the use of reason for human benefits, the economic revolution of science and technology, the political revolutions of France and America — forces like these were now all compressed in intercontinental, rapid social change.[29] "Modernity" appeared to be the distillate of them all. The entrance into modernity on the part of the traditional societies involved "nation building," itself a modern concept, and that signified a transformed sense of identity.

Basically, this transformation took place through the constant oscillation of dilemma and opportunity. Among many dilemmas and opportunities, none was more pervasive than the opportunity afforded by the injection of technology into the nontechnical societies. The opportunity was obvious: a dam promised electricity which promised great benefits. The dilemma was formidable: could societies adjust creatively to the multiple revolutions which that dam symbolized and through which the peoples were passing almost simultaneously?

What promise, hope, and help did Christians perceive? One reply was simple and direct: "With confidence in emancipation goes the challenge to men and women to help each other through the difficulties that accompany social change, and the responsibility to share the benefits it offers." That suggested a common bond and cause, a mutual helpfulness on the basis of a common humanity, citizenship, suffering, and aspiration. In more specifically Christian terms: "Social change is a medium through which God acts to awaken the world anew."[30]

That sounded a fundamental note. As Christians looked together at their involvement in multiple revolution, their faith did not channel them into a ghetto, but impelled them into the mainstream. Christian faith grounded its sense of social responsibility in the revelation of God's reign in Christ. This reign involved all of human history, not merely personal or religious affairs. More particularly, the biblical revelation of love of neighbor became urgent when it was understood that the neighbor is affected for good or evil by social institutions, the behavior of nations and other groups, and the decisions of citizens. Especially, the biblical revelation emphasized God's care of the victims, the "least of these." Moreover, the scriptural call to repentance was directed to whole persons, for whom personal sin included involvement in the corporate sins of their groups. This biblical revelation set the church in

29. *Ibid.,* p. 7.
30. *Ibid.,* p. 8.

motion, in the midst of the world, with responsibility for all people as children of God. Indeed, the church seemed to have a charter:

> In all its activity and in every social situation, the Church exists to bear witness to the present role of God, to set forth the sovereign demands of holiness and righteousness. Sometimes it is a small minority within a nation; sometimes it is numerically strong. But it should never be a political association using religion as a means to a political end. We are the servants of Christ. Our political concern springs from the imperatives of the Gospel, and through our political service we seek to serve His Kingdom.[31]

THE BASIC THRUST

From Amsterdam's delineation of the Responsible Society to the 1959 analysis of dilemmas and opportunities in rapid social change, it was clear that ecumenical thought was advocating and formulating a Christian thrust into society. Unconsciously but definitely, it rejected both sectarian withdrawal from the surrounding world and triumphalism.

This aspect of ecumenical thought concerned morality and ethics. It affirmed duty, but it was not an ethics drawn particularly from a sense of duty. It was hopeful, but it was not primarily an ethics of aspiration. It saw a profound utility in freedom and justice, but it was not a utilitarian ethics. It drew ultimately on love, but its interpretation of love was neither sentimental nor utopian. It demanded emancipation and rejoiced when it was achieved, but it did not present either an ethics or a theology of liberation.

Overall, ecumenical thought on church and society was neither an "ethics" nor a "theology," but an ethical, moral thrust, a component of the emerging ecumenical tradition. That component had various dimensions—a method, a distinctive character, and a conception of witness.

The first step in the method was the discovery of people who were able to combine Christian insight with expertise in some aspect of social analysis or action. These included laypeople — educators, trade unionists, economists, politicians—and younger church leaders, among them some from Asia and Africa and Latin America whose Christianity had been learned in the exhilarating atmosphere of the struggles for freedom and the new modernity. Attention had to be paid to representativeness: of church traditions, broad theological perspectives, and

31. *Ibid.*, p. 43.

opinion on major social issues, as well as of country, sex, and race. This process of selection went on continuously and was subject to general review by the leaders of the churches involved and by the WCC.

Once these resource people were identified, it was necessary to secure their cooperation (itself a time-consuming process) and then to organize occasions of dialogue and consultation. For this a set of questions had to be outlined or perhaps a paper presented by one of the participants, and the discussion was underway. There was no vestige of clergy proclaiming to laity, of Westerner "telling" third world people, or vice versa. Thought emerged on the ground, to be challenged, tested, refined, and recorded. The written materials required from all consultations (many of them organized nationally or regionally) were especially valuable because they were not necessarily "consensus statements" but frequently reports and analyses of discussions.

Practiced worldwide over a period of many years, this method produced a series of contributions that was fed into WCC governing bodies and disseminated to member churches and interested people. This method involved more laity—women and men—than any other aspect of ecumenical work, because the laypeople were the experts on society.

Chairing the team that conducted the "rapid social change" enterprise was Egbert de Vries, a Dutch social scientist of high competence and astonishingly comprehensive grasp. With him worked Oxford economist Denys Munby and M. M. Thomas, with Paul Abrecht and Daisuke Kitagawa of the WCC staff. The success of the method was due in large part to Abrecht, who had joined the WCC staff in 1949, and been responsible for developing thought concerning the Responsible Society.

"Genial and a genius" (in Philip Potter's phrase), Abrecht inherited the method in Church and Society in embryo from J. H. Oldham, but far outstripped the progenitor in the development and use of it. His genius lay in a capacity to understand, interpret, and synthesize; his geniality attracted cooperation from people worldwide.[32] Through Abrecht and his colleagues much of the Life and Work movement was adapted to the WCC, continuing to provide a major contribution to the growing ecumenical tradition.

Along with a distinctive method went a distinctive character. To call this thrust of ecumenical thought "Christian social ethics" does not do it justice. "Witness" is usually used in the sense of evangelism, of

32. See *Church and Society: Ecumenical Perspectives. Essays in Honor of Paul Abrecht*, special issue of *Ecumenical Review*, XXXVII, No. 1 (1985).

preaching the gospel. One of the contributions of the phases of Responsible Society and Rapid Social Change in the WCC was to broaden the concept of witness to include ethics and to broaden the concept of ethics to include witness.

The evangelistic purpose of those engaged in the Rapid Social Change enterprise was especially noteworthy. Here, too, M. M. Thomas's contribution was substantial. As his voice carried and rose in emphasis, his intellect penetrated in analysis and soared in imagination. "The Rapid Social Change study," he told the Central Committee in 1958,

> confronts the churches with the challenge to emerge from their own world and to confront this world in a missionary way. The basic meaning of the Rapid Social Change study is therefore evangelistic. The Church can preach the Gospel effectively only if it is a whole Gospel. . . . In this era Communism is too often the heir of Christian hope when the latter fails to show the way in society.[33]

A third component of this ethical-moral thrust of ecumenical thought was its conception of witness. We noted that ecumenical thought did not advocate withdrawal into some kind of updated "missionary compound." On the contrary, although ecumenical thought arose from the tiniest of minorities—the usual figure was less than one-half of one percent of the populations of the great continents in turmoil—it mobilized the intellectual energy of those minorities to fight injustice and reach out to human need and misery.

The center of this impulse was the trinitarian faith, enunciated in the claim that Christ is Lord over the world and the church. Sometimes Christ as both Savior and King was confessed; and the faith that God (or Christ) was at work in human history was affirmed again and again. The urgency of this appeared in the Christian sense of the importance of history, as over against attempts to deny and escape from history or to dismiss it as merely cyclical. Indeed, one function of the church was affirmed to be a corporate participation in society, in order to discern more clearly the hidden meaning of history and the manner in which Christ is at work in it.

This faith in the triune God at work in history had consequences for the Christian community. In Niebuhr's terms, as we have used them earlier, it produced the sense of a "church of the center." Sometimes this took the form of a prophetic calling, in the sense of moral and spir-

---

33. Report of the Department on Church and Society, in Central Committee minutes, 1958, p. 15.

The Rapid Social Change Team (l. to r.): M. M. Thomas, Paul A. Abrecht, Egbert de Vries, John Karefa-Smart, and Daisuke Kitagawa (WCC Photo)

itual attack; more often, it focused on bringing about a transformation of the societies in which it was set. In neither mode was this mission triumphalistic. Rather, mission in society was called forth most creatively and decisively by the note of discerning the work of God already taking place.

As the problems of rapid social change in traditional societies claimed attention, the Responsible Society broadened, although its basic categories remained. In particular, "the human" came to the fore as a category of thought. Here a positive engagement with Western culture was evident, for to accent "the human" was to recognize humanism, the secular at its best, and the Christian background of that tradition. The human appeared in the dignity of nationalism as opposed to the indignity of colonialism; in mutual respect as opposed to the indignity of racism; in economic improvement as opposed to the indignity of poverty. The "human" signified the dignity and freedom of the person as seen in Christ, in contrast to other forces—whether Western or not—which overrode that dignity and confined that freedom. Thus God was at work, Christ was at work, to produce the human; and where the human appeared, there God was at work.

This was bold doctrine. It was also dangerous, for it could lead far afield from the central affirmation of God-in-Christ as the Lord of history. Its boldness was augmented and its danger diminished, however, by the repetition again and again, in many different forms, and in the thought of the Christian minorities in three continents, of the point made in 1947 by M. M. Thomas. He argued forcefully that the doctrine of creation and the doctrine of redemption were both required in order to understand the predicament of modern humanity and to perceive the true humanity of the gospel. That made clear, he proceeded to describe this humanity, "the human," in communal terms.

Emphasizing that the personal interpretation of modern social reality must arise out of a visible, personal community in society, Thomas continued:

> I submit that the missionary movement, and the small congregations of the Christian Church founded in different parts of Asia, whatever they may appear in the eyes of the rational historian, are in their *essence* the one personal reality in all Asia. Proclaiming the gospel, and confronting every man with a responsible decision to repent and enter the historical community of the redeemed, the Church in Asia stands as the one community of persons. Knowing every man as a "brother for whom Christ died," and as destined to a personal destiny beyond the natural order in the order of grace, the fact of the Church is the clue to a personal understanding of man and his history.[34]

To place the discernment of God acting in history in the setting of the church and the church in the setting of God acting in history was perhaps the boldest and most significant stroke of all. In the tempestuous movements of the period, the church was the arena in which Scripture, doctrine, different traditions, and the problems of the time were thought through, and their significance understood. Amid the bewildering dilemmas besetting whole peoples and in the constant presence of far-reaching opportunities for them, church, in the sense of the people of God, was understood to be the communal reality that enabled Christians to discern the manner of God's working in history and gave authenticity to Christian serving-by-witnessing and witnessing-by-serving in society.[35]

---

34. M. M. Thomas, *op. cit.*, p. 76.
35. Hendrikus Berkhof, "The Calling of the Church to Witness and to Serve," in Central Committee minutes, 1957, p. 88. See also the reports of the sections on Witness, Service, and Unity, received by the Third Assembly; *New Delhi Report*, pp. 77-135.

13

The Sexes: Cooperation between Men and Women

Our rented house in Geneva was located in Veyrier, on the French border, the last property in Swiss territory. One evening shortly after settling in, we sat with Madeleine Barot after dinner, drinking coffee on the veranda, overlooking the orchard on our property. "Bob, I know that land down there better than you do," Madeleine said. I was inclined to protest, and did, since I had been working hard on it to make it presentable.

"Yes, but you see, I crawled through it, from there to there, on my hands and knees, often inching along on my stomach. In the days of the Resistance, I came up from France to the top of the Salève," she said, pointing to the landmark mountain that towered above our house. "Then I came down, to just over there. I had to be careful. The German sentries in France walked back and forth; the Swiss sentries here walked back and forth, and I had to slip through them both just at the right moment. When I got to your orchard, I was fairly safe, but I had to crawl. I did it many times."

At that time, Madeleine Barot was director of the WCC Department on the Cooperation of Men and Women in Church and Society, but she was no stranger to the Council's work. She had heard with some amazement of the plan to have a meeting of the Provisional Committee of the World Council in February 1946, only a few short months after the end of World War II.

I thought it was mad! I had often been in Geneva during the

war years. I regularly crossed the frontier in secret, taking Jewish children to safety from deportation. I was in close touch with the resistance networks of the churches in Western Europe. I was aware of all the contacts maintained by Visser 't Hooft. But we in Europe, from the Atlantic to the Urals, victors and vanquished alike, were physically and psychologically exhausted; morale was at a low ebb. Would a committee meeting in February 1946 even be capable of doing creative work? . . . As it turned out, on the morning of 20 February, in the chalet in the route de Malagnou in Geneva to which the office had just moved, there were sixty delegates representing 16 countries.[1]

She was there, and together with D. T. Niles was appointed co-chair of the new Youth Department of the WCC. "One of its first achievements was in obtaining places for one hundred young people to attend the Amsterdam Assembly in 1948 in addition to the ushers. This decision caused as big a furor at the time as the decision, many years later, to allocate a specific number of seats to women delegates at the Nairobi Assembly."

She had been active in ecumenical refugee work from the beginning, including a spectacular trip to Shanghai in 1946 to register the many Russians who had fled the revolution and were refugees there. The French government had said it was ready to receive them provided that the operation would be managed by the Comité Inter-Mouvements auprès des Evacués (CIMADE), of which she was director. At the time, all transportation from Europe eastward was commandeered by the military, so she journeyed to China by way of a ship across the Atlantic, a train to San Francisco, and a US battleship across the Pacific. But a typhoon damaged the ship and it was put in drydock in Yokohama for repairs. Suddenly she was "ordered to disembark."

> A military car was waiting for me on the quayside and an hour later, somewhat bewildered, I found myself at the headquarters of the US forces in the Pacific, at General MacArthur's base.
>
> The general's chief-of-staff had received the battleship's passenger list. His son, a young pastor from Boston, had just arrived in France to work for CIMADE, so he was one of my staff. His father saw my name and made the connection. I spent many fascinating days observing the Americans' occupation methods.

---

1. This and following quotations are from Madeleine Barot, "1946: Its Significance for the WCC" (mimeographed transcript of an address to the Central Committee, January 1987).

Madeleine Barot (WCC Photo)

Madeleine Barot had learned about the cooperation of men and women in church and society not only theoretically, but in the French SCM, the WSCF, and at the risk of death in the French Resistance as the leader of CIMADE. That extraordinary organization had a long, creative, and ecumenically powerful life, beginning with a ministry in internment camps and assisting Jews to escape the Nazis.[2] Arranging for the latter had brought her to Geneva, through our orchard. Throughout, men and women had cooperated with one another, at high risk and performing great service.

The SCM had also given me a background of mutuality in men/women relationships. In the Presbyterian Church women were ordained as ministers and ruling elders. On the face of it, the whole issue did not seem to me to be much of a problem, but I could understand that it might need emphasis elsewhere in the WCC membership. But Madeleine Barot, assisted by a pioneering working committee for her department—chaired first by Kathleen Bliss of the Church of England and then by Walter Muelder of Boston University and the Methodist Church—penetrated to realms of which I had scarcely been aware.

2. Marc Boegner, *The Long Road to Unity*, pp. 181f.

Kathleen Bliss (WCC Photo)

A swelling movement of social change made the issues of men/women relationships unavoidable in the ecumenical movement. In preparation for the First Assembly, Kathleen Bliss, whose brilliance and depth would contribute strongly to ecumenical thought, pointed to a profound distinction between "bourgeois society" and "technical society." In the former, women do what is "consistent with a continuous cycle of conceiving, childbearing and nursing, and men do the rest." In the latter, an increasing range of work is shared by men and women, in science, factories, transport, agriculture, and engineering. Large opportunities were open to women in education, health, and welfare in the community. World War II had given immense stimulus to this development.

The influence of technical society on women had a profound impact on marriage. Technical society stressed the likeness between men and women; marriage, by contrast, is not based on likeness but difference. In technical society home becomes a kind of "operational base" from which members go out. Little holds partners together except the biological function of sex, "and they find that sex for all its powerful cohesive qualities is essentially vagrant if isolated from all other factors in human relationships." A whole generation thus looks for new meaning in marriage.[3]

It was not only a Western problem. In the traditional societies of Asia, Africa, and Latin America, the rapidity of social change liberated women and at the same time put enormous pressure on them.

I could not forget the long lines of women carrying dirt out of the excavation for the dam in southern India, while their babies slept in hammocks in the nurseries nearby, and in the villages and homes from which they had come. Nor could I forget the mines of Johannesburg, where multitudes of men from South Africa's "homelands" and surrounding countries came for months at a time, leaving village and home, living in segregated compounds and sending back paychecks.

Madeleine Barot said of women in Africa:

Nothing stops them, neither the weight of tradition nor their elders' lack of understanding, nor the need of constantly inventing a new style of life to suit unprecedented situations. They are rarely helped by the men, who are themselves too occupied with their own evolution. They are on the march with bewildering speed like all Africa. Their obedience, or their disobedience, concerns not only Africa, but the whole Church.[4]

A similar note was struck by the concluding international meeting of the study of social change in Asia, Africa, and Latin America. Rapid social change "affects women perhaps more than men, changing relations between the sexes as well as bringing material improvements in living which ease the drudgery of the daily round; and releasing women for education and training so that they can serve more fully both their families and communities in the changing pattern of urban and rural life."[5]

Even so, there was a marked similarity of the problems in the relationship between men and women everywhere. After years of exploration, the Third Assembly provided a catalogue of problems that were worldwide:

3. Kathleen Bliss, "Personal Relations in a Technical Society," Amsterdam Vol. 3, pp. 84, 86.
4. Quoted by Paul Abrecht, *The Churches and Rapid Social Change*, p. 162.
5. *Dilemmas and Opportunities: Christian Action in Rapid Social Change*, p. 8.

sex relations before and after marriage; illegitimacy; in some cultures polygamy or concubinage as a social system sanctioned by law and custom; in some Western cultures short-term marriages, or liaisons, easy divorce; in all parts of the world mixed marriages (interfaith, inter-confessional and inter-racial) with the diminishing of caste and class systems of racial prejudice.[6]

The New Delhi language was mild. The churches would "have to discover what position and action to take" in regard to these matters. From one's own experience and knowledge, one could expect that scarcely anyone present was untouched by most of these issues; and that the movements of social change they reflected were forcing individual Christians and churches to provide answers, whether by silence or explicitly, whether wise or not.

The beginning of the WCC's involvement in responding to changing men/women relationships and their meaning for the life of the churches was modest, but met with a surprising response. On the initiative of church women's organizations in the US, a questionnaire had been produced and circulated in 1946 and 1947 by Twila Cavert, under the auspices of the embryonic WCC. It produced substantial results. No such comprehensive inquiry had ever before been done on this major subject. People and groups from 58 countries sent in memoranda, often as much as 100 pages, with supporting documents. Besides Anglican and Protestant responses, there were replies from Orthodox churches, not only in Greece, but also from a large group of churches not represented in Amsterdam. It was clear that this was among the most urgent concerns of the churches, and it was so registered at the First Assembly.[7]

The announced subject was "The Life and Work of Women in the Church," but in response to the concerns registered by delegates and the questionnaire results, the Assembly made a broad, fundamental affirmation:

> The Church as the Body of Christ consists of men and women created, as responsible persons, together to glorify God and to do His Will. This truth, accepted in theory, is too often ignored in practice. In many countries and churches it is evident that the full co-operation of men and women in the service of Christ

6. New Delhi Report, p. 212.
7. Revised Interim Report of a Study on the Life and Work of Women in the Church (Geneva: WCC, 1948). See also Kathleen Bliss, *The Service and Status of Women in the Church* (Geneva: WCC, 1952); Madeleine Barot, *Cooperation of Men and Women in Church, Family and Society* (Geneva: WCC, 1964), p. 10.

through the Church has not been achieved. Yet the Church as a whole, particularly at the present time of change and tension, needs the contribution of all its members in order to fulfil its task.[8]

This affirmation was based on an understanding of creation and of redemption. As to the former, there was no hint of the subordination of woman to man or vice versa; and the reference to "responsible persons" gave a basis for the guiding concept of "cooperation." By placing the whole in the context of the Body of Christ, redemption was implied. There was no evidence that this affirmation was consciously constructed in this way; it was significant that it came naturally, not as a reflection of a system. Even so, the affirmation arose from a substantial biblical basis.

Scripture and Theology

The conditions in which women and men found themselves at the time made it all but inevitable that a main ecumenical contribution would be in the realm of scriptural interpretation and theology. There was the sharp novelty of change in the position of women in society, challenging women and the relation of men and women. The churches were divided, not only by society but within themselves, concerning the role of women in their life. An understanding of Scripture was imperative, not least because what the Bible said about the relation of men and women seemed to be confusing.

A major problem was that at crucial points Genesis 1:26-28 and Genesis 2:18-24 presented different accounts. One was the creation of humanity; the other the institution of marriage. Close scrutiny in the ecumenical setting, however, revealed certain fundamentals. Both passages revealed men and women to be created in the image of God and thus to be of the same nature, equal in dignity and in value in God's sight. Also, man and woman were created one for the other. There was mutuality and purpose in the creation of women and men. Men and women were called to "complete one another, to multiply and to reign over creation."[9]

But historically these passages had been interpreted differently. This traditional interpretation — still maintained in some circles — had begun with creation itself, discerning "orders of creation," among them

8. Amsterdam Report, p. 146; for the work of the Department on Cooperation, see *The First Six Years*, pp. 53ff.; *Evanston to New Delhi*, pp. 84-90.
9. Madeleine Barot, *op. cit.*, p. 4.

the state and marriage. Approached in this fashion, the creation of men and women implied the subordination of women to men as part of the "order." This static hierarchy in the account of creation was applied to the man/woman relationship generally and in the church.

Ecumenically, it was argued that this hierarchical view owed too much to a Judaic theology of ancient times.[10] This had maintained a natural inferiority of woman and progressively degraded the status of women among the Jewish people. By the time of Christ, woman was considered an inferior being. Moreover, that interpretation of Genesis was transmitted through St. Paul to the church fathers and adopted by them.

"Christ made a spectacular break with this attitude."[11] Freed from the view that orders and hierarchy were built into creation itself, the import of Christ for human relations took on new meaning. The relation of men and women found its fulfillment in the Kingdom Christ inaugurated, whose power could enter and transform any society. Moreover, the apostle Paul was equally revolutionary: "There is neither male nor female; for you are all one in Christ Jesus" (Gal. 3:28).

On this last point, the dilemma was clear. Obviously the "subordination tradition" was present in the Pauline writings. The question remained, For what purpose was that tradition there? The answer to that raised a further question: Did the Galatians 3:28 tradition stand alone, or was there more?

Further search shed more light. Chapter 7 of 1 Corinthians, where it is clear that woman's destiny has to do with her relation to Christ, was seen as fundamental. This relation may be fulfilled not only in marriage and motherhood, but also in celibacy. "In marriage, the wife does not have sole authority over her own body, but the husband; similarly, the husband has not sole authority over his own body, but the wife" (1 Cor. 7:4).[12] Even the Ephesians passage (5:22-24) which recommends that women be subject to their husbands as unto the Lord because the husband is the head of the woman is preceded (vs. 21) by "Be subject one to the other out of reverence for Christ," and followed (vs. 25) by "Husbands, love your wives, as Christ loved the Church and gave himself up for her." Furthermore, a Christian wife may save her pagan husband. A profound mutuality was apparent.

But how could one reconcile this line of Paul's thought with the "subordination line" which he advocated to guide the behavior of

10. *Ibid.,* pp. 12-15; cf. Francine Dumas, *Man and Woman: Similarity and Difference* (Geneva: WCC, 1966), pp. 22- 41.
11. Madeleine Barot, *op. cit.,* p. 14.
12. *Ibid.,* p. 14.

women in public assemblies and elsewhere? Did the existence of the "conservative" passages, based on the then-current interpretation of Genesis, cancel out the revolutionary conviction of Galatians 3:28? "It is possible to think not."[13] The answer lay in response to another question: What was the tension between these passages really all about?

The tension between the revolutionary and the conservative passages in the Pauline writings reflected the life-and-death passion of Paul's life — to preach the gospel. The conservative passages concerning women's behavior reflect Paul's desire that women behave according to demands of the contemporary culture in order to help, or at least not to hinder, the preaching of the gospel. These "subordination passages," it was pointedly argued, "are all addressed to married women and concern their participation in public meetings."[14] In that setting the Apostle demanded that the women accept the customs of the day rather than do something that would hinder the preaching, hearing, and accepting of the gospel. The basic point was: accept the cultural facts and use them to witness to Christ.

Ecumenically there was no desire to ignore the difficult passages or reject them. Rather, a principle of interpretation was employed which allowed the demonstrably more fundamental aspects of scriptural thought to explain and transcend the less fundamental. Even so, it was argued, prudence was more important than quick rejection of difficult passages, as the conservative churches showed, because "the Word of God is an ever new power of life which nothing can shackle."[15] Today, it was important to do what Paul did, namely to use the customs. If Paul did not want women to speak in assemblies and if he wanted them to wear veils, we did the opposite; yet both worked with customs.

For ecumenical thought, the definitive perspective was gained by looking through and beyond these passages to the new creation in Christ. Hendrik Kraemer made the point vigorously in his exploration of the theology of the laity, which, he strongly insisted, included men and women. There was nothing, he said, on which the "Christian church has been so retrograde, so subject to non-Christian, pagan notions of the sexes and to patriarchal thinking as in regard to women and their place in the Church."[16] Disagreement about biblical interpretation raised difficulties, he conceded, but "behind these debates about disobedience or obedience to the divine Word there are, of course, hiding themselves

13. *Ibid.*
14. *Ibid.,* p. 15.
15. *Ibid.*
16. Hendrik Kraemer, *A Theology of the Laity,* p. 69.

also all the sociological and psychological inhibitions which together build up the deep entrenched masculine superiority assumption." But when both men and women were viewed as "the new creature in Christ," all the other arguments became irrelevant.[17]

In this new creature, the order of creation itself was restored, for in Christ there were cosmic dimensions. *All things* were made new. Men and women must live within their sex, but the new liberty, given in Christ, allowed them to transcend these limits. As this liberty provided for celibacy as well as marriage, was it not true that new forms of cooperation between men and women might be found also?

> The new life in Christ remains mysterious and hidden — it is constantly given anew, it escapes all definition; but it seems, however, that interdependence, mutual submission, complementary equality between the sexes, correspond better with what we can perceive of it than do hierarchy, authority, and subordination.[18]

Cooperation

The WCC began its work under the heading of "The Life and Work of Women in the Church," but the concern was soon broadened to "The Cooperation of Men and Women in Church and Society," and from this to "The Cooperation of Men and Women in Church, Family and Society." Throughout, ecumenical thought centered on "cooperation" as a fundamental category for the relation of men and women. An analogy can be drawn between the concept of cooperation in this area and the concept of the Responsible Society in regard to society as a whole. "Cooperation" performed the function of a penultimate category of thought. On the one side, it was derived from the gospel; on the other side, it was a norm for masculine and feminine relationships in society.

Moreover, cooperation bore on the church. Responses to the questionnaire of 1946-47 had shown that the economic and political emancipation of women had reached to the center of the churches' life and calling: "A great hope was born: would not a better use of these new feminine capabilities give birth to new forms of witness and service?"[19] "Cooperation," it was felt, would go far to enable, guide, and express the development of such new forms.

17. *Ibid.,* p. 71.
18. Madeleine Barot, *op. cit.,* p. 15.
19. *Ibid.,* p. 3.

Man and Woman

Ecumenical experience among men and women made it clear that women now held a deep mistrust of "myths once woven into a prison for her kind. . . . She is born an autonomous person."[20] This led, in turn, to understanding a profound shift in male and female consciousness.

For the first time in history, men and women faced one another aware of a dual character of similarity and dissimilarity. They were consciously similar because they were fully human; they were consciously different because they were male and female. In this way the two sexes were discovering themselves as part of the same race but different and strangers to one another. Within this duality, they were attempting a common adventure of freedom.[21]

In this situation, men seemed more affected by present changes than they were ready to admit. Even those convinced of the need for women to change had difficulty in accepting the same need for themselves. Understanding that women were finding new ways of expressing feminine personality, men were driven to recognize that they also needed new ways of expressing masculine personality.

That went further than equality between the sexes, at least in the juridical sense. It went to the depths of personal identity. The point of cooperation was clear: mutual help among men and women in finding new ways of expressing their respective gifts;[22] and that was psychologically, spiritually, and socially revolutionary.

Society

Cooperation of women and men, based on the biblical revelation, also had consequences for society itself. Inequalities of many kinds needed redress. Men were no doubt astonished to see how many realms of Western society this involved: ways of life, customs, legislation, opportunities for education, vocational training, the organization of work, the practice (as distinguished from the theory) of having women in civic life, the gap between the right to vote and the election of women to public office, prejudice among women, and the fear of women in public office to innovate as they wanted lest they fail. If, as Kathleen Bliss rightly observed, technical society drew women from the home, it was also sadly true "that the work of the mother in the home, whatever the

---

20. Francine Dumas, *op. cit.,* p. 16.
21. *Ibid.,* p. 11.
22. Madeleine Barot, *op. cit.,* p. 48.

compliments showered upon her, has never by itself raised the legal, political or social status of woman."[23] As "cooperation" pointed to the ultimate freedom of the new being in Christ, it pointed also to the transformation of society.

The Churches

Cooperation also had implications for the churches. The issue of the life and the work of women in the church and of the role of women in society had been gaining attention since the nineteenth century, and especially since the turn of the twentieth century. By the time the Amsterdam Assembly met, the movement for the equality of women in church and society could not be denied.

At the same time, there was difference and division within the churches. Most critical were divisions over the ordination of women. Orthodoxy, Roman Catholicism, and at that time most of Anglicanism were opposed to women's ordination; much (though far from all) of Protestantism accepted it. By the time of the Third Assembly in 1961, two strands in the ecumenical tradition were joining forces. Those concerned for cooperation among men and women and for unity in faith and order were collaborating in a focus on the division in the churches concerning the ordination of women.

A Ministry

I have left until this point mention of an aspect of the work of much of the WCC staff—and occasionally of some committee members as well — which amounted to a special ministry. I have done so because Madeleine Barot's work was particularly effective in this respect.

All of the problems, issues, and specific programs discussed in this book demanded work that came to a form of ministry. Whatever the specific interests—assisting refugees, speaking to youth conferences, organizing consultations, or other—WCC staff especially found themselves engaged in an extensive one-on-one correspondence, in discovering new people and cultivating their interest, in organizing large and small occasions of ecumenical consultation, and in speaking to small groups or large audiences. Worldwide travel was essential. Always, there was the personal element of relating to individuals, as well as the conceptual element—biblical, theological, sociological, psychological—lest one run around the world empty-handed. In each realm of concern, the

23. *Ibid.*, p. 26.

objective was to stimulate interest, encourage the pioneer, and provide a sense of support and worldwide fellowship to those who felt alone or nearly so. It was a distinctive, ecumenical ministry.

The work of the Department on the Cooperation of Men and Women in Church, Society and Family entailed incessant travel on the part of Madeleine Barot, in part because of the pioneering aspect of the work and in part because of people's needs. Cooperation had to be demonstrated in an ecumenical mode of caring, moving from the greater fellowship to the various parts and back again.

That showed itself as the Department on Cooperation drew from, and built into, other aspects of WCC work. Interchurch aid and refugee service engaged men and women in the *koinonia* of giving and receiving, of sharing. The constituency of the Youth Department was men and women. The Ecumenical Institute was diligent in securing women and men to take part in its courses and consultations. The work of Hans-Ruedi Weber in the Laity Department and of Madeleine Barot exhibited a virtual partnership in a mutual focus on the laity. Everywhere, the Rapid Social Change study engaged the participation of women and men and confronted the problems of their cooperation in church and society and family. I was constantly impressed with the combination of intellectual energy and cooperative activity in pursuit of Christian man/woman relationships around the world.

Many conditions cried out for such a ministry. Frustrated and anxious men and women needed to find healing in a new relationship. Society separated the home from work, straining the family. Women in many societies did not play a sufficient role in family life, and in traditional societies the patriarchal and extended family were giving way to the pressures of the city. Such conditions could scarcely be helped by simply announcing "cooperation," however well conceived. They required the extensive exercise of ecumenical ministry.[24]

Four convictions animated the work as a whole. Three have been suggested above: (1) that the relations between the sexes and the ethics governing them are a fundamental element of Christian teaching about human beings and their societies; (2) that "the nature and qualities peculiar to men and women cannot be specifically defined"; (3) that "the richness of the complementary relationship of man and woman, and their incompleteness when either is alone, extend to all fields of life."[25]

24. Memorandum: "Comments on the Task of the Department on the Cooperation of Men and Women in Church and Society," *Ecumenical Review*, XI (1958); cf. *Evanston to New Delhi*, pp. 84-87.
25. Madeleine Barot, *op. cit.*, pp. 8f.

Hans-Ruedi Weber (WCC Photo)

The fourth conviction concerned need.

A long history of ignorance and unconditional submission on the part of the woman, the temptations of one sex to exploit the other, the peculiar vulnerability to sin of any relationship between man and woman — all make it difficult to understand what true cooperation can be. The traditional teaching of the churches and the divergent interpretations given by theologians of what the Bible tells us about man and woman add further to the difficulty of breaking familiar patterns of paternalism and of feminism.[26]

That conviction could only be carried through by an ecumenical ministry.

26. *Ibid.,* p. 14.

"The Christian gospel," said Mollie Batten, principal of William Temple College in England, "with its revolutionary insights, is still bursting upon the world, and the cooperation of men and women has only been under serious consideration for much less than a century. In New Testament times, there is the astounding new community in which women were received from the beginning as equal members with men, something quite new in the ancient world, so revolutionary that we have never really grasped it or caught up with it. Nor has there been in this new community, the Christian Church, an unbroken, golden tradition. The golden moment is ahead, because we are stretching after the implications of the unique revelation which came in Jesus Christ."[27]

27. Mollie Batten, in *Obstacles to the Cooperation of Men and Women in Working Life, in Public Service. Report of the Consultation Held at Odense, Denmark, August 8-12, 1956* (Geneva: WCC, 1956), p. 17.

14

The Races

I started to feel tension in my stomach as the plane left what was still known in 1960 as Salisbury, Southern Rhodesia. As we circled over Johannesburg a short time later, it grew. We landed, and came to a stop. Someone entered the plane. "Is Mr. Bilheimer on board?" he asked loudly. Turning in my seat, I saw a uniformed officer. At my signal he approached and said: "Your hosts wish to know whether you will meet the press now."

I replied that I had no special need to see the press but would do so if my hosts desired it. I asked the officer to repeat my message and sank back in relief. Fear that I was being arrested before I got off the plane gave way to anxiety that I might have to meet the press before I had anything to say. At home in Geneva, my wife heard on the BBC that I had arrived safely in Johannesburg on a one-person "mission of fellowship" on behalf of the WCC to its South African member churches.

What had led to this mission and journey?

My responsibility in planning the Evanston Assembly in 1954 had given me a specific opportunity that I deeply desired. The great ecumenical conferences had not given substantial attention to race relations since 1928. It was high time for a contemporary treatment of the subject. On a visit to Geneva in the early 1950s, I proposed race relations to Visser 't Hooft as a major topic for the Second Assembly.

He knew of — and shared — my concern. He had preached several times at the small black church in New York City where I had learned to see "race" not only through the relatively theoretical eyes of my SCM experience, but through the eyes of close black friends.

"OK," Wim said, "go ahead and develop a proposal. But you will have to demonstrate that 'race' is a world concern and not just a matter of South Africa and the southern part of the USA." He understood the European mentality which did not understand Europe's complicity in the racism of the colonial era and its current aftermath. Nor, at that time, had there been enough attention to ethnic conflict and its meaning.

The precedent of previous ecumenical meetings provided a starting point.[1] The experience of J. Oscar Lee of the US Federal Council of Churches helped, as did that of Hans Hoekendijk, who had been to South Africa and who knew Indonesia. The Executive Committee meeting in 1952 and the Central Committee in Lucknow in early 1953 were convinced by the proposal. One of the six major topics at Evanston would be "Inter-Group Relations: the Churches Amid Racial and Ethnic Tensions." The advance survey, comparable to those prepared for each of the Assembly topics, established beyond any doubt that racism was a world issue.

My pastorate in Queens had unexpected benefits. I was able to persuade Carol Brice, a member of the church and one of the great concert voices of the time, to sing with the Chicago Symphony at the Assembly. Sybil Caine, who sang in "Lost in the Stars," the Broadway musical adaptation of Alan Paton's *Cry, The Beloved Country*, gave us tickets for the opening night performance. At the cast party afterwards, standing next to a quiet man, I introduced myself. "How do you do," he said; "Paton's my name, Alan Paton." Subsequently, he agreed to help us prepare for the Assembly treatment of race relations.

Although I could participate in the preparatory work, my responsibilities for Assembly organization kept me from its discussions. When the report was read in plenary session, I was moved by vision and gratitude. Roswell Barnes of the USH as chair, Peter Dagadu of Ghana, and Oscar Lee as fellow officers, Benjamin Mays of Atlanta, Alan Paton, and others had produced an acknowledged classic.

Recognizing the restlessness of peoples, the hunger of millions for status and recognition, the search for meaning in life, and the poverty of whole populations, the statement moved quickly to the root problem. "The hatreds, jealousies and suspicions with which the world has always been afflicted are deepened by racial prejudices and fears, rooted in the sinful human heart and entrenched in law and custom. In some situations, men come to accept race conflict as inevitable and lose hope of peaceful solution."[2]

1. See Jerusalem Vol. 4; Oxford Report, pp. 60-61; Madras Report, pp. 106-109; Amsterdam Report, p. 81.
2. Quotations in this and following paragraphs are from the Evanston Report, pp. 152-57.

Hope lay in Jesus Christ, who revealed God as Father and who died for all, reconciling them to God and to each other by his cross. That faith was the clear foundation of everything else. Briefly stated, it led to a further implication.

> From every race and nation a new people of God is created, in which the power of the Spirit overcomes racial pride and fear. So far from being without hope or purpose, God's people now as new creatures are co-workers with Him, and are filled with joy, and assured His final victory. So to us is given the gift of sharing in and working for the Kingdom even now. Assured that the final victory is Christ's, we can work actively, continually repentant and continually forgiven, for that reconciliation which we believe to be God's will.

As that was read out at the Assembly, one recognized a cogent statement of the essence of the faith, its historical embodiment, the hope it contained, and its demands on life.

The Evanston report drew three consequences concerning the church's witness. First, the church was to witness within itself to the kingship of Christ and to the unity of his people in him, thus demonstrating the power of God-in-Christ to transcend racial diversity. The churches, in other words, must embody what the church is. Second, Christians are to witness to the kingship of Christ and the unity of all humanity, striving through social and political action to secure justice, peace, and freedom for all. One noted here the import of the word "striving." It was strung tight between vision and historical limitations, giving timbre and strength to "witness." Third, the calling and the striving yielded "a foretaste of that Kingdom into which the faithful shall be gathered." The witness, in orther words, did not depend on approval or success but on the gift of a foretaste now of God's future for humanity.

The precondition of all was repentance for

> something far deeper than our disunity and our offences. We need to repent of our separation from God, from which these spring, and of our feeble grasp of the truth of the gospel. . . .
> When we are given Christian insight the whole pattern of racial discrimination is seen as an unutterable offence against God, to be endured no longer, so that the very stones cry out. In such moments we understand more fully the meaning of the gospel, and the duty of both Church and Christian.

Where the churches gave segregation the status of a principle, it was their duty "to search themselves continually whether their theology is not the child of fear, and meanwhile to test every application of segregation by the standard of Christian love." Upon all churches lay a constant twofold duty: obeying and proclaiming the word of judgment, repenting and calling to repentance.

That directed attention to society. The churches' task was to "challenge the conscience of society," and to keep open every line of communication in societies riven by racial strife. The pressure of South Africa and the US showed in the emphasis on supporting church members who stood against segregation.

Developing a principle that had been a general ecumenical assumption since Oxford 1937 had recognized the Confessing Church in Germany, the Evanston Statement spoke of the law and breaking the law. Being the conscience of society requires the church to protest any law or arrangement that is unjust to any human being or makes Christian fellowship impossible. Some church members might be led to break the law: "The church does not contemplate lightly any breaking of the law, but it recognizes the duty of a Christian to do so when he feels that he has reached that point where the honour and glory of God command him to obey God rather than man."

More specifically, "the Church cannot approve any law" which discriminates on the ground of race, restricts the opportunity of any to acquire education, prepare for, procure, or practise employment in the pursuit of a vocation, curtails the exercise of the full rights and responsibilities of citizenship, or forbids racial or ethnic intermarriage.

Reports of this nature were not adopted by the Assembly but received and commended to the churches. They did not express a policy of the WCC, but were signposts registering the "mind" of the Assembly and contributions to the growing ecumenical tradition.

On race relations the Second Assembly wanted to go further and to establish formal WCC policy. That was done by adopting two Resolutions—one on antisemitism and one on segregation.

The basic opposition to antisemitism was formulated at the First Assembly and adopted as resolutions in specific actions by the Second and the Third Assemblies. The First Assembly formulation read: "We call upon all the churches we represent to denounce antisemitism, no matter what its origin, as absolutely irreconcilable with the profession and practice of the Christian faith. Antisemitism is sin against God and man."[3]

The Evanston resolution on segregation read:

> The Second Assembly of the World Council of Churches declares its conviction that any form of segregation based on race,

3. Amsterdam Report, p. 161; cf. Evanston Report, p. 159; *New Delhi Report*, p. 148.

colour or ethnic origin is contrary to the gospel, and is incompatible with the Christian doctrine of man and with the nature of the Church of Christ. The Assembly urges the churches within its membership to renounce all forms of segregation or discrimination and to work for their abolition within their own life and within society.

In doing so the Assembly is painfully aware that, in the realities of the contemporary world, many churches find themselves confronted by historical, political, social and economic circumstances which may make the immediate achievement of this objective extremely difficult. But under God the fellowship of the ecumenical movement is such as to offer to these churches the strength and encouragement to help them and individuals within them to overcome these difficulties with the courage given by faith, and with the desire to testify ever more faithfully to our Master.

From its very beginning the ecumenical movement by its very nature has been committed to a form of fellowship in which there is no segregation or discrimination. The Assembly of the World Council of Churches rejoices in this fact and confirms this practice as the established policy of the Council.[4]

SOUTH AFRICA

"Sharpeville" became, after March 1960, the symbol of revolt and suppression, of protest and killing in South Africa. There had been many "disturbances" (as the language of the time had it) — protesting crowds eliciting police reaction and control. At Sharpeville, somewhere between 5,000 and 20,000 — depending on who did the estimating — gathered on March 21, with 67 blacks killed and 167 wounded, 30 shots entering from the front and 155 from the back.[5] Uprisings spread and killings increased. On March 24, the government banned public meetings of all races, and six days later declared a state of emergency. The events aroused world opinion.

At Amsterdam there had been five member churches from South Africa; at Evanston eight. Some were all black (African), some "colored" (mixed descent), some all white (European origin), and some were inclusive of all three. All existed in the rigidly segregated society

4. Evanston Report, pp. 158f. Visser 't Hooft gives an account of negotiations leading to this resolution; *Memoirs*, p. 282.
5. Muriel Horrell, *A Survey of Race Relations in South Africa* (Johannesburg: Institute of Race Relations, 1961), pp. 57f. The discrepancy in totals is not accounted for.

organized under the principles of apartheid. Three of the member churches were composed of Afrikaners (whites of Dutch descent); the Anglican (Church of the Province of South Africa), Congregational, Methodist, and Presbyterian churches were composed of whites, mostly of English descent, and blacks (living in segregation). The Bantu Presbyterian Church was black.

The Evanston report and resolution on race relations had been widely publicized in the South African press and discussed among the churches. And since 1948, WCC representatives had made a number of visits to South Africa—notably Hoekendijk, Cavert, Goodall, and Visser 't Hooft.

Clearly, the WCC had to make some response to the violence of Sharpeville and the consequent worldwide outcry. But everyone agreed that a mere statement to the press would not suffice at this point. Moreover, the Anglican Archbishop of Capetown, Joost de Blank, had told the *New York Times* that the WCC should expel the Dutch Reformed South African member churches. That demand began to clarify an essential aspect of the problem.

How could the WCC maintain the integrity of both its covenant and its position on race? The covenant meant that the WCC existed to draw churches out of isolation into conversation and *koinonia*. To accede to de Blank's proposal would have meant an immediate denial of the WCC's basic purpose. At the same time, integrity demanded that the Council could in no way downplay or compromise its conviction on race relations. The WCC officers proposed a "mission of fellowship" to all the member churches in South Africa, in the form of one person. I was asked to undertake the mission—and I was sent without instructions. "See what you can do," Wim had said, "and God bless."

In South Africa in 1960, as now, blacks and coloreds were severely oppressed, and whites lived in privileged opulence, though some of them clung to the illusion of an idealistic form of apartheid—a sort of South African equivalent of the American "separate but equal." Black South Africa had determined leaders—Nelson Mandela was still free—but the African National Congress and the Pan African Congress were banned, and the Black Consciousness movement had not yet taken shape.

Even so, there was surprising freedom of the press and surprising readiness to talk, even with one's opponents, about the evils or supposed virtues of apartheid. The continuing explosions of violence, save for Sharpeville, had not yet appeared. At the same time, the hardness was there: apartheid governed every aspect of South African life. All of the ingredients of the unfolding tragedy were there, but, in the weird calm following Sharpeville, warily quiescent.

Mine was a mission of fellowship through diplomacy. Its overall objective was to maintain—and restore where broken—the *koinonia* of the covenant. "Do we still intend to stay together?" was the explicit and implicit question to both blacks who suffered and whites who exploited. That implied the full WCC position on race. I was grateful that the Assembly had left no room for interpretation: it was an ironclad policy that segregation "is contrary to the gospel and is incompatible with the Christian doctrine of man and with the nature of the Church of Christ." At this point, the nature of the covenant came into play. Did all concerned really believe in the absolute need to avoid isolation and embrace *koinonia*?

The morning after my arrival in Johannesburg (I had not met the press at the airport), I met with the executive committee of the Dutch Reformed Church of the Transvaal. I said that I first wanted to hear what they had to say. They went around the table: confessing their faith, justifying apartheid, believing themselves misunderstood, but giving me a tiny glimmer of a way out. They appreciated that the WCC had sent a person, not a message through the mail or a reaction in the press. That was the clue. At the end, they asked me what I had to say.

I proposed that the personal dialogue continue with a serious consultation in Johannesburg between a major WCC delegation and representatives from each WCC member church in South Africa, interracial in membership and living accommodations. They agreed, but asked, "What about Archbishop de Blank?" Politely, I told them that that was my problem.

In Capetown, Archbishop de Blank received me at tea in Bishopscourt. The pleasantries of the English tea over, de Blank stated his case. I tried one argument, namely that people of British descent in South Africa, including church members, bore stains of segregation — as was evident from their stake in the economic structure — and thus had little ground to stand on in asking the WCC to expel the Dutch Reformed. The archbishop did not take kindly to this argument, but I think it did convey something to him. Still, he reiterated his demand: prove that you stand by the Evanston statement by expelling the Dutch Reformed Church.

I decided that the moment had come, and said, "Archbishop, if I agreed to that here, I would then have to say that an archbishop of the Anglican Communion desires to turn the World Council of Churches into a super-church, with power over its member churches." I did not need a verbal response to know I had won the argument. We discussed my alternative — the full consultation — and the archbishop agreed, joined the Planning Committee, and attended.

Various other issues came up, and it took three round trips between Geneva and Johannesburg and one to Lambeth Palace in London to get the problems settled and the conference planned. In London, I discovered that the Archbishop of Canterbury wanted to postpone the conference for six months or a year. Since I had no authority to do that, we arranged a further discussion the next morning. Consultation by phone with Visser 't Hooft gave me the grounds to refuse. There I saw Visser 't Hooft's willingness to take risks for what he believed in; defying the Archbishop of Canterbury is not an easy thing to do.

In December 1960 the consultation met at Cottesloe, a residence in the University of Witwatersrand. Lodging, work, and worship were on a totally interracial basis. Eight churches sent delegations of ten people each; the WCC delegation numbered six. The meeting was chaired by Franklin Clark Fry, moderator of the WCC Central Committee.

Cottesloe was a microcosm of South Africa as a whole. The tensions there arose from anger, suspicion, long history, theological division, divergences of culture, language, tradition and loyalty, prejudice outspoken and prejudice rationalized. Fry's extraordinary gifts of intelligence, commitment, fair play, and experience, which we had often seen in the Central Committee, were taxed to the full. Hour by hour it was evident that the achievement of a good moderator goes far beyond keeping order in a discussion. Chairing a meeting is a highly creative act in which the essence of leadership lies in the ability to produce leadership from and by the group.

The language of Cottesloe's basic attack on apartheid was so muted that on the last day I expressed my near total disillusionment to Wim and Frank Fry. But that afternoon when I met with the press, one of the true radicals present told me that the work of the conference was a "miracle." I realized I was wrong. In the center of Afrikanerdom, an interracial group of people had in the name of Christ mounted a telling witness against apartheid.

The statements, each agreed upon by at least 80% of the conference, made three fundamental points. The first concerned loyalty.

> The Church of Jesus Christ, by its nature and calling, is deeply concerned with the welfare of all people, both as individuals and as members of social groups. It is called to minister to human need in whatever circumstances and forms it appears, and to insist that all be done with justice. In its social witness the Church must take cognizance of all attitudes, forces, poli-

cies and laws which affect the life of a people, but the Church must proclaim that the final criterion of all social and political action is the principles of Scripture regarding the realization for all men of a life worthy of their God-given vocation.[6]

The two critical words were "final criterion." The interracial ecumenical group had insisted that this lay in Scripture and that it applied to the life and destiny of all people.

The criterion was elaborated more specifically in regard to nationalism, a word with a special force in South Africa, where the Afrikaners, identifying themselves politically as the National Party, were in power.

> In so far as nationalism grows out of a desire for self-realization, Christians should understand and respect it. The danger of nationalism is, however, that it may seek to fulfil its aim at the expense of the interests of others and that it can make the nation an absolute value which takes the place of God. The role of the Church must therefore be to help to direct national movements towards just and worthy ends.

The second point zeroed in on South Africa and apartheid. The white government had reserved an overwhelming proportion of the best land for whites. They numbered at that time about 3,000,000, or 21% of the population, with blacks, colored (mixed), and Indians numbering about 12,000,000 (79%).

The conference recognized "that all racial groups who permanently inhabit our country are a part of our total population, and we regard them as indigenous. Members of all these groups have an equal right to make their contribution towards the enrichment of the life of their country and to share in the ensuing responsibilities, rewards and privileges."

This was elaborated in strong affirmations about land ownership and employment. The right to own land, said the statement, "is part of the dignity of the adult man, and for this reason a policy which permanently denies to Non-White people the right of collaboration in the government of the country of which they are citizens cannot be justified." Moreover, "the present system of job reservation must give way to a more equitable system of labour which safeguards the interests of all concerned."

The third fundamental point concerned the church and its unity

---

6. Quotations of the Consultation statement are from *Mission in South Africa* (Geneva: World Council of Churches, 1961); cf. Visser 't Hooft, *op. cit.,* pp. 283-88; *Evanston to New Delhi*, pp. 322-25; A. H. Luckhoff, *Cottesloe* (Johannesburg: Tafelberg, 1978).

as the Body of Christ: "Within this unity the natural diversity among men is not annulled but sanctified. No one who believes in Jesus Christ may be excluded from any church on the grounds of his color or race. The spiritual unity among all men who are in Christ must find visible expression in acts of common worship and witness, and in fellowship and consultation on matters of common concern." This, combined with the point concerning the authority of Scripture, made possible a single sentence concerning mixed marriage: "There are no Scriptural grounds for the prohibition of mixed marriages."

What did Cottesloe accomplish? There was a moment of euphoria. Church leadership was encouraged, and the extraordinary publicity given to the conference reached to the pews. Some unity had been demonstrated. Blacks, colored, and Indians were encouraged. Clearly, the effort made an impact on South Africa.

The consultation adjourned on December 14. On January 1, Prime Minister Verwoerd made his usual New Year's address to the nation. In it he publicly denounced the Cottesloe Consultation and demanded that the Afrikaner participants retract their agreement to the Report. All but one did.

The one who refused to recant was C. F. Beyers Naudé. Within three years he resigned a brilliant career in the church to devote his life to a fundamental challenge to apartheid in the name of Christ and the church. Through the 1960s and into the 1970s he would head the Christian Institute of Southern Africa, which he founded, and would then be banned. After the banning, he resumed the struggle, eventually serving as general secretary of the South African Council of Churches. A world figure, Naudé has been a leader and a symbol of an interracial confessing church movement which gathered power and influence, giving hope and strength as the struggle intensified.

I stayed in touch with him during the period of his work with the Christian Institute, but did not write. I knew that he was in danger and that letters from me in his files would not help. When the Institute was closed down, its files confiscated, and Naudé himself banned, I was glad that there was nothing there from me. In 1985, after his banning was lifted, we had a reunion in New York, and the moment of rejoicing was profound indeed.[7]

*　　　　　*　　　　　*

7. Naudé's own account is admirably set forth in an hour-long documentary film, "The Cry of Reason," produced by Worldwide Documentaries, Inc.

C. F. Beyers Naudé (AFRAPIX/P. Weinberg)

The Evanston resolutions clearly had implications for the ecumenical movement elsewhere as well. Everywhere, racial tension was a component of rapid social change. In Ceylon, Tamils and Sinhalese fought. The racist aspects of the British Raj in India were alive in the Indian memory.

Racism and its effects were especially marked in Africa. Ongoing witness to justice in racial relations was urgent. In a book on the indigenous church in the Copper Belt, John V. Taylor spoke of the racial intolerance that had characterized missionaries, governments, and companies since the beginning of the nineteenth century. He noted that "the African complaint against colour prejudice—what Mr. Van der Post has called 'the wrong look in the eye'—is not a new thing; and that it has continuously fostered disillusionment towards Christianity."[8]

8. John V. Taylor, *The Growth of the Church in the Copperbelt* (London: SCM Press, 1960), p. 177; the Van der Post phrase is from *The Dark Eye in Africa* (London: The Hogarth Press, 1955).

Over the ferment of Asian, African, and Latin American peoples hung the harsh and terrible contrast between the rich white North and the poor South, of many colors. In that world, every extension of the *koinonia* of the ecumenical movement was a probe into the racism and the racial tension of the time.

Establishing a position, as the WCC did at Evanston, and responding to crisis, as it did in Cottesloe, were accompanied by a long process of consciousness-raising and reconciliation. A significant contribution came from Daisuke Kitagawa, an American who began his work in the Japanese-American internment camps in the US in World War II. He started a unique ministry especially in Africa and North America, patiently seeking the means of communication and break-through amid racial alienation.[9]

The basic function of the WCC was to help make the whole Christian world conscious of white racism everywhere, of ethnic tension and its basis, and to initiate or augment processes of reconciliation. New occasions would teach further duties. Of the latter-day Programme to Combat Racism, Visser 't Hooft wrote that it was the "unavoidable consequence" of these beginnings.[10] I agreed, and was grateful.

9. See Daisuke Kitagawa, *Race Relations and Christian Mission* (New York: Friendship Press, 1964).

10. Visser 't Hooft, *Has the Ecumenical Movement a Future?* (Belfast: Christian Journals Limited, 1974), p. 91.

CONCLUSION

15

The Emerging Ecumenical Tradition

In 1963 I was 46, and had spent virtually the whole of my working life in the WCC. Visser 't Hooft would retire within two years. It was time to leave. I did so in the autumn, not without misgivings; though these were tempered by the certainty of friendships that would last and the deep *koinonia.*

The turmoil of the 1960s appeared quickly. I arrived in Rochester, New York, where I had accepted the pastorate of Central Presbyterian Church, from Geneva on a Monday. On Thursday President Kennedy was assassinated. My first service at Central Church was on the next Sunday, when most of the US population, it seemed, attended church. In the summer of 1964, some seven months later, the first of the race riots of the 1960s occurred in Rochester.

Two-and-a-half years later, I reluctantly accepted a "draft" by Eugene Carson Blake and Edwin Espy to provide staff direction for the peace effort of the National Council of Churches, with a focus strongly on the Vietnam War.

The ecumenical struggle was acute. In the church in Rochester and later in the NCC, the fundamental problem of the ecumenical movement came to the fore daily: how to create conditions which would enable the Body of Christ, the People of God, the Church, to be evident within the churches, whether in the city of Rochester or on the national scene. The essence of the struggle appeared in two modes.

One of these had to do with the meaning and vitality of Christian faith itself — the vitality of the Bible in the lives and thought of people, the manner of worship, and the quality of Christian living. At this point, there was a marked contrast, both locally and nationally, with the biblical theology and direction of life that had been the essence of things in the WCC. At this point, too, I began to understand the urgent need for liturgical renewal. At the same time, there were always those for whom "the church" was the great reality, invigorating church in its lesser, highly institutionalized sense. Struggle between the two formed a large part of the scene.

The other mode in which this decade revealed ecumenical tension was external—in the relation between church and society. When I looked at the Rochester congregation as a whole, and later at the constituency of the NCC, the "church of the center" appeared to be a distinct minority. My long international experience left me unprepared for this. Theoretically, of course, I knew that US Protestantism was heavily influenced, even dominated by American culture (however one defined it). But I was not prepared for the extent and depth of the hold that the "church of culture" had on the lives and witness of the church members. Nor, in the area of race relations, was I prepared for the virulence with which the church of white culture was prepared to defend itself.

At the same time, there was a restive and influential core, both in Rochester and in the NCC constituency. In Rochester the issue was race. Although hundreds of people mostly stayed away from church (though without withdrawing their membership), a core of some hundreds stayed and bore strong witness. In the NCC the issue was US nationalism. The principal reason I had left the church in Rochester was that I felt the ecumenical need to assist those who sought to transcend the nationalism of the time. Here again, there was a core of those whose commitment went beyond nationalism.

During my years at the NCC, the results of the Second Vatican Council became strikingly evident. There was optimism, even euphoria, over the sudden flood of associations—as if a pent-up longing on both sides had been suddenly released. Post-Vatican II collaboration for me came by the activist route. Theology would come later. I encountered the Roman Catholic peace movement, or parts of it, both in its grassroots manifestations and at the headquarters of the US Catholic Conference.

In 1974 an invitation came to be executive director of the Institute for Ecumenical and Cultural Research in Collegeville, Minnesota. The Institute was started by Fr. Kilian McDonnell, O.S.B., a monk of St. John's Abbey. Its small, lovely buildings are located on the grounds of the abbey and of St. John's University, founded by the abbey in the nineteenth century. St. John's is a Benedictine monastery, now the largest in the world, immensely vital. It was a spearhead of the Roman Catholic liturgical movement and had substantial influence at Vatican II.

The Institute is not governed by the abbey but by a board of directors, lay and clergy, drawn from the main branches of Christianity. They wanted a Protestant director, and working there as a Protestant I found that I had an extraordinary entrée to the churches, to theological circles, and to lay leadership. For the first time I had an opportunity to gain some understanding of Roman Catholicism, not from books, but from living in the atmosphere of a Roman Catholic institution and among Roman Catholic friends.

Work at the Institute also gave me a chance to reflect on the ecumenical tradition. People spent their sabbatical leaves — whether from academic or other institutions—at the Institute to do research and writing on a topic relevant to "ecumenism." A liberal construction of the term permitted a wide variety of "Fellows" in residence. Most were younger than I, and many had scant awareness of the fact of an ecumenical tradition. Explaining it required reflection. Moreover, the Institute reached out into differing theological circles, including those of evangelical connection, and into the churches in Minnesota. From all sides, there was stimulus to consider post-Vatican II "ecumenism" and its US setting and task.

*   *   *

In conclusion I want to reflect on what is permanent in the emerging ecumenical tradition that we have examined. I shall take account of only one event in the period since 1963, namely the basic ecumenical work of Vatican II, and the entrance of the Roman Catholic Church into the ecumenical movement. Since I cannot draw on personal experience, I shall not speak of further developments in the WCC, nor attempt any analysis of the enormous ecumenical activity initiated by Rome. Rather, I shall comment on three questions: (1) What are the basic ingredients that can be distilled from the ecumenical tradition as it emerged between 1948 and 1963? (2) What is the significance of the dominant thrust of the ecumenical tradition? (3) What consequences may be drawn for the present and future?

THE EMERGING ECUMENICAL TRADITION: BASIC INGREDIENTS

The Faith

The root of all was living faith in the living triune God. Expressed again and again, this faith was the explicit and implicit ground of ecumenical thought and action. It was confessed in the modes of God's work of creation, redemption, and consummation; and each of these modes was to be seen in the created world, in humanity and human history, and in the person.

This faith might well have been shaken by the change in the milieu in which the Western church had lived. Over three centuries the *corpus Christianum* of Europe and the special form of it in predominantly Protestant America had been increasingly eroded by secularism. Finally, at the historic center of its life, the church had been threatened unto death by the brutalizing terror of racist totalitarian forces. Moreover, from its earlier position within the imperial center reaching out into the world, the Western church began to develop a minority consciousness in its own territories as well as among other peoples of the world, in this respect becoming akin to the Eastern Church. Such change of milieu might have weakened the essential faith of the Western church.

Instead, this faith burst forth. My experience of power meeting power was in the ecumenical movement. First, I met it vicariously—in Kenneth Latourette's classroom and in books, especially biographies of pioneer missionaries in Asia and Africa. Amid the terrors of loneliness, hardship, discouragement, disease, the threat of death, and death itself, the power of their faith was greater than these: hence, "The Great Century" which made Christianity ecumenical. Then I met that power in the ecumenical circles of Europe, Asia, and, somewhat later, Africa and Latin America. The people who created the ecumenical movement there were those who had met the powers of the world in their ultimate evil and had not been silenced, but had defeated their strength. For these pioneers and warriors in Christ, the gospel was not a truth among others, but news, a word about reality, *the* power among all other powers. From its beginning, the ecumenical tradition was based on faith in the triune God, Father, Son, and Holy Spirit, one God.

The Church

The second element in the emerging ecumenical tradition was the perception of the church as the Body of Christ and the People of God. Paul

Minear's work showed the scope and meaning of New Testament images of the church and their importance for a full understanding of the church.[1] Similarly, ecumenical perceptions of the church were cast strongly in terms of images.

Two stand out: the Body of Christ and the People of God. Together, they illumined one another, giving substance to the ecumenical tradition. The use of them both suggested that in a sense the church can be the Body of Christ because it realizes that it is the People of God among all the peoples. No one suggested that these two images exhausted the biblical possibilities, but in the highly charged history of the times, they arose. And one remembered the thought of Georges Florovsky at the beginning: the Church is "depicted rather than defined," and only from within, because "the Mystery is apprehended only by faith."[2]

Ecumenical thought about the church thus affirmed a core, expressed not in doctrine but in image, which was toughened by four implications:

The first was "renewal." Far from downgrading the churches, this accent registered the high degree of seriousness with which the churches were taken. Renewal implied the recognition of sin in the churches. That did not mean that "the church sins" (which is another proposition altogether and not acceptable); it did mean that in the churches in which all were nurtured, there was sin. "We must," wrote Visser 't Hooft, "avoid the 'angelic fallacy' which St. Augustine repudiated when he said that the Church here on earth is not without spot or wrinkle and needs to pray: 'Forgive us our sins.'"[3]

The Roman Catholic experience was different. In it, ecumenism did not produce the need for renewal, but renewal — *aggiornamento* — drove Vatican II to ecumenism and the ecumenical movement.

Hindsight makes me wonder why there was no emphasis on liturgical renewal in the 1948-63 period. Why did the Faith and Order project on "Ways of Worship" come to very little, if anything?[4] The sort of explosion which took place concerning "Christ and the church" and "Tradition and traditions" never took place concerning worship. There is little use in exploring the "why."

1. Paul Minear, *Images of the Church in the New Testament* (Philadelphia: Westminster Press, 1959).
2. Georges Florovsky, "The Church—Her Nature and Task," Amsterdam Vol. 1, p. 44.
3. Visser 't Hooft, *The Renewal of the Church* (London: SCM Press, 1956).
4. P. C. Roger and Lukas Vischer (eds.), *The Fourth World Conference on Faith and Order* (New York: Association Press, 1964).

I had first been made aware of the influence of the Roman Catholic liturgical renewal by Fr. Thomas Stransky. He was speaking of the growing influence of the Newman Centers on campuses across the nation, and when I asked him what he thought explained this growth, he replied "the liturgical renewal." Recalling this, and in the light of my experience at the Institute in Collegeville, I have taken increasing note of this lack in the early ecumenical tradition.

The second implication of "the church" in the emerging ecumenical tradition was that of a universal mission to proclaim salvation to all humanity, throughout all history. Even at the height of European colonial expansion that mission was not perceived as civilizing the world, although it did include a mission to help improve human life and to seek justice and peace. That mission was always understood, even through the fog of human preoccupations, as to "declare the wonderful works of him who called you out of darkness into his marvellous light" (1 Peter 2:9). However heatedly its meaning was debated, the mission was not only assumed but proclaimed. It was foundational, growing from the core of the faith. It was universal, belonging to every Christian and every church. It was final, pertaining to all of humanity and all of human history.

Third, "church" in the ecumenical tradition implied a calling to Christians and the churches to witness together to the unity of humanity in the purpose of the triune God. The answer to the question of how, over against all other claims about the meaning of life, we know about the finality of Christ and the church, rested first on our redemption, hence upon the incarnation, the Word becoming flesh, taking the form of a servant, and being obedient to death. In the incarnation one saw the unity of humanity with God, the decisive foretaste of the promised unity of humanity as a whole in God. On that "future which is now" and that "now which is the future" rested the vision, the promise, the expectation, gathered in the supplication: "Thy kingdom come."

Fourth, as the ecumenical tradition saw it, "church" implied a distinctive function in all societies. The faith required loyalty to God, love of neighbor, anticipation of the Kingdom of God, and the demonstration of these in the life of the Body of Christ amid the circumstances of human history. This implied a rejection of tendencies to withdraw from society, or to become submerged by society, or to rule over society.

Instead, as we have said, the ecumenical tradition affirmed the historical "church of the center." That required prophetic criticism of existing societies, constructive thought, and collaborative action with all. The steady goal was the continual transformation of society by means of some workable synthesis, compatible with the Christian revelation, that would provide — in Reinhold Niebuhr's familiar word — "tolerable" justice, freedom and peace in society, and relief to acute human need.

A four-point summary, of course, inevitably takes the life and dynamism out of the ecumenical tradition. Let us look at the emerging tradition from another viewpoint.

THE EMERGING TRADITION: SIGNIFICANCE

An unmistakable sense of "moment" and of "momentousness" accompanied nearly every stage of my own ecumenical experience. It seemed that God was giving the church new equipment for its work in the world. That meant a new thing, a new dimension in "church" that was in being and coming to be at the same time. The ecumenical movement became less and less an option, more and more an inescapable "given."

I began to notice the language of others. Visser 't Hooft: ". . . a new reality begins to emerge." Outler: "the priority of Christian community over the principle of 'pure doctrine,' so that the mutual recognition of Christians as Christians is the *precondition* of ecumenical work rather than the goal." Tomkins: "God has given his people in our days a new insight into what He wants them to do; one fruit of it is the official, organized ecumenical movement, with the World Council as its chief expression; but the essence of it, ecumenicity, is something which happens in the souls of Christians. It is a new understanding of the Body of Christ, . . . a deep spiritual traffic, a bond of spirit so strong that it will not allow to fly apart those who are under great pressure to become separated."[5] That language conveyed an affinity with what a later generation would call "praxis."

And the formal report to the Third Assembly: "There are things which the Spirit says to the churches when they submit themselves together to the revealed truth of God. When the churches speak and act together there is that 'plus,' that new dimension which belongs to the mystery of the Church's unity and fellowship and through which the divine truth is seen in fuller proportion."[6]

It was not, however, until I had come to understand the shift that had taken place in the Roman Catholic Church at Vatican II that I

5. Visser 't Hooft, "What Can We Say Together About the Meaning of Membership in the World Council of Churches?", in Central Committee minutes, 1963, p. 138; Outler, *The Christian Tradition and the Unity we Seek* (New York: Oxford U.P., 1957), p. 10; Tomkins, *The Wholeness of the Church* (London: SCM Press, 1949), pp. 13-15.

6. *New Delhi Report*, p. 191.

could articulate the meaning of "ecumenical" in a way that did justice to its momentousness, newness, and meaning.

The emerging ecumenical tradition was not, so to speak, up for a point-by-point review by the Second Vatican Council. But the Council did take a position in the "Decree on Ecumenism"[7] which affirmed the essence of the ecumenical tradition in a way that was remarkably reminiscent of that taken in 1950 in Toronto as Protestants and Orthodox and Anglicans struggled with the ecclesiology implied in WCC membership. There the problems were resolved by affirming that a church could recognize other churches in the ecumenical body without compromising its own ecclesiology. The recognition at Vatican II that those who believe in Christ and are baptized are "brought into a certain though imperfect communion" with the Roman Catholic Church gave the basis for its participation in the ecumenical movement.

This recognition opened a floodgate through which has poured a vast stream of exploration, dialogue, and collaboration. Clearly, the nascent ecumenical tradition would be transformed. At the same time, the Faith and Order study on *Baptism, Eucharist and Ministry*[8] gave evidence that the transformation would not mean a radical break with the tradition which had begun to emerge, but rather a development of its claims as to the essential nature and function of the church.

I had once described the ecumenical movement as analogous to the monastic reformation(s) and the Protestant Reformation.[9] Now this seems insufficient to me. The significance of the emergence of a developing ecumenical tradition is more far-reaching. A better analogy, I think, is with the processes that led to the Councils of Nicea (325), Ephesus (431), and Chalcedon (451). These had provided a definitive and thus irreversible formulation of faith in God. Similarly, the emergence of the ecumenical tradition provided for the first time an irreversible formulation of the nature of the church. What the patristic discussion, Nicea, and its successors did to state the essence of the faith in the triune God, the ecumenical development did to declare the essence of faith in the church.

One could not compare any ecumenical event with Nicea, but one could point to the process which began at Edinburgh in 1910, was

7. Austin Flannery, O.P. (ed.), *Vatican Council II: The Conciliar and Post-Conciliar Documents* (Collegeville, Minn.: The Liturgical Press, 1975), "Decree on Ecumenism," pp. 452-64. The quotation below is from "Decree on Ecumenism," para. 3.

8. *Baptism, Eucharist and Ministry,* Faith and Order Paper No. 111 (Geneva: World Council of Churches, 1982).

9. Robert S. Bilheimer, *What Must the Church Do?* (New York: Harper and Brothers, 1947), pp. 63-107.

brought to a focus at Amsterdam in 1948, and came to its first conclusion with the adjournment of Vatican II in 1965. There were of course doctrines of the church prior to the ecumenical movement, but there was no commanding, unifying concept. That was the condition which the ecumenical tradition began to address. In this sense, its work has seemed to me to be not only an observable "first," but also definitive.[10]

"Church" was ill-defined when vast blocks of Christians would not grant a mutual recognition to one another as belonging to Christ. "Church" was ill-defined by any church which confined itself to one civilization when there was the opportunity to penetrate to other civilizations; or left its world mission to a few pioneers, sometimes even opposing them. "Church" was ill-defined when it allowed itself to become submerged within one society or any part of society. And it was the trinitarian faith of Nicea which, in the final analysis, enabled one to judge all three cases as ill-defined.

It is easier to say that Nicea is irreversible because it has lasted over a millennium and a half, but ultimately such an affirmation is based on the knowledge provided by faith. To say that the basic affirmation of the ecumenical tradition—mutual recognition to some substantial degree in the Body of Christ—is irreversible is also a statement of faith. I believe it, because I believe that "ecumenism," meaning the inauguration of an "ecumenical tradition," is what God has been doing with the church during this half century of extraordinary change in world society.

CONSEQUENCES FOR THE FUTURE

What might be the meaning of the ecumenical tradition for the future? It is nonsensical to forecast developments, but one may point to some crucial elements in the growth of the ecumenical tradition for what light they may shed.

Above all, it appears to me that "the local" has rare importance. I do not mean "local" simply in the sense of a village or town or even city in contrast to the international world, nor in the sense of "local congregation" or "local parish" in contrast to the ecumenical church. I mean it rather in the sense of the Third Assembly of the WCC, which spoke about "all in each place." At the moment I am especially concerned with the concept of "each place" as being "local." Each place may be a na-

10. I am indebted to John Long, S.J., Douglas Meeks, Margaret O'Gara, Thomas Stransky, and Michael Vertin for assistance in formulating this analogy, which occurred to me in reading Jaroslav Pelikan, *The Emergence of the Catholic Tradition 100-600* (Chicago: U. of Chicago Press, 1971).

tion. It may be a small place in a nation. It may be a small group or a large group in a place for a short time, or a long time.

The power of God-in-Christ, formed and located by the Holy Spirit in "places" and in each "place," is indispensable to the ecumenical tradition. One saw that in the students volunteering for foreign missions, in the Confessing Church in Germany and elsewhere in Europe, and now in South Africa, South Korea, the Philippines, and Latin America. One saw that in the Concertgebouw in Amsterdam on the morning of August 23, 1948, and at Vatican II, and in every formative moment in the development of the ecumenical tradition, including when official and unofficial bodies and agencies of churches voted to join ecumenical agencies. But is there reason to take ecumenical hope and vision from contemporary "places"? Does the concept of "the local" have genuine contemporary relevance? I suggest that it does.

Of course, it would be foolish to try to speak comprehensively or dogmatically about "the future," as though any of us could know the consequences of what God is doing in the vast expansion of Christianity in Africa, as well as Asia and Latin America. With the "weight" of Christianity shifting from north of the Equator to south of it, especially under the present economic and political conditions of both, who can forecast a future?

Who could do such forecasting even for the US alone? At the Institute we undertook an extensive survey of Christianity in Minnesota.[11] National comment showed that it probably mirrored the country in the main outlines. This gave a picture of enormous vitality in church life, accompanied by the predominance of a fundamental subjectivism in the appropriation of Christian faith by church members—a pick-and-choose, do-it-yourself religiosity that left one wondering where the center is. Ecumenism in the sense of mutual recognition of Christians across denominational lines ran high. Who would forecast a future in relation to these conditions?

Granted that contemporary conditions make forecasting absurd, what makes "the local" important for the future? In reply, one can point to a phenomenon that runs through the churches everywhere. It is more than a mere phenomenon. I believe that we have before our eyes a priceless gift. *Is it not a fact that the ecumenically oriented Orthodox, Roman Catholic, Anglican, and Protestant Christians have more in common with one another than they have with the non-ecumenically oriented persons and insti-*

11. See Joan D. Chittister, O.S.B., and Martin E. Marty, *Faith and Ferment*, ed. Robert S. Bilheimer (Collegeville, Minn.: The Liturgical Press, and Minneapolis: Augsburg Publishing House, 1983).

tutions within their own confessions? A very substantial number of Christians in all four of these historic and historically divided confessions are bound together across confessional lines more strongly than to people who are strictly confessional or institutional in their loyalties. I believe that is true and that it is a worldwide fact. It is a new form of the ecumenical *koinonia.*

Moreover, *what ecumenical Roman Catholics, Protestants, Anglicans, and Eastern Orthodox have in common with each other is more fundamental than what they have in common with the non-ecumenical membership of their own communions.*

The underlying factor in these affirmations is the existence in all four confessional groupings of the fundamental ecumenical glue. That consists of a realization, empowered by the Holy Spirit, that in some recognizable measure "church" exists in the other groupings. When that recognition bursts on people across confessional lines, the result is a new bond, stronger than the bond previously known. The new bond does not obliterate the older, confessional bond; it transforms it, because the Spirit has enlarged it.

For the existence of this modern-day gift, one offers prayers of gratitude. At the same time, the dynamism of the gift does not allow a mere acquiescence. A sense of calling accompanies the gift.

This calling focuses on Christian life within the church and the churches. It is a calling to make this new bond visible, to demonstrate its power, to speak the truth that comes from within it. One notes with some amazement that there has never been a tendency in the ecumenical movement to found a new church composed of those who have all these things in common. The universal ecumenical experience has been to seek renewal of the confessions within which the bond has been formed.

How may the ecumenical calling be exercised? It will first need to bear the historic—and productive—ecumenical tension. Throughout its whole history, the ecumenical enterprise has been strung between "movement" and "structure." It owed its existence to the foreign missionary *movement,* the Student Christian Movement, the *movement* of Life and Work, the *movement* of Faith and Order, the development of biblical scholarship and the *movement* of biblical theology, the *movement* of the confessing churches, the liturgical *movement,* and the *movement* among the Roman Catholic pioneer theologians. These movements invariably turned their vision and directed their energy toward the existing structures, the churches.

Tension resulted—the tension of restlessness, the tension of a double loyalty, on the one hand to the vision of the ecumenical movement, and on the other to the spiritual, institutional, theological, historical structure of the church.

"Movement" and "structure" in the church, and the tension between them, did not, of course, originate in the ecumenical enterprise. It has appeared in a thousand guises in church history, affecting and benefiting all the great branches of Christianity, mostly in connection with renewal, or missionary or social outreach.

Its reappearance in the ecumenical tradition suggests that the movement-structure tension can play a large part in the future of ecumenism. In particular, the commonality of ecumenically minded Roman Catholics, Protestants, Orthodox, and Anglicans will be far more fruitful if its members recognize the requirement of the church for structure, its need for movement, and the benefit that accrues from the tension between the two. That means that the local groups—the group "in each place"—need to express that commonality not merely in "movement" meetings, functions, and actions, but also in the role that their members play in the structures of their respective churches. That will require considerable engineering! But that may be the basic engineering task as the emerging ecumenical tradition develops.

The ecumenical calling, however, has a further aspect also extrapolated from history. It insists on the ceaseless orientation of the church toward the world. In the ecumenical tradition, unity among Christians and churches is oriented to witness in the world; message and task are world-oriented; the identity of the church is to be in but not of the world. Furthermore, the ecumenical movement has spoken for and embodied the "church of the center." The terms, issues, and crises of the church and world will differ, as will the answers. The ecumenical calling requires not only that the structure-movement tension be kept, but that the whole be oriented toward the world's peoples and the world's societies, and the world's sin, in the name of one God, Father, Son, and Holy Spirit.

*   *   *

Toward the end of the Toronto meeting of the Central Committee in 1950, Bishop Stephen Neill had to make a report. He was in a difficult position: the excitement of responding to war in Korea and to the threat to the WCC's existence had all but exhausted the attention span of the Committee members.

Neill's report concerned the nascent *History of the Ecumenical*

Movement, on which he and Ruth Rouse were then at work. Quite aware of his difficult position, Neill typically seized the initiative. Speaking of the history, he said: "It is a matter of life and death. A man who has lost his memory is to all intents dead. So is a movement."[12]

Memory gives life and life evokes memory. This book is intended as an act of memory for the sake of life, in the hope that the ecumenical tradition may be drawn upon, and contribute to the developing sense of ecumenical identity. And so I conclude with a remark drawn, appropriately, from Visser 't Hooft which points to future life for the ecumenical tradition: "We need the impatient people who call for boldness, imagination and forward-looking hope in action. But there is an impatience which gives up and an impatience which builds up."[13] The ecumenical tradition today needs the second impatience.

12. Central Committee minutes, 1950, p. 55.
13. Visser 't Hooft, *Has the Ecumenical Movement a Future?*, p. 53.

Official Ecumenical Corpus

Modern ecumenical history is frequently viewed as the convergence in the World Council of Churches of three streams of ecumenical activity: world missions, faith and order, and life and work (or church and society). The following list is organized according to this pattern.

WORLD MISSIONS

The Edinburgh Volumes of 1910

Each of the Edinburgh volumes contains substantial reports, prepared by an international commission on various aspects of the overall subject of the volume, and an account of the discussion of the report at the Conference.

World Missionary Conference, 1910; Edinburgh: Oliphant, Anderson & Ferrier, and New York: Fleming H. Revell Company, 1910.
    Vol. I Carrying the Gospel to All the Non-Christian World
    Vol. II The Church in the Mission Field
    Vol. III Education in Relation to the Christianisation of National Life
    Vol. IV The Missionary Message in Relation to Non-Christian Religions
    Vol. V The Preparation of Missionaries
    Vol. VI The Home Base of Missions
    Vol. VII Missions and Governments
    Vol. VIII Cooperation and the Promotion of Unity
    Vol. IX History and Records of the Conference

The Jerusalem Volumes of 1928

Each of the Jerusalem volumes contains chapters written by missionary leaders, followed by the Council's Statement on the subject of the volume.

The Jerusalem Meeting of the International Missionary Council, March 24– April 8, 1928; New York and London: The International Missionary Council, 1928.

Vol. I *The Christian Life and Message in Relation to Non-Christian Systems of Thought and Life*

Vol. II *Religious Education*

Vol. III *The Relation between the Younger and the Older Churches*

Vol. IV *The Christian Mission in the Light of Race Conflict*

Vol. V *The Christian Mission in Relation to Industrial Problems*

Vol. VI *The Christian Mission in Relation to Rural Problems*

Vol. VII *International Missionary Cooperation*

Vol. VIII *Addresses on General Subjects*

The Madras Series of 1938-39

The contents of the Madras volumes vary, with papers, notes on preliminary papers, or special reports on particular subjects used in different combinations depending on the volume. Each volume also contains the findings of the Conference on the subject of the volume; the final volume here listed contains all the findings of the Conference.

The Madras Series; New York and London: The International Missionary Council, 1939.

Vol. I *The Authority of the Faith*

Vol. II *The Growing Church*

Vol. III *Evangelism*

Vol. IV *The Life of the Church*

Vol. V *The Economic Basis of the Church*

Vol. VI *The Church and the State*

Vol. VII *Addresses and Other Records*

The World Mission of the Church: Findings and Recommendations of the International Missionary Council, Tambaram, Madras, India, December 12th to 29th, 1938; London and New York: The International Missionary Council, 1939.

The two following volumes record the final meetings of the International Missionary Council before its integration with the World Council of Churches in 1961.

The Witness of a Revolutionary Church: Statements Issued by the Committee of the International Missionary Council, Whitby, Ontario, Canada, July 5-24, 1947; New York: International Missionary Council, 1947.

Missions under the Cross: Addresses Delivered at the Enlarged Meeting of the Committee of the International Missionary Council at Willingen, in Germany, 1952; with Statements issued by the Meeting; Norman Goodall, ed.; London: Edinburgh House Press, 1953.

FAITH AND ORDER

Faith and Order published the reports of its world conferences. Varied methods were used for their preparation. (See below, *A Documentary History of the Faith and Order Movement. . . .*)

Faith and Order: Proceedings of the World Conference, Lausanne, August 3-21, 1927; H. N. Bate, ed.; Garden City and New York: Doubleday, Doran & Company, Inc., 1928.

The Second World Conference on Faith and Order Held at Edinburgh, August 3-18, 1937; Leonard Hodgson, ed.; New York: The Macmillan Company, 1938.

The Third Conference on Faith and Order Held at Lund, August 15th to 28th, 1952; Oliver S. Tomkins, D.D., ed.; London: SCM Press, 1953.

A Documentary History of the Faith and Order Movement, 1927-1963; Lukas Vischer, ed.; St. Louis: The Bethany Press, 1963.

LIFE AND WORK

The Stockholm Conference on Life and Work in 1925 did not publish preparatory volumes and its report is minimal. See *The History of the Ecumenical Movement,* listed below.)

The Oxford Conference Volumes, 1938

Each of the Oxford Conference volumes is a symposium on its particular subject, the respective chapters throughout being contributed by a recognized authority on the theme. The Official Report contains the findings of the Conference.

The Official Oxford Conference Books; Chicago and New York: Willett,
 Clarke & Company, 1938.
  Vol. 1 *The Church and Its Function in Society*
  Vol. 2 *The Christian Understanding of Man*
  Vol. 3 *The Kingdom of God and History*
  Vol. 4 *Christian Faith and the Common Life*
  Vol. 5 *Church and Community*
  Vol. 6 *Church, Community, and State in Relation to Education*
  Vol. 7 *The Universal Church and the World of Nations*

The Oxford Conference: Official Report; J. H. Oldham, ed.; Chicago and New
 York: Willett, Clarke and Company, 1937.

THE WORLD COUNCIL OF CHURCHES

*The Ten Formative Years, 1938-1948: Report on the Activities of the World
 Council of Churches during its Period of Formation;* Geneva: World
 Council of Churches, 1948.

The Amsterdam Volumes, 1948

Each of "The Amsterdam Assembly Series" is a symposium of chapters
contributed by recognized authorities on the respective subjects. The
Official Report contains Assembly reports on the subjects of Vols. I-IV
and other actions, lists of Assembly membership, etc.

Man's Disorder and God's Design, The Amsterdam Assembly Series; New
 York: Harper and Brothers, 1948.
  Vol. I *The Universal Church in God's Design*
  Vol. II *The Church's Witness to God's Design*
  Vol. III *The Church and the Disorder of Society*
  Vol. IV *The Church and the International Disorder*
  Vol. V *The First Assembly of the World Council of Churches: The Of-
   ficial Report*

The Evanston Volumes, 1954

*The First Six Years–1948-1954: Report of the Central Committee of the World
 Council of Churches on the Activities of the Departments and Secretar-
 iats of the Council;* Geneva: World Council of Churches, 1954.

The Christian Hope and the Task of the Church: Six Ecumenical Surveys and the Report of the Advisory Commission on the Main Theme; New York: Harper and Brothers, 1954. (Surveys on Faith and Order, Evangelism, Church and Society, International Affairs, Intergroup Relations, and the Laity; Report on "Christ—The Hope of the World").

The New Delhi Volumes, 1961

Evanston to New Delhi 1954-1961: Report of the Central Committee to the Third Assembly of the World Council of Churches; Geneva: World Council of Churches, 1961.

Jesus Christ—The Light of the World (Bible Studies in Preparation for the Third Assembly); Geneva: World Council of Churches, 1961.

The New Delhi Report: The Third Assembly of the World Council of Churches, 1961; London: SCM Press, 1961.

Other Records

Minutes of successive meetings of the Central Committee of the WCC, 1948-1963.

The Ecumenical Review, published quarterly by the World Council of Churches.

The International Review of Missions, published quarterly by the International Missionary Council prior to 1961 and thereafter by the World Council of Churches.

A History of the Ecumenical Movement, Vol. I, Ruth Rouse and Stephen C. Neill; Philadelphia: Westminster Press, 1967; Vol. II, Harold E. Fey; Philadelphia: Westminster Press, 1970.

The World Council of Churches publishes numerous bibliographies on the subjects of its concerns.

Index